British Radical Culture of the 1790s

Edited by Robert M. Maniquis

Huntington Library
San Marino, California

Cover illustration

William Blake, *Europe a Prophecy*, plate 14. Reproduced with permission from the collection of Robert N. Essick.

Also published as the *Huntington Library Quarterly*, volume 63, number 3, edited by Susan Green.

Library of Congress Cataloging-in-Publication Data

British radical culture of the 1790s / edited by Robert M. Maniquis.
    p. cm.
"Also published as the Huntington Library quarterly, volume 63, number 3."
Includes bibliographical references.
    ISBN 0-87328-196-9 (alk. paper)
  1. Radicalism—Great Britain—History—18th century. I. Maniquis, Robert M.
    HN400.R3 B75 2002
    306.2'0941'09033—dc21

                             2002002633

Contents

Contributors

Robert M. Maniquis, the editor of this volume, teaches English at UCLA, and he is a research associate of the Centre d'Etude de la Langue et de la Littérature Française du XVIIe et XVIIIe Siècles at the University of Paris, Sorbonne (Paris IV). He is the author of *Lonely Empires: Personal and Public Visions of Thomas De Quincey* and the editor of collections of essays on eighteenth- and nineteenth-century British and French culture. He is currently working on a study of violence and sacrifice in late-eighteenth-century European culture.

❧ ❧

John Barrell, a codirector of the Centre for Eighteenth-Century Studies at the University of York, is the author of many books and articles on eighteenth- and nineteenth-century art, literature, culture, and politics. His most recent book is *Imagining the King's Death: Figurative Treason, Fantasies of Regicide, 1793–1796* (2000).

Frederick Burwick is a professor of English at UCLA and has written and edited a number of books on Romanticism. His most recent are *Mimesis and Its Romantic Reflections* (2001) and *Thomas DeQuincey: Knowledge and Power* (2001). He is coeditor of the journal *European Romantic Review*.

Nigel Leask is a fellow of Queen's College, Cambridge University, and the author of *British Romantic Writers and the East: Anxieties of Empire* (1992). He has also published on comparative mythography and on the relationship between literature and science in the Romantic period. His book *Curiosity and the Aesthetics of Travel Writing, 1770–1840* is forthcoming from Oxford.

Philippe Roger is a director of research for the CNRS (Centre Nationale de la Recherche Scientifique), a member of the Centre d'Etude de la Langue et de la Littérature Française du XVIIe et XVIIIe Siècles at the University of Paris, Sorbonne (Paris IV), and a professor at the Ecole des Hautes Etudes en Sciences Sociales. He is the author of many studies on eighteenth-century culture and he is working presently on a book about anti-Americanism in France.

Michael S. C. Smith recently completed his Ph.D. in history at the University of California, Riverside. He teaches at California Polytechnic University, Pomona.

Fredrika J. Teute is Editor of Publications at the Omohundro Institute of Early American History and Culture. She has published articles on Margaret Bayard Smith and the new American nation, most recently in the *Cambridge Companion to Ninteenth-Century American Women's Writing* (2001), edited by Dale M. Bauer and Philip Gould. She has served as documentary editor on *The Papers of James Madison* and *The Papers of John Marshall.*

Introduction

Robert M. Maniquis

British radical culture of the 1790s has received in recent decades a great deal of scholarly attention. Hundreds of books, monographs, and articles have raised new questions and reexamined old ones, and many writers have been refigured in terms of the continuities and clashes between political "cultures" of the 1790s. Anyone studying this period today has at hand a rich body of inquiry into many subjects: the connections between Continental, British, and American writing; the late-eighteenth-century's expanding consumerist culture; the works of once neglected female writers; clandestine writing and political activity; the audiences of underground, popular, political, economic, scientific, and belletristic literature; the overlapping of bourgeois and philosophical "radicalism" with utopianism and millenarianism; the shared discourse in the rhetorics of Protestant dissent and reactionary organicism on the one hand and, on the other, the connections between radical Toryism and the earliest stages of working-class culture. The essays in this volume, based on talks presented at the William Andrews Clark Library, UCLA, in March of 1999, testify to our continuing interest in this decade of continuity and contradiction. Each essay focuses on political problems comprehensible only in the cultural matrix of the 1790s and its particular mix of political, aesthetic, and philosophical "languages." Each of these essays engages one or another aspect of those languages.

Our first essay begins with the subject of how language is found at the heart of concrete political fears. Most early sympathizers of the Revolution in the 1790s faced constant repression, and some were confronted with judicial threats to their lives. Frederick Burwick considers those threats in the famous treason trial of Thomas Hardy, Horne Tooke, and other radicals of Edinburgh. Most of these men stood accused of capital offenses, all the more striking when we consider Horne Tooke's argument that his freedom and, technically, his life were at stake in an accusation that rested on "two prepositions and a conjunction." Attacking the terror wielded by the law in prepositions and conjunctions was an eighteenth-century commonplace. We remember Burke's assertion, in *A Vindication of Natural Society,* that the misuse of an "and" or a "for" could mean prison for a father and "beggary and famine" for his family. Moreover, this was not the first time in history that lives were threatened or actually extinguished because of slippery parts of speech. Early Christian assassination and massacre, as Gibbon liked to remind readers of *The Decline and Fall of the Roman Empire*, often turned upon such words as "in," "for," or "with" in claims about the true relation of Christ to God. The 1790s in Britain did not suffer anything like the bloodshed occasioned by Christian grammar, but it certainly bristled with linguistic menace and paranoia. In the 1790s, words were taken to signify not only, as in Christianity, fundamentals of belief but also acts, equivalent juridically to actual violence. Burwick discusses the apprehension of the violence of language in the trial and in the writings of Horne Tooke. The essay reminds us of how cultural battles of the 1790s often reposed on linguistic "acts" and the attempts of a frightened government to catch traitors not in what they did but also in what they said. This famous trial of 1794 was, of course, an important event in the legal history of free speech in Britain. It also suggests how the government shared with its critics a belief in the sheer force of mentality—or of what today we would call psychology and ideology—in political struggles.

The revolutionary seizing of power, it is often argued, is first achieved in cultural mentalities—an idea that leads some historians to argue that the French Revolution, for instance, was essentially accomplished in the Enlightenment. But if today it is common to see ideological presence even before its social manifestation, such a notion was unfamiliar in the 1790s. Hence it is all the more striking that in one cultural and political area, it was not only the radicals who sought to instrumentalize imagination as an act of power but also the government itself. This is the subject of John Barrell's essay on the government's imagining of the political act of "imagining." The government of Pitt infused new life into a clause of a medieval law of treason in order to apprehend radicals in supposedly dangerous acts of imagination. This legal maneuver is not fully comprehensible, as Barrell points out, without seeing how it was "infected" by uses of the word in various extralegal discourses. Both prosecutorial and defense strategies in the world of realpolitik were clearly affected by late-eighteenth-century aesthetics. Barrell's essay traces the intersection of aesthetic, psychological, and authoritarian discourses down to the concrete setting of the courtroom, where lives were at stake not only for what was said, as discussed in Burwick's essay, but also for what could be conceived in the imagination that produced the words. Imagination—that exalted late-eighteenth-century and Romantic concept—was turned juridically into a threatening mental place, where murder had not even quite to be said in order to be done. Readers of Barrell's essay will want to go on to the full exposition of his ideas in his book *Imagining the King's Death: Figurative Treason, Fantasies of Regicide, 1793–1796* (Oxford, 2000).

Honored and treacherous words are the subject also of Philippe Roger's essay. The many conferences and publications occasioned by the bicentennial of the French Revolution gave us a well-known story in new detail—the influence of French Siècle de Lumières and the French Revolution upon British radicalism. And those bicentennial conferences also helped us to see more clearly how many British ideas prominent in the French Enlightenment had an influence upon the Revolution. But was there any significant influence across the Channel the other way, from Britain to France, during the Revolution? Roger begins by suggesting that the story of British influence on the French in the 1790s may have been a historical *rendez-vous manqué*. Indeed, his essay may remind us at first of what Roland Barthes called the *histoire plate*—the flat story that begins in excited anticipation, after which nothing really happens. Yet, as Roger's essay proceeds, we discover that quite a lot happened, though often of a chiefly rhetorical and semantic complexity, and even of self-interested deviousness—a story that is anything but flat. Publishing epistolary exchanges between radical British societies and French revolutionaries in the *Assemblée nationale* was an important radical political gesture in the 1790s. It was one of these cross-Channel salutations that occasioned Burke's writing of the *Reflections on the Revolution in France*. Roger emphasizes how, in these epistles of mutual admiration, the British saluted the French as if their revolution was an extension of the British revolutionary élan of the seventeenth century, while the French took these congratulations as the sentiments of merely sympathetic followers. Considering the political language that complicated these exchanges, Roger offers us the fascinating example of *constitutionnel* and *constitutional*, grand institutionalizing words that sound similar but actually harbor significantly different concepts—*faux amis*, as the French call such pairs. In the ritual exchanges of correspondence between the British and the French, there came a moment after 1793 when the most radical of French revolutionaries accused the British of having indeed been false friends. But even in the heady days of celebration in 1789 and 1790, when British radicals and French revolutionaries exchanged friendly greetings, their different languages suggest that they often did not understand each other's slogans and did not always know exactly what sort of friends they were.

Fredrika J. Teute writes about a more homogeneous radical friendship, as manifested in a group in Philadelphia that called itself the Friendly Club. Members of this group were middle-class intellectuals—ministers, writers, doctors, lawyers, even a senator, and their highly intellectual wives. They were deists, abolitionists, and freethinking republicans. These were intellectuals living in a country that could rightfully claim to be more advanced than any other in the ways of establishing a republic based on Enlightenment ideas. And yet the allegiances of the Friendly Club also suggest how America still looked for guidance in furthering American reformist thinking in the works of British philosophical radicals such as William Godwin, feminist writers such as Mary Wollstonecraft, and one of the most popular scientists or "natural philosophers" of the 1790s, Erasmus Darwin. This group of American enlightened thinkers is also interesting to consider in relation to such a towering figure as Tom Paine, British radical, capitalist entrepreneur, and fervent anticlerical writer. Tom Paine lived in a whirlwind. He fled from England to America, where he became the most important propagandist of the American Revolution; on to France, where he had been imprisoned under the Terror; and back to America, where he died a poor and lonely man, despised by many because of his virulent attacks on orthodox religion. Compared to Paine, who lived and died in intellectual fury, the committed intellectuals of the Friendly Club seem to have lived quiet lives. They read, they thought, they discussed, and they wrote, committed to the Enlightenment ideal of spreading truth. Yet, was it not the French Revolution that convinced them also of the wisdom of gradual amelioration? They were clearly fascinated by what today we would call sexual politics, at least as it was implied in Erasmus Darwin's *Loves of the Plants* and *The Botanic Garden*. In their cautious exploration of the political and sexual elements of natural and social organization, we see the inhibited aspect of philosophically radical culture. As Teute explains, the group shepherded the American edition of the tantalizing *Loves of the Plants* through the press in an expensive format. This common publishing practice among philosophical radicals in Britain and America was its own kind of ideologically complicated strategy, designed both to avoid censure and to keep dangerously imaginative literature out of the hands of those who might not understand—or perhaps might understand all too clearly—the implications of what they were reading. As in the essays of Burwick and Barrell, in Teute's discussion we come upon that sense, in both radicals and reactionaries, of how socially dangerous both imagination and utterance could be.

Among the intellectuals of the Friendly Club surely the eeriest person to be found was Charles Brockden Brown. His novels—*Wieland, or The Transformation, an American Tale* (1798) and the unfinished *Carwin the Biloquist* (1798, 1803–5)—are the subject of Nigel Leask's essay. Here we are treated to a rich complex of connections between French revolutionary, British radical, American republican, and utopian ideas. The political critique embodied in Brown's novels carries us immediately from the Enlightenment conception of a small, systematized, utopian community to the social reality of the young American republic. American society and its republic turned out to be more complicated than most Continental and British radicals and reformers could accept or understand. In America, a number of achieved freedoms—of the press, for example—could be seen, in both American multiplicity and American mass, to serve a new kind of bodiless control of public opinion. Hence the manipulating ventriloquist Carwin, who plays a crucially destructive role in both novels of Brown. Carwin is an intriguing figure with which to portray what could already be imagined in the 1790s—mass, mediatized culture, where the key to power was to institutionalize the ideas and values of a controlling political and intellectual class in public culture. Leask sets the scene of late-eighteenth-century Philadelphia, placing both Charles Brockden Brown and the Irish revolutionary Wolfe Tone—one of those radicals who actually did lose his life in political struggle. The story Leask tells is of the clash between Enlightenment, rationalist, revolutionary culture and the newly developing culture of mass politics. Tone was disgusted with the American version of "freedom," which seemed to him obsessed with the self and self-enrichment. He returned to Europe and, inspired by the French Revolution and many of its utopian ideals, actually tried to achieve a free Ireland based on the "higher principles" of liberty, not the self-centered, material achievements of American freedom and the treacheries of orchestrated mass politics. An important part of the fascinating and suggestive story that Leask has to tell is how Wolfe Tone, driven to suicide after his revolutionary failure, may lie behind the dark, eerie, gothic imagination of Charles Brockden Brown and his ventriloquist.

In my own essay, I discuss some aspects of the political rhetoric of the sublime. The eighteenth-century sublime has been much studied in the last twenty years. Yet it is so pervasive in reformist, revolutionary, and reactionary discourse that there are still many things to be learned about its rhetorical conventions and ruptures. My concern is to explore particular accommodations of fear and terror to the sublime, both before and after the Revolution. I emphasize how eighteenth-century connections between metaphysical terror and metaphysical majesty were more frighteningly dangerous than anything imagined by medieval or seventeenth-century theologians. A delicate rhetorical balance, established principally by Edmund Burke, guaranteed a self-controlled meditation upon and acceptance of psychological terror, necessary to both the empowering and the institutionalizing of the self in imperial imagination. That delicate balance played an important part in the eighteenth-century political imagination of terror, and it is essential to understanding the theorized political policy of French revolutionary Terror. But it was also the French Revolution that guaranteed the rupture of eighteenth-century connections between the sublime and terror. The rhetoric of the British radicals of the 1790s was significantly affected, and the poetic rhetoric in the traditions of Protestant dissent were forever changed. These rhetorical shifts in the balance of terror and the sublime are also important in our understanding of nineteenth-century political rhetoric. Philosophical and psychological elaborations of emotion in both political theory and literature would seek a variety of new ways to incorporate fear, terror, and violence into a complete vision of the self and society. Such new visions were, however, usually marked by a self-conscious inability to surmount the effects upon the imagination of the violence, both real and imagined, of the French Revolution.

With the hope that this volume may complement the knowledge of specialists but also be helpful to readers seeking more background for this rich historical period, we have added a review essay by Michael Smith. This essay leads the reader through some important recent books in what has become a huge bibliography of studies of 1790s political culture. Two presentations first given at our conference were already committed for publication elsewhere: Anne Mellor's paper on Hannah More's role in stabilizing moral and social values in an age of revolution and reform, now part of her book *Mothers of the Nation: Women's Political Writing in England, 1780–1830* (Indiana University Press, 2000); and Kevin Gilmartin's talk on political reaction, now "In the Theater of Counter-Revolution: Loyalist Association and Conservative Political Opinion in the 1790s," forthcoming in the *Journal of British Studies*.

Finally, I want to thank all those who had a hand in organizing the conference "British Radical Culture of the 1790s," from which these essays arose. Peter Reill, the director of the Center for 17th and 18th Century Studies, UCLA, along with the planning committee of the Center, enthusiastically supported our research and discussion. The staff of the Center, Candis Snoddy, Nancy Connoly, Marina Romani, Kathryn Sanchez, and Fran Andersen, all contributed to the success of the event. To those who presided over sessions—Michael Merzanze, Reginald Foakes, Margaret Russett, and Paul Sheats—and to those who attended and participated in the discussions of the conference, I am deeply grateful. Their questions, objections, and arguments are not recorded here, but they were important in the formulation and sometimes reformulation of ideas presented in these essays. Lastly I want to thank the staff of the Huntington Library Press, and above all its chief editor Susan Green, who has accepted with equanimity and kindness some necessary delays in the publication of this volume. Her editorial expertise and smart advice have made my work easier.

University of California, Los Angeles

The Language of High Treason: Thomas Hardy, John Horne Tooke, and the Edinburgh Seven

—————————————————— FREDERICK BURWICK

In tracking the effects of the French Revolution in Great Britain, historians have usually been disposed to give more attention to political events than to discriminations about language, but charges were leveled and cases tried on the basis of the uses of words. Charged with high treason because of the language of *The Rights of Man*, Tom Paine was indicted in May 1792; his counsel argued, to no avail, that to express opinions on the problems of political philosophy was not a criminal act. In cases of conspiracy, however, "Acts and Words" were routinely taken as equally valid evidence of criminal intent.[1] When charged with sedition for his words, John Horne Tooke informed the court that the case against him rested on "two prepositions and a conjunction." In particular, the role assumed by the Corresponding Societies during the 1790s made the uses of language central to both popular agitations and the agitations for constitutional reform. At the same time that the documents of the Corresponding Societies were subjected to legal scrutiny during the trials for sedition and treason, the language of politics and the politics of language gained nuance and subtlety. As letters were exchanged among the Corresponding Societies, panic increased among conservatives, who believed that a conspiracy to overthrow the government was underway, and the government instituted far-reaching measures. The Habeas Corpus Acts were suspended on 23 May 1794. "I hope you will be cautious in writing or expressing your political opinions," wrote Richard Wordsworth to his brother William on that very day, warning, "By the suspension of the Habeas Corpus Acts the Ministers have great powers."[2] In 1795, the

---

1. *The English and Empire Digest, with Complete and Exhaustive Annotations* (London, 1919–81), vol. 15, pt. 1 (c): "*Acts and Words of Co-Conspirators,*" par. 987 (the Hardy trial, 1794); par. 1002 (the Horne Tooke trial, 1794); pt. 1 (f): "*Speeches and Writings*" (on "spoken words" and "publication of writings" as sufficient evidence), par. 7128; "Words may be an overt act of high treason," par. 7141 (the Hardy trial, 1794); par. 7142 (the Horne Tooke trial, 1794).
2. *The Letters of William and Dorothy Wordsworth: The Early Years, 1787–1805,* ed. Ernest de Selincourt, rev. Chester L. Saver (Oxford, 1967), 121n.

following year, a Statute of Treason was passed, dispensing with the need for proof for any overt act of treason, as well as a Seditious Meetings Bill, which made it a criminal offense for any group of fifty persons or more to gather without prior approval by the magistrate. Any person publicly uttering words that tended to excite contempt of the government was subject to immediate prosecution.[3]

In November 1792, the French Republic issued its Edict of Fraternity, encouraging democratic agencies in every nation to follow the French example. In response, the Corresponding Societies in England actively rallied supporters of political reform, organizing a British Convention of the Delegates of the People to be held in Edinburgh the following year. The purpose was to petition for universal suffrage and annual parliaments. Joseph Gerrald and Maurice Margarot were sent to the convention as delegates of the London Corresponding Society. The delegates addressed one another as "citizen" and generally adopted the language of the French Revolution. Because of his speaking abilities, Gerrald rose to prominence among the delegates, drawing great crowds to his talks at the Black Bull Inn. On 5 December 1793, he and Margarot were arrested for sedition. By the time Gerrald's case came to trial in March 1794, Margarot and William Skirving, secretary of the convention, had already been tried and sentenced to transportation. Also found guilty and sentenced to fourteen years transportation, Gerrald was kept in prison for an entire year before he was abruptly shipped to Botany Bay in May 1795. He was not allowed to make any preparations for the voyage and consequently suffered severe exposure. He arrived in Sidney on 5 November 1795; five months later, at age thirty-three, he died.[4]

Because the court decision had gone decisively against members of the Corresponding Societies for their appropriation of revolutionary language, there was good reason to fear the outcome of the trials held later that year. The London Corresponding Society, which sent Gerrald and Margarot to Edinburgh, had been founded in January 1792 by Thomas Hardy, a London bootmaker, and a group of friends. Nine persons attended the first meeting, held at the Bell Tavern in Exeter Street, Strand. Hardy was the wordsmith of the society: he served as secretary, delivered speeches, and authored the handbills that were distributed in London. On 27 September 1792 he issued his congratulatory address to the National Convention of France. Hardy was no master of impassioned rhetoric. His papers were concerned, rather, with defining terms: the meaning of "free-

3. H. D. Traill and J. S. Mann, eds., *Social England: A Record of the Progress of the People*, 6 vols. (1902–4), reprint ed. (Westport, Conn., 1969), 5:666–70.

4. To commemorate the struggle for parliamentary reform, 1794–1844, "The Martyr's Monument" was erected on Carlton Hill, Edinburgh, with Gerrald's name inscribed on the obelisk; see the *Dictionary of National Biography.*

dom," "liberty," "representation," "rights."[5] From London, Hardy maintained correspondence with "every Society in Great Britain which had been instituted for the purpose of obtaining legal and constitutional means of Reform in the Common's House of Parliament."[6] The British Convention of the Delegates of the People in Edinburgh was conceived as a way of bringing about that change. When it was dispersed, and the London delegates Margarot and Gerrald were arrested, Hardy resolved that another convention should be held in England to which the Scottish Societies could send their delegates. To prevent such a convention from assembling, however, a warrant for Hardy's arrest was issued. On 12 May 1794, his papers were seized and he was brought to jail on charges of high treason. After being interviewed by the Privy Council, he was committed to the Tower on 29 May. His wife died on 27 August. His trial commenced on 28 October.

Four days after Hardy's arrest, Horne Tooke, an active member of the Society for Constitutional Information, deliberately implicated himself in the case against Hardy. Jeremiah Joyce, another member of the society, had been accused of "treasonable practices" on 4 May, but no "practices" other than letter writing were alleged by the Privy Council. Because he was denied legal counsel during his interrogation, he refused to answer questions. Joyce wrote to Horne Tooke to inform him that "Citizen Hardy" had been arrested. Joyce then added the question, "Is it possible to get ready by Thursday?" It was a deliberately cryptic question, encoded by members of the society, who knew what it meant (of which more later). If the authorities who were intercepting correspondence were looking for concealed meanings, then it was fitting and proper that meanings should be concealed. To those who were anticipating an uprising, the implication of the question "Is it possible to get ready by Thursday?" seemed obvious. Horne Tooke was arrested on 16 May and delivered to the Tower. Imprisoned for the next six months, he awaited the trial that—if he were found guilty—would eventuate not in transportation, as in cases of sedition, but in execution for high treason.

Twenty years earlier, Horne Tooke had been charged with sedition for his support of the American Revolution. A resolution of the Constitutional Society was printed in London newspapers calling for funds to aid "our beloved American fellow subjects," who had "preferred death to slavery" and "were, for that reason only inhumanly murdered by the king's troops" at Lexington (19 April 1775). The notice was ignored until after war was declared. On 4 July 1777,

---

5. Thomas Hardy, "The History of the London Corresponding Society, British Library, Add. MS. 27814; the letters of Thomas Hardy, Add. MS. 27818; and the Place Collection of the London Corresponding Society, Add. MS. 27811–17.

6. Hardy, *Memoir of Thomas Hardy* (London, 1832), 24.

Horne Tooke was formally charged with "seditious Libel tending to disquiet the minds of the People."[7] Thus his words were seditious acts in themselves, and sought to stir others to similar acts. He was found guilty and sentenced to a year's confinement in the King's Bench prison. Horne Tooke thereupon launched his battle against "grammatical" ignorance. He wrote that the case against him "afforded a striking instance of the importance of the meaning of words; not only (as has been too lightly supposed) to Metaphysicians and Schoolmen but to the rights and happiness of mankind in their dearest concerns—the Courts of Justice" (1:79).

In the first volume of *Epea Pteroenta, or The Diversions of Purley* (1786), Horne Tooke had argued that language, as the system for expressing thought, had evolved modes of expression aimed at efficiency and speed.[8] Whereas some words could be explained as immediate signs for ideas of things, other words "are merely *abbreviations* employed for dispatch, and are the signs of other words" (*Diversions of Purley*, 27). Words in the first group, the immediate signs, are made up exclusively of nouns and verbs. All other parts of speech, he held, were particles, or abbreviations of nouns and verbs. Horne Tooke did not develop his theory of language as a private speculation, as mere after-dinner diversions to while away the time at William Tooke's estate at Purley. He derived it from his active engagement in courts of law.

Just as his trial for sedition and year-long imprisonment gave rise to the deliberations on language that were the subject of the first volume of *Diversions of Purley*, his six months in the Tower awaiting trial for high treason helped fuel his deliberations for the expanded two-volume edition published in 1798. In his training for the bar, Horne Tooke had learned to regard language as an objective and pragmatic instrument. His first maneuver as his trial opened was to request the judge's sanction for removing him from the prisoner's box and placing him with his legal counsel "for the purpose of making my defence."[9] Because the evidence consisted of the written documents of the London Corresponding Society and the Constitutional Society, Horne Tooke wanted the advantage of ready reference to the language of those texts. Indeed, words were held to be acts in terms

7.   *The Trial of John Horne* (London, 1777).
8.   Horne Tooke, *Epea Pteroenta, or The Diversions of Purley* (1786); cited henceforward in the text.
9.   *The Trial of John Horne Tooke, for High Treason, taken in short-hand by Joseph Gurney*, 2 vols. (London, 1795), 1:4–5; cited henceforward in the text (*HT*). See also *The Proceedings in Cases of High Treason (King versus Thomas Hardy [and others]) under a Special Commission . . . opened Oct. 2, 1794 . . ., taken in short-hand by W. Ramsey* (London, 1794); Thomas Erskine, *The speeches at Large of the Honourable T. Erskine and V. Gibbs, esq., in defence of Thomas Hardy, and John Horne Tooke, esq., tried by special commission, on a charge of high treason*, 4 vols. in 1 (London, 1795); *The Prison Diary (16 May–22 November 1794) of John Horne Tooke*, edited with introduction and notes by A. V. Beedell and A. D. Harvey (Leeds, 1995).

of the indictment presented by the prosecution: "any act done, the consequence of which may endanger the life of the King, is taken to be an act done in pursuance of an intent to compass the death of the King, demonstrated by the act, and is the crime of High Treason" (*HT* 1:22). "Conspiring to depose the King" is an act of high treason (see John Barrell's essay in this volume). "Conspiring, in any degree, to deprive the King of his Royal Authority, so that those who ought to be subject shall command" is therefore also an act of high treason. It follows that it is an act of high treason to conspire to bring about a change in the government, so that "the King shall be compelled to obey authorities which the Constitution of the Government has not required him to obey" (*HT* 1:22). To advocate a change in government "is a conspiracy to depose the King." The written word is therefore an act. "I attribute to the prisoner, together with others," declared the prosecutor, "a conspiracy to depose the King, a deliberate plan to subvert the Constitution of the Sovereign Power as by law established, and to execute that plan by his own force, and by the force of those whom he hoped to draw to his assistance" (*HT* 1:23).

Thus, words are not merely acts, they are acts that wield power, a power drawn from a contagious sympathy with events then unfolding in France and a rampant disaffection in Britain. "Governments can only subsist in the opinion and in the love of people," acknowledged the prosecutor, confident that "the British Government is a Government firmly and deeply rooted in the hearts of the people." Within his constituency, Horne Tooke, like a vile Iago, began to disseminate words designed to alienate the loyal affections of the British people: the conspirators, it was charged, "determined to destroy that attachment, that opinion, which they themselves stated to be the security of the British Constitution, and to constitute the difference between the situation of this Country and the situation of France." The constitution itself is a text, a compilation of words, vulnerable to the effects of other words.

The conspirators endeavored to bring forth new words and to substitute new meanings for old words: "[T]hey taught that no Government could be lawful, but that which was founded on what they called the Rights of Man; which they interpreted to include, among other things, the right of equal, active citizenship." Aghast at the implications of a concept such as "equal, active citizenship," the prosecutor went on to point out that it "was inconsistent with the principles of British Government; for the right of equal, active citizenship, cannot exist with an hereditary King, or an hereditary House of Lords; the moment therefore it was said, that equal, active citizenship was a right of man, an indefeasible, imprescriptible right of man, that no Government could lawfully exist, which was not founded on the principles of the Rights of Man, it was said that the British Government was unlawfully constituted" (*HT* 1:25–26). Speaking these words, "that equal, active citizenship was a right of man," was the act of high treason. And these words were abetted by other words telling the people that the existing government "was a complete system of slavery and oppression; . . . that from this slavery and oppression they must emancipate themselves" (*HT* 1:26).

Here is the crux of the Crown's case against Horne Tooke: "If this doctrine had been established in the minds of the people, a great length would have been gone . . . towards the absolute subversion of the existing Government." The prosecutor thus summed up his indictment against the prisoner: "he meant to use the propagation of those principles as a means to destroy the existing Government, and . . . he did propagate those principles" (*HT* 1:27). With words as his weapons, Horne Tooke led an assault that must be punished by his execution for high treason.

The arguments of the defense counsel were very different from those of Horne Tooke himself. Erskine, his counsel, attempted to disassociate words from acts; Horne Tooke was quite content to grant that words did indeed correspond to mental acts. This disparity might well have undermined their defense had Horne Tooke not also made the case that the implication of words may be reconstituted. The prosecutor, after all, had spoken the very words for which the prisoner had been indicted. Is repeating what someone else has said an act equally punishable? If the import of words cannot be properly understood without reference to the situation in which they were written or spoken, then they certainly will be misunderstood if presumed to refer to some very different situation.[10]

The prosecution emphasized the effect of words on readers and auditors; the defense turned attention back to the situation in which words are used.[11] If the prosecution chose to repeat words attributed to the defendant and averred to be treasonous, then presumably the prosecution's use of the very same words was no longer treasonous because they were being presented for discussion rather

---

10.   The debate over the relationship between words and acts in the court trials of Hardy and Horne Tooke, no less than in the subsequent discussion of Paine's *Rights of Man* in the second volume of *Epea Pteroenta* (1798), clearly anticipates the issues addressed in the speech-act theory of John Austin and John Searle; see John L. Austin, *How to Do Things with Words* (Cambridge, 1965); and John R. Searle, *Speech Acts: An Essay in the Philosophy of Language* (London, 1969). Another anticipation of speech-act theory is John Cleland's *The Way to Things by Words, and to Words by Things* (London, 1766).

11.   The legal status of words as acts obviously makes court records a rich source for documenting basic premises of speech-act theory. See, for example, Dennis Kurzon, "A Speech Act Approach to 'Dead Letter' Legislation," in Hanneke van Schooten, ed., *Semiotics and Legislation: Jurisprudential, Institutional, and Sociological Perspectives* (Liverpool, 1999), 123–37; Christian Schnoor, "Wurzeln des Rechts in der Sprache: Eine Entdeckung des Sprechaktes im Jahre 1909," in *Jahrbuch für Recht und Ethik* 1 (1993). Schnoor argues that the German lawyer Rudolf Henle (1879–1941) should be credited with having discovered and expounded speech-act theory in 1909–10, when he explained legally binding declarations of will, uttered by contracting parties, as constituting actions.

than with the insistence that they be adopted or enforced. Such was precisely the practice, Horne Tooke maintained in his defense, of the Corresponding Society and the Constitutional Society, where passages from Paine's *Rights of Man* were distributed and discussed.

Among the witnesses called by the defense were Charles James Fox[12] and Richard Brinsley Sheridan, as members of Parliament, and Prime Minister William Pitt. The purpose of their testimony was to show that, because Horne Tooke supported parliamentary reform within Parliament, he would be unlikely to seek to overthrow the very process of governmental legislation in which he was actively involved. For many in the conservative establishment, however, Fox and Sheridan were nothing better than co-conspirators. In a series of political cartoons, James Gillray translated their words into images where, precisely as the prosecution contended, Sheridan, Fox, and Horne Tooke were portrayed as Jacobin revolutionaries bent on deposing the king.[13]

Among the many documents the prosecution brought before the court as evidence, which included the proceedings of the London Corresponding Society and of the Constitutional Society, none was decisive in proving Horne Tooke's guilt. Two texts, however, were significant in revealing the complexity of the presumed causality of words as acts. One was *The Rights of Man*, copies of which had been circulated among members of the societies. The other was the letter of Jeremiah Joyce announcing that "Citizen Hardy has been imprisoned" and raising the ominous query "Is it possible to get ready by Thursday?"

In introducing Paine's *Rights of Man* as evidence against Horne Tooke, the prosecution endeavored to show that the defendant was associated with Paine, that copies of the work had been published by members of the defendant's society, and that copies were distributed by the society. Three London publishers and booksellers were called as witnesses: Thomas Chapman, Jeremiah Samuel Jordan, and Joseph Johnson (*HT* 1:147, 215–18). All three testified that they had published and sold copies of Paine's book; Jordan acknowledged that he was the publisher of one of the two editions of *The Rights of Man, Part the Second* (*HT* 1:220). The prosecution requested that sections of *Part the Second* be read into the court record as evidence. Horne Tooke then requested that the preface be read as "not the less suitable to this sort of evidence" (*HT* 1:221). In his summing up, Lord Chief Justice Eyre acknowledged that "the object of reading the

---

12. The relationship between John Horne Tooke and Charles James Fox had not always been congenial; see *Proceedings in an Action for Debt, between the Right Honourable Charles James Fox, Plaintiff, and John Horne Tooke, Esq., Defendant* (London, 1792).

13. *The Works of James Gillray* (1852), reprint ed. (Bronx, N.Y., 1968). See Thomas Wright and R. H. Evans, *Historical and Descriptive Account of the Caricatures of James Gillray* (1851), reprint ed. (Bronx, N.Y., 1968).

preface . . . was to shew that it was written in consequence of Mr. Burke having made some publication, which provoked Mr. Paine to give this answer." Horne Tooke's defense was not simply that Paine wrote in response to Burke's *Reflections on the Revolution in France* (1790) but that Paine and Burke were both addressing a topic being debated throughout Britain (*HT* 2:338–39). Paine's *Rights of Man* had been judged "a direct attack upon the Monarchy of England, and upon the Constitution of the Government of England." Disagreeing with the court case against Paine, Horne Tooke's Constitutional Society had passed resolutions defending civil rights. The prosecution objected specifically to this resolution: "Resolved, That the right of investigating principles and systems of Government, is one of those rights; and that the works of any author, which cannot be refuted by reason, cannot, on principles of good government, and common sense, be made the subject of a prosecution" (*HT* 2:339). The prosecution also presented as evidence against Horne Tooke his part in a plan of the society to distribute six thousand copies of *The Rights of Man*. Horne Tooke did not refute his continuing endorsement of the resolution, and he argued that the *The Rights of Man* was not a covert publication circulated only through the Corresponding Societies but was a book that had been read and discussed by a wide audience (*HT* 2:339–40). Clearly, if this book had the power to enact its own arguments, then the revolution must have already taken place among its many readers.

William Sharpe, the engraver, was called by the prosecution as a member of the Constitutional Society. During the cross-examination, Horne Tooke asked him if he knew of the letter that had been addressed to him by Jeremiah Joyce but that he never received. Once Sharpe confirmed that such a letter was written and sent, Horne Tooke could presume that "it was for this plot that I was apprehended the next day." He revealed the circumstances, noting

> that a letter was intercepted, which should have came by the post to me, on the Wednesday previous to my apprehension—that it was produced before the Privy Council, and made the subject of a very serious examination; that great alarm, and great apprehensions, were entertained from the particular way of wording that letter—and it is for the purpose of cross-examination that I wish to have the letter produced.

In terms of the distinction set forth in *Epea Pteroenta*, "Is it possible to get ready by Thursday?" is a question composed of words referring to other words rather than directly naming specific things and action. Their meaning, as Sharpe explained, was no cause at all for alarm: "there were to be extracts made from the red book, of the sinecures and pensions which Mr. Pitt and his family received from the public." Sharpe continued: "Mr. Joyce called upon me the day Hardy was taken up, and told me he had sent a letter to you, to acquaint you that Hardy was taken up, and desired you to be ready at Spitalfields on Thursday next, with those extracts." The intercepted letter, Horne Tooke revealed to the court, "contained the horrible plot of taking from the Court Calendar a list of large sinecure places and pensions enjoyed by Mr. Pitt, his family and creatures." Yet these words had been mistaken for the words of insurrection (*HT* 1:348–49).[14]

Words that equivocate, contended the prosecution, are as dangerous as words that act immediately. It was on the grounds of equivocation that the prosecution objected to the testimony of Fox and Sheridan, who had testified that Horne Tooke supported parliamentary reform:

> [T]he intent avowed . . . is a Reform of the Commons House of Parliament, and that intent is innocent; but the prosecutors undertake to shew you that this is not the true intent; they say that the words ought not to be so understood; they remark that there is an equivoke in the words which these persons use; that the words Parliamentary Reform are used—radical Reform is used—full representation of the people in Parliament is used—full and free representation of the people in general, without saying in Parliament, is used; all of which, they say, are words that have in them an equivoke. (*HT* 2:417)

The prosecution claimed that in strict reference to the constitution of England, the words "reform" and "representation" might be used "without any equivoke in them, as applied to the Commons House of Parliament." However, the argument continued, these words have a very different import when applied to the activities of the Corresponding and Constitutional Societies.[15]

In summarizing the arguments put forth by prosecution and defense on determining "the context of these words" and "the true interpretation of the words," Lord Chief Justice Eyre instructed the jury "that this interpretation of words, this intent of the party accused, ought not to be left to be made out by nice and verbal criticism." Eyre went on to instruct the jury not to consider the words alone but the words in relation to the other actions of those who use them:

14. That Horne Tooke engaged in "words of insurrection" was documented in other evidence presented by the prosecution: "Mr. Horne Tooke, the prisoner at the bar, is found actually dealing with these subjects, by his intercourse with Hardy, by his interference with the papers of the Society, but, above all, by those more public demonstrations to be collected from the Address to the Jacobins, from the Address to the National Convention, and from the unfortunate publication [letter of 9 November 1792 to the editor of the *Patriot*] in which, in his own hand, he says 'That Liberty is making Herculean efforts, and those vipers, Monarchy and Aristocracy, are panting and writhing under its grasp' "(*HT* 2:433–34; 1:256, 2:352).

15. Dolf Sternberger, "A Controversy of the Late Eighteenth Century Concerning Representation," *Social Research* 38 (Autumn 1971): 581–94.

> [W]here the words are "representative Government," that representative Government, in the strict sense, does not accord with the idea of a Government by King, Lords, and Commons, but that people may express themselves not with grammatical correctness, and that they may mean the very things that they ought to mean, though they use the words "representative Government"; and that, therefore, you are to look further. When you found, in that same declaration, the words "equal and active citizenship," you might then begin to doubt what the parties meant by these words—"representative Government." Therefore, you will consider the words which these men have used, with their context; and you will look at the conduct of the parties who use this words;—for the conduct of the parties will best explain and fix the meaning of anything which is equivocal in the language they use. (*HT* 2:417–18)

In his instructions to the jury, Eyre was clearly aware of how much this entire trial had been about words as acts (acts that incited riots, instigated insurrection, or legislated reform); and about words as words (words that equivocated, or deliberately disguised context and reference).

At the opening of the second volume of *Epea Pteroenta*,[16] Horne Tooke describes an after-dinner conversation that occurs when a guest at Purley, unfamiliar with the house rule laid down by William Tooke, proposes that they discuss Paine's *Rights of Man*. Tooke's rule was quite simple: there shall be no discussion of politics (*EP,* 1:3). As he explained in the first volume, Horne Tooke found his way around this restriction by proposing that their diversions be devoted instead to language. Therefore the dialogue of chapter 1 addresses not the politics of *The Rights of Man* but the meaning of the words "rights of man." Upon determining that Johnson's *Dictionary* provided no satisfactory explanation of the meaning of "rights," the speakers ("H" and "F," that is, Horne Tooke and Sir Francis Burdett) attempt to draw its meaning from its etymology. From historical references, it is concluded that "right" and "right-handed" meant "just," "ordered," "commanded." These meanings, worries one of the speakers ("F"), seem at odds with notions of "freedom" and "liberty":

16. The second volume of *Epea Pteroenta* is dedicated to the members of the jury in his trial for high treason: "To you, Gentlemen, my Jury, I present this small portion of the fruits of your integrity; which decided in my favour the Bill of Chancery filed against my life." A note is added: "The fears of my printer [Joseph Johnson] (which I cannot call unfounded, in the present degraded state of the press) do not permit me to expose the circumstances producing, preceding, accompanying, and following my strange trial for six days for High Treason: or to make any remarks on the important changes which have taken place in our criminal legal proceedings; and the consequent future of the lives of innocent English subjects."

F. Now what comes of your vaunted RIGHTS of man? According to you, the chief merit of men is obedience: and whatever is *Ordered* and *commanded* is RIGHT and JUST! This is pretty well for a Democrat! And these have always been your sentiments?

H. Always. And these sentiments confirm my democracy.

F. These sentiments do not appear to have made you very conspicuous for obedience. There are not a few passages, I believe, in your life, where you have opposed what was *Ordered* and *commanded*. Upon your own principles, was that RIGHT?

H. Perfectly.

F. How now? Was it *Ordered* and *commanded* that you should oppose what was *Ordered* and *commanded*? How can the same thing be at the same time both RIGHT and WRONG?

(*EP,* 2:12–13).

As in his trial, Horne Tooke uses words "that have in them an equivoke." The "RIGHT and WRONG" established by government and court may be at odds with human rights. He uses, that is, the paradox of the word "right"[17] to advocate civil disobedience as obedience to a human right.

> I have always been most obedient when taxed with disobedience. . . .The RIGHT I revere is not the RIGHT adored by sycophants; the *Jus vagum*, the capricious *command* of princes or ministers. I follow the LAW of God (what is *Laid down* by him for the rule of my conduct) when I follow the LAWS of human nature; which, without any testimony, we know must proceed from God: and upon these are founded the RIGHTS of man, or what is *ordered* for man. (*EP,* 2:14)

The concept of civil disobedience, forwarded by Paine and by William Godwin, is articulated by Horne Tooke with the stubborn attention to literal meaning that informed all of his writings on the politics of language and the language of politics.

William Hazlitt, in *The Spirit of the Age* (1824), describes Horne Tooke as literal-minded and unimaginative: "[T]he same shrewdness, quickness, cool self-possession, the same *literalness* of perception, and absence of passion and enthusiasm, characterised nearly all he did, said, or wrote." These were the qualities that

---

17. To illustrate the verbal paradox Horne Tooke cites the following case: "In an action for damages, the Counsel pleaded—'My client was travelling from Wimbledon to London: he kept the LEFT side of the road, and that was RIGHT. The plaintiff was travelling from London to Wimbledon: he kept the RIGHT side of the road, and that was WRONG'"(*EP,* 2:13).

made him "an expert public speaker, a keen politician, and a first-rate grammarian." What was often taken as his wit, Hazlitt declares, was rather "a rigid and constant habit of attending to the exact import of every word and clause in a sentence." His great accomplishment was "his work on Grammar, oddly enough entitled *The Diversions of Purley*. . . . It is, in truth, one of the few philosophical works on Grammar that were ever written." Hazlitt himself had earlier composed *A New and Improved Grammar of the English Tongue* (1810), which he candidly declared to be based on "the Discoveries of Mr. Horne Tooke."[18] Not surprisingly, few subsequent grammarians adopted Horne Tooke's principles of language, except to redress the dangerous implications of the author's account of an extensive class of words as "abbreviations."[19]

Thanking the jury, who had found him not guilty and thus "afforded a just protection to my life," Horne Tooke declared, "We shall both have done good to our Country." He had risked his life on the charge of treason to uphold his belief in freedom of speech: "To prevent the prosecution of other persons for libel, I have suffered a prosecution for high treason." He was confident that the acquittal would be a legal landmark: "I am sure we shall never see such a trial as this again" (*HT* 2:429–31). Unfortunately, the acquittal of Hardy and Horne Tooke failed to curb reactionary oppression. In 1797 Fox moved for the repeal of the 1795 Statute of Treasons and the Seditious Meetings Bill, arguing that "in proportion as opinions are open they are innocent and harmless." Fox's effort was no more successful than Horne Tooke's. Although the fear of revolution in England had subsided, industrial disturbances continued. Bad harvests and the closing of foreign markets had raised the price of corn. Increasing prices were accompanied by rising unemployment. Radical agitation became all the more vigorous. Therefore, rather than acts of suppression being repealed, new acts were adopted. In 1799 the Corresponding Societies Act was passed against all groups that sought to meet in private, declaring unlawful any proceedings that required members to take an oath. Also in 1799 and 1800 came the Act against Combinations, directed against trade unions, specifically against the efforts to organize the textile workers in Yorkshire and Lancashire.

The turmoil of the 1790s produced changes in the language and in the awareness of language. In reaction to the events of the French Revolution, some

18. *A New and Improved Grammar of the English Tongue* (London, 1810), in *The Complete Works of William Hazlitt*, ed. P. P. Howe, 21 vols. (London, 1930–34), 2:1–110.

19. John Fearn, *Anti-Tooke; or An Analysis of the Principles and Structure of Language*, 2 vols. (London, 1824–27); for a very different response, see Charles Richardson, *On the Study of Language: An Exposition of "Epea Pteroenta, or the Diversions of Purley by John Horne Tooke"* (London, 1854); and for an excellent summary of Horne Tooke's work, its context and reception, see Hans Aarsleff, *The Study of Language in England, 1780–1860* (Minneapolis, 1983), 13–14, 44–114.

politically concerned individuals founded a network of Corresponding Societies; in the reaction of the British government to the Corresponding Societies, the members were arrested, charged either with sedition, to be sentenced to transportation to Botany Bay, or with high treason, to be sentenced to execution. The records of the court trials make it evident that the Crown's charges of treason and sedition depended upon equating words with acts and intentions to act. There emerged during the 1790s a vocabulary with new meanings for such words as "citizen," "representation," "rights"; there emerged, as well, circumstances that made the very use of these words ground for imprisonment. Horne Tooke, advocate for the spirit of the age, built his defense on the uses of language.

University of California, Los Angeles

Figure 1. James Gillray, *A Keen-Sighted Politician Warming his Imagination* (London, 13 June 1795); Huntington Library copy.

"Fire, Famine, and Slaughter"

John Barrell

Lord Grenville, the foreign secretary in the government of William Pitt, was famous for the hugeness of his bottom. In this caricature of 1795, *A Keen-Sighted Politician Warming his Imagination* (figure 1), by James Gillray, he has turned his most famous attribute to a roaring fire while he studies a pamphlet entitled, with a nudge and a wink, "The Fundamental Principles of Government."[1] He is preparing to address the House of Lords, where, the suggestion is, he will speak not with his mouth but his arse. Later in this essay I will return to the association between the fundament, or arse, and the imagination; for the moment I use this image simply to introduce the point that, in the discourses of politics and the law in the 1790s, the faculty of the imagination fell on very hard times. Almost no one but Burke had a good word to say for it; and it was Burke's imagination, as displayed especially in his *Reflections on the Revolution in France* of 1790, that had crystallized the sense that in the discussion of politics, the imagination had no place. In the numerous replies to Burke's *Reflections*, the character of Burke's imagination was qualified by a bewildering range of epithets. It is "fine" and "poetic," "lively" and "vivid," "rich" and "luxuriant," "creative" and "prolific." It is "powerful," "boundless." It is "warm," "glowing," "heated," "combustible," "volcanic." It is "debauched," "libertine," "ungoverned," "distempered," "haunted," "frantic," "wild, malevolent." But the variety of these adjectives conceals a high degree of unanimity among Burke's opponents about the nature both of his own imagination and of the imagination itself.[2]

Virtually without exception, those who reply to the *Reflections* in the early years of the decade, even if they admire Burke's imagination, represent it as inappropriately exercised in a work of political theory. The case is made most powerfully in the most powerful replies—those by Catharine Macaulay,

---

1. No. 8659 in Dorothy George, *Catalogue of Satires in the British Museum*.
2. For full citations on these brief quotations, readers are referred to the introduction to my book *Imagining the King's Death, 1793–1796: Figurative Treason, Fantasies of Regicide* (Oxford, 2000).

David Williams, Thomas Paine, Mary Wollstonecraft, Joseph Priestley[3]—but it is made in almost every reply. Repeatedly, the use of the imagination in the *Reflections* is adduced as evidence of a failure on Burke's part to observe the supposedly clear divisions between different forms of cultural and intellectual endeavor: those that are properly undertaken by the imagination, and those that must be pursued by reason, method, and laborious historical inquiry. The "facility" with which ideas are associated in Burke's "lively" imagination, "absolved from the laws of vulgar method," disables him from undertaking "the drudgery of close reasoning."[4] The imagination is on the side of sensibility—of passion, even—and is hostile to reason, judgment, understanding. It is infantile, a symptom of intellectual and political immaturity. It is "extravagant" in the literal sense of the word, for the path of reason is straight, direct; but the imagination has a propensity to err, to wander. It is implicitly feminine or effeminate, with a habit of leaping the uncertain boundary between sensibility and sensuality. It is womanish, too, in being easily terrified, the dupe and prey of alarms, horrors, specters, phantoms—"imaginary dangers" that it has itself conjured up. The alarmism of Burke is frequently described as the effect of a "wild," "distempered," "disordered," "deranged," or "diseased" imagination, with the implication that he was mad or infatuated when he wrote the *Reflections*.

"In this battle of books," writes Tom Furniss of the pamphlet war initiated by Burke's *Reflections*, "both sets of antagonists make virtually identical assumptions about the relation between imaginative discourse and reality; while each relies on the persuasive power of visionary rhetoric, each condemns the other for doing so."[5] This is perhaps to overstate the case—few of the participants in the battle, on either side, are quite as "visionary" in their rhetoric as Burke. It is certainly true, however, that in the pamphlets written in the early years of the 1790s to defend the *Reflections*, and usually therefore to attack *The Rights of Man*, the imagination is not much less frequently evoked—and condemned—than it is by the critics of Burke. Those who wrote against the supporters of revolution in

3. [Catharine Macaulay], *Observations on the Reflections of the Right Hon. Edmund Burke, on the Revolution in France, in a Letter to the Right Hon. the Earl of Stanhope* (London, 1790); [David Williams], *Letters to a Young Prince, by an Old Statesman*, 5th ed. (London, 1790); Paine, *Rights of Man* (1791, 1792, numerous editions); Mary Wollstonecraft, *A Vindication of the Rights of Men, in a Letter to the Right Honourable Edmund Burke* (London, 1790); Joseph Priestley, *Letters to the Right Honourable Edmund Burke, occasioned by his Reflections on the Revolution in France* (1791), 3d ed. (Birmingham, 1791).

4. *Short Observations on the Right Hon. Edmund Burke's Reflections* (London, 1790), 10; James Mackintosh, *Vindiciae Gallicae* (London, 1791), vii; Wollstonecraft, *Vindication* 132, 67, and see 3, 19; and Macaulay, *Observations*, 93.

5. Tom Furniss, *Edmund Burke's Aesthetic Ideology: Language, Gender, and Political Economy in Revolution* (Cambridge, 1993), 257.

general and against Tom Paine in particular tend to argue that to reason on questions of politics from first principles rather than from experience was to make the same use of the imagination as Paine had charged against Burke. The visionary and distorted imagination of Paine is seen to condemn him to inhabit a world no less imaginary than he himself had accused Burke of inhabiting: a world in which "imaginary Systems" of government are supposed capable of redressing "imaginary grievances" or of guaranteeing (by far the most frequent use) "imaginary rights."

The vilification of the imagination, by radical and loyalist alike, continued in the years after the *Reflections* and *The Rights of Man* had ceased to be central to political debate. To radical writers and Opposition M.P.s, Burke's imaginary alarms, his mistaken application of the imagination to the science of politics, became a characteristic of the mentality of all who deplored the revolution in France and defended the unreformed constitution of Britain. To loyalists, not only Paine but also the entire campaign for universal manhood suffrage seemed a kind of disorder or hypochondria of the imagination. And the dangers associated with the imagination became still more salient when, in 1794, the government of William Pitt attempted to suppress the movement for parliamentary reform in Britain by charging its leaders with high treason. They were charged, under the first clause of the medieval law of treason, with having "compassed or imagined" the king's death.

〜 ✌

What did this strange clause mean? and what could or might it be taken to mean in 1794? I can begin to explain by pointing out that in English law you cannot be charged with murdering the king or queen. Indeed, you could murder them with perfect impunity, if only you could prove that you had not previously compassed or imagined their death. The fact that you have murdered them is judicially cognizable only as evidence that you had thus compassed or imagined their death, which is the whole crime; and if you have compassed or imagined their death, you have committed high treason, whether or not you have murdered them or made any attempt whatsoever on their life.

The verbs "compass or imagine" in the law of treason both seem originally to have meant "design" or "intend," and since at least the second half of the seventeenth century, indictments for this species of high treason had begun to include words such as "design" or "intend," or "contrive," "devise," "purpose," alongside "compass or imagine"—apparently indicating that the words of the statute were by then thought to be in need of a gloss. By the second half of the eighteenth century, however, legal authorities were repeatedly commenting on the strangeness of using "imagine" in the purposive sense of "intend"—even "design"—at a time when almost every usage of "imagine" and "imagination" seemed to stress the spontaneous, even the involuntary, nature of imagining.

The meaning of "compass," as used in the statute, occurs in no other context except when the word is implicitly borrowed from the statute itself; this meaning of "imagine" was one that the word had retained in only one other context, the King James Bible, where it had long ceased to be generally understood, even by learned commentators. Indeed, the use of "imagine" and "imagination" in the Bible, which might have been expected to lend the legal meaning of the words a degree of stability, probably did the opposite, by supplying lawyers with such ready-made oratorical phrases as "wicked imaginations" and "evil imaginations," whose meaning in the Bible was by then imperfectly understood. In trials of radicals for high treason in the 1790s the lawyers for the Crown frequently use such phrases to attribute a dark and gothic cast of mind to those they are prosecuting. They speak of the "wicked imaginations" in the heart of the traitor, the "desperate imagination" of the supposed revolutionary, and may well have been thought to be accusing the defendants not of intending the king's death but merely of imagining it in the weak sense—by an association of ideas however involuntary.[6] To these lawyers, of course, the legal meaning of "imagine" was clear enough, at least in theory; the difficulty was to preserve that meaning in actual usage, in the heat of courtroom argument. By the 1790s "imagine" and "imagination" were keys that turned the locks of a number of different discourses. Under pressure from a host of other meanings of "imagination"—in the familiar sense of "picturing in the mind," in the discourses of aesthetics and of psychiatry, in controversial political writings—the fence protecting the legal meaning of "imagine" was broken down, and the word lost all definition, a victim of the instability that is liable to occur whenever such a polyvalent term is required to function as a term of art.

Partly, I am suggesting, those charged with the responsibility of describing the crime of imagining the king's death fell victim to the uncontrollably porous nature of all supposedly "closed" discourses. Partly, however, the instability of the word "imagine" seems to have been the result of the deliberate inflection of its legal meaning with all those meanings supposed to lie outside the discourse of law. The generosity with which the word "imagine" lent itself to figurative and analogical manipulations invited and facilitated a confusion about the nature of the crime of imagining the king's death, a confusion that was differently exploited by prosecuting and defending counsel. The extralegal connotations of the word

6. *State Trials*, 33 vols., comp. T. J. Howell (London, 1811–26), 24:133, 209, 271.

"imagine" could be exploited by the enemies of the reform movement so as to loosen the notion of what it meant to "devise" or "intend" the king's death; in turn, the accusation of "imagining the king's death" could in one way or another be retorted against the accusers by a similar exploitation of the extralegal meanings of the word.

This development had been prepared for by generations of legal authorities who had extended the law of treason by extending the notions of what it meant to intend, or imagine, the king's death and of what was meant by the "death" thus imagined. Early commentators had defined the treason of imagining the king's death as referring to manifest designs to do something by which the king's life would inevitably be endangered; by the mid-eighteenth century it was represented as referring to manifest designs to do anything at all that might threaten the king's life. By the 1790s it was possible for Crown lawyers to charge defendants with intending the king's death on the grounds that, though they were conscious of no such intention, the king's death, or deposition, or at least a change in his constitutional position, would have been the likely, or at least the possible, outcome of their actions.

This progressive loosening of the meaning of the treason of imagining the king's death was justified as a proper and necessary response to what had become over the centuries a defect in the law. The statute had been framed at a time, it was argued, when it made complete sense to identify the survival of the constitution with the survival of the king. The law therefore took no account of what came to be known as "modern treasons" and had to be extended by construction to catch those who, though having no direct designs on the person of the king, had designs against the constitution that, if successful, would arguably be far more dangerous to the safety of the state than the execution or assassination of a king would be. Equally, however, this extension of the statute by construction was to be deplored, by radical and liberal writers, as an attempt to represent as high treason actions that could be represented as such only figuratively or analogically, only by confusing the king's actual body with his political body, his head with his hat. These actions were, in short, "imaginary treason," treasons imagined not by the defendants but by those who were accusing them.

In the trials for high treason of English and Scots radicals in the mid-1790s, this point was made time and time again. It is as if, once the indictment has released the word into the courtroom, a subject has to be found for it. *Someone* has been imagining treason. The defendant, by pleading not guilty, insists that it is not him; who else, then, can it be but his accusers?—who on the basis of actions that import no apparent intention to kill the king have conjured up an imaginary scene of regicide. The government, whether hysterically or maliciously, has lost all grip on the difference between the spirit of democracy and threats to the king's life. The point was made most economically by Richard Newton, the most economical of caricaturists, in the print *Treason!!!* of 1798 (figure 2),[7] which perhaps reveals its full meaning only when juxtaposed with Gillray's image of Grenville's imagination. John Bull points his own generously rotund imagination at the king's picture and farts; Pitt accuses him of treason—it can only be the treason of imagining the king's death, presumably by asphyxiation. Pitt had, according to Coleridge, no imagination at all, and famously had no bottom: indeed, he was known by satirists as "Mr Bottomless Pitt."[8] But bottomless or not, it is evidently Pitt here who is doing the imagining. In the treason trials, this retort—it isn't me, it's *you* who's doing the imagining—seeks to repel the charge of imagining as intending with a countercharge of imagining as picturing in the mind; it then ushers into the court, and into the newspaper and pamphlet commentary on the trials, the various meanings of "imagine" and "imagination" from writings on aesthetics and psychiatry and from the pamphlet attacks on Burke's *Reflections*. The imagination of the prosecution and the government is under the sway of passion, not of reason; it is wildly associating ideas without end; it is inventing "impossible existences," it is disordered, deranged. The English law is boasted to be "the perfection of reason"; surely then it is inappropriate, ungrammatical, to allow its application to be dictated by the imagination. The imagination that framed the charges is identical with the imagination that has manifested itself in the loyalist alarm; either it is inflamed by imaginary fears, terrified by phantoms of its own creation, or it is foul and malevolent, coolly imagining the death of those it has falsely accused of imagining the king's death.

Arguments like these, and the frequency with which they were made in the mid-1790s, are the signs of a struggle for ownership of the languages of law and politics. In the crisis of the mid-1790s, the word "imagine" became a symbolic trophy that the Opposition in and out of Parliament, the writers of radical pamphlets, the defendants in treason trials and their counsel, repeatedly attempted to wrest from the government, its lawyers and its loyalist supporters, and to use against them. To the defendants in trials for high treason, ownership of the word appeared to bring with it the power to bend and blunt the most dangerous weapon in the armory of the government, the statute by which it hoped the

7.   George 9188.
8.   For "Mr. Bottomless Pitt," see the broadside *A New Tragedy, entitled Another Campaign* ([London, 1795]), first published in the *Telegraph*, 16 July 1795. The phrase refers to Pitt's natural home (in Hell); to his lack of any ideological baggage, and hence of sound principles ("bottom"); to his inscrutability and talent for political intrigue ("Deep Will"); to his capacity for alcohol; to his extravagance in pursuing the war (throwing money into a bottomless pit); but also, more literally, to his physique.

Figure 2. Richard Newton, *Treason!!!* (London, 19 March 1798). Copyright, The British Museum.

popular movement for parliamentary reform could be destroyed. The arguments I have sketched out helped in the characterization of loyalist alarmism as a disorder of the imagination, a kind of hysteria by which every demand for political change was imagined as a threat to the king. These arguments helped focus attention on the antique language of law and on the need to purge the statute book of ambiguity. For proponents of popular sovereignty they facilitated the accusation that the government was itself imagining the destruction of the democratic part of the constitution and even of the king himself. And these arguments about imagination may need to be understood also as part of the context in which Coleridge developed his account of the poetic imagination.

❧ ❧

In a letter to the *Moral and Political Magazine* of the London Corresponding Society written in November 1796, a pseudonymous contributor who signs himself "Paramythion" warns his fellow citizens of the dangers of attending "public dinners, free and easy clubs, and other societies wherein singing is introduced as a relaxation from serious business." He has in mind the singing especially of indecent songs and where it might lead:

> Whoever should throw oil on a consuming fire, would, with great justice, be denominated a mad-man; and what name can be more proper for the person who takes the reins of a fiery imagination from reason, to place them in the hands of an inflamed sensibility: yet every one does this, who, by improper discourses raises licentious images in the minds of his hearers, which, by banishing judgment, suffers them to become an easy prey to the inducements of glowing passion. How many of our youth owe their dereliction from virtue to this detestable behavior. Heated by figures, conjured up by the fervor of fancy, and every particle of consideration for future consequences destroyed by the ebullition of the active spirits, they rush heedless into the chambers of the wanton—"Whence without guilt they never more return."[9]

The imagination, escaping the control of judgment, catching fire, heating the figures by which it finds expression, inciting the passions into vicious action— the language here is familiar from loyalist denunciations of licentious radicalism, from radical denunciations of loyalist alarmism, or, as here, from the concern of a radical for the moral purity of the reform societies.

9.   *Moral and Political Magazine* 1 (November 1796): 264–65.

But compare the anxiety of Paramythion with Coleridge's discussion, in *Biographia Literaria*, of how the poetic imagination is manifested in *Venus and Adonis*, and in particular of how Shakespeare's apparently most erotic poem avoids inflaming the sexual appetites of its readers, so that, "though the very subject cannot but detract from the pleasure of a delicate mind, yet never was poem less dangerous on a moral account." For "Shakspeare," Coleridge explains, precludes "all sympathy" with "the animal impulse"

> by dissipating the reader's notice among the thousand outward images, and now beautiful, now fanciful circumstances, which form its dresses and its scenery; or by diverting our attention from the main subject by those frequent witty or profound reflections which the poet's ever active mind has deduced from, or connected with, the imagery and the incidents. The reader is forced into too much activity to sympathize with the merely passive in our nature. As little can a mind thus roused and awakened be brooded on by mean and indistinct emotion, as the low lazy mist can creep upon the surface of the lake, while a strong gale is driving it onward in waves and billows.[10]

The imagination, by this account, is what tames passion rather than what inflames it; the figures it produces are as water, not oil, to the fire. The synthesizing power of the imagination is also a neutralizing agent, which by harmonizing "discordant qualities" disarms them, disarms the passions, of their disruptive force. It does not escape the control of judgment, as Coleridge had explained in the previous chapter, but reconciles it with enthusiasm and vehement feeling, itself remaining under the "irremissive, but gentle and unnoticed controul" of "the will and understanding."[11]

I suggest that one of the numerous origins of the effort, in the second part of *Biographia Literaria,* to "sublimate," as Nigel Leask has put it, the "poetic symbol from the civic or political realm"[12] may be looked for in the arguments about the use of imagination in political discourse and in the quarrels about imagining the king's death, which seem to have helped make the imagination such a dangerous faculty in the mid-1790s. If the imagination was a sublimating and synthesizing power in the *Biographia*, in the political disputes of the 1790s its appearance in political discourse was almost always recognized as a symptom of

---

10. Coleridge, *Biographia Literaria*, vol. 7 of *The Collected Works of Samuel Taylor Coleridge*, gen. ed. Kathleen Coburn, ed. James Engell and W. Jackson Bate (London and Princeton, N.J., 1983), 2:22; henceforward cited in the text as *CC*.

11. *CC* 7; 2:16–17.

12. Nigel Leask, *The Politics of Imagination in Coleridge's Critical Thought* (London, 1988), 160.

division—between itself and the faculty of judgment, between words and intentions, between illusion and reality. But the gap between the bad imagination I have been discussing and the good imagination of the *Biographia* was not as great as it appears. At one moment in his life, Coleridge crossed it with a single step; in one instance, at least, the theory of imagination developed by the "mature" Coleridge in the mid-1810s can be shown to have developed directly out of the arguments about regicidal imaginings of twenty years before.

In January 1798, Coleridge published pseudonymously in the *Morning Post* the poem "Fire, Famine, and Slaughter," which he described as a "War Eclogue," and which is set in "a depopulated tract in La Vendée" where the army of the French Republic was mercilessly putting down the remnants of the ill-fated and British-aided Royalist revolt. Ernest Hartly Coleridge suggests that the poem had been written two years earlier, for in both his pamphlet *Conciones ad Populum* of late 1795 and his periodical, the *Watchman*, in early 1796, Coleridge had deplored the bloodshed in La Vendée and Britain's share of the responsibility for it.[13] There is no reason to doubt that the germ of the poem should be traced to that period, but it was probably being revised and added to right up to the date of its publication, for the poem also describes the atrocities of the British army against the Catholics in Ireland, which first became of concern in Coleridge's political writings in the same month as the poem was published.[14] In the column of the *Morning Post* adjacent to Coleridge's poem there appears Arthur O'Connor's "Address to the Irish Nation," in which those atrocities are also described.

The poem recounts a meeting between the three personifications named in its title, which are seemingly based on the three witches in *Macbeth*. All three, it transpires, had been sent there to do their terrible work of destruction by a man whose name is so terrible, so unspeakable, they dare not pronounce it. They are willing only to hint at his identity, each whispering to the others that "Four letters form his name." Toward the end of the poem the three chant in unison:

> He let us loose, and cry'd Halloo!
> How shall I give him honour due?

13. *The Complete Poetical Works of Samuel Taylor Coleridge*, ed. Ernest Hartley Coleridge, 2 vols. (Oxford, 1912) 1:237n; see Coleridge, *Conciones ad Populum. Or, Addresses to the People* ([Bristol], 1795), 13, 46; and *Watchman, CC,* vol. 2, ed. Lewis Patton (London and Princeton, N.J., 1970), 213.

14. The essay on Ireland of 9 March 1796 in *Watchman, CC* 2:75–77, is concerned with the persecution of Catholics by the "Orange Boys"; military persecution seems not to be discussed until the articles "Ireland and La Vendée," *Morning Post,* 17 January 1798 (attributed to Coleridge by David Erdman); Coleridge, *Essays on his Times, CC,* vol. 3, ed. David Erdman (1978), 11–12; and "Lord Moira's Letter," *Morning Post,* 20 January, *CC* 3, 1:13–17.

Famine and Slaughter answer this question in terms suggesting that "he," whoever he is, cannot hope to escape the forces he has so rashly set in motion. "Wisdom comes with lack of food," chants Famine;

> I'll gnaw, I'll gnaw the multitude,
> Till the cup of rage o'erbrim:
> They shall seize him of his brood.

And Slaughter eagerly interrupts to round off the quatrain:

> They shall tear him limb from limb!

Fire pretends to be shocked by the ingratitude of her companions toward a man who ever since the start of the revolution in France has, as she puts in, "richly catered" for them both. Is it fair, she asks, to repay his repeated favors so peremptorily and so treacherously? For her part, she will remain faithful: she will "Cling to him everlastingly!"—offering him perpetual damnation and a death infinitely prolonged in the unquenchable flames of hell.

Within a few years of the publication of "Fire, Famine, and Slaughter," Coleridge's attitude to the French Revolution had undergone a total change, and he was becoming increasingly embarrassed at being reminded of his recent radical past. In 1817 Coleridge republished the poem in the collected edition of his poetry, *Sibylline Leaves*, explaining in an "Apologetic Preface" that he was doing so because it had been attributed at various times to other poets—as David Erdman suggests, to Robert Southey in particular—"and what I had dared beget, I thought it neither manly nor honorable not to dare father."[15] *Sibylline Leaves* had been printed, but not released, in 1815; when it appeared, in July 1817, the preface must have been read as part of the embarrassing controversy provoked by William Hone's unauthorized publication earlier that year of Southey's regicidal and conventionist dramatic poem *Wat Tyler*, written in 1794.[16] Coleridge, in the second of four articles in defense of Southey in the *Courier*, had absolved Southey—now a true blue Tory—from responsibility for the political beliefs expressed in his poem in terms closely borrowed from those in which, in the "Apologetic Preface," he had just excused the radicalism of "Fire, Famine, and Slaughter."[17]

---

15.   Coleridge, *Sibylline Leaves* (London, 1817), 98, 88; Erdman in *CC* 3, 3:270.
16.   Robert Southey, *Wat Tyler; a Dramatic Poem. A New Edition* (London, 1817).
17.   Compare *CC* 3, 2:458–59, with *Sibylline Leaves*, 95–96; and see Hazlitt's withering attack on Coleridge's *Courier* articles in "*The Courier* and *Wat Tyler*," *The Complete Works of William Hazlitt*, ed. P. P. Howe, 21 vols. (London, 1930–34), 7:196, noting that Southey had himself published a poem apparently in praise of king killing, an inscription "For the Apartment in CHEPSTOW-CASTLE where HENRY MARTEN the regicide was imprisoned Thirty Years"; see *Poems by Robert Southey* (Bristol and London, 1787), 59–60.

ᴪ ᴥ

The "Apologetic Preface" is introduced by two epigraphs, one from Ecclesiasticus, the other adapted and misprinted from Claudian's abject but perhaps ironic apology to the prefect Hadrianus, whom in a previous poem Claudian had imagined, if not dead exactly, at least in a perpetual coma.[18] Together these epigraphs represent Coleridge's poem as an impetuous outburst of his youth, one that it would be ungenerous not to forgive. The preface itself is an attempt to justify the poem by recounting a conversation that had taken place, possibly in 1803, at a dinner party attended by, among others, Sir Walter Scott and Sir Humphrey Davy.[19] According to Coleridge, Scott had recited the poem from memory earlier that morning, and was now asked by one of the dinner guests to recite it again. Scott, the preface points out, was "not only a firm and active anti-Jacobin and anti-Gallican, but likewise a zealous admirer of Mr. Pitt, both as a good man and a great Statesman," and by this remark the preface acknowledges, not as if revealing a secret but as if confirming the obvious, that the four letters that spelled the name of the guilty man—the man whose death the poem had imagined— were *P, I, T, T.* Scott, the preface suggests, must certainly have detested the sentiments of the poem; but as a poet he had been considerably impressed by it and he recited it in such a way as did full justice to its quality. When the recitation was over, however, the host of the party, the scholar and man of letters William Sotheby, suggested to Scott that he had overestimated the poem's merits; and added that even had they been ten times greater than they were, "they would not have compensated," as he put it, "for that malignity of heart, which could alone have prompted sentiments so atrocious": sentiments which, by representing Pitt as an object of detestation, incited the death which the poem had imagined.[20]

To this observation Coleridge was bound to make some kind of reply. One of the company at dinner, Sir Humphrey Davy, "knew, or suspected" the identity of the poem's author,[21] and it would certainly have seemed to him an act of cowardice on Coleridge's part not to engage with Sotheby's judgment or to

---

18. Ecclesiasticus 19:16; the epigraph from Claudian is made up of lines 6–8 and 12 of the "Apology to Hadrian"; see *Claudian*, ed. and trans. Marice Platnauer, 2 vols. (London and Cambridge, Mass., 1963), 2:196–99; for the insulting epigram for which it apparently apologizes, see 2:196–97. Both poems had been made famous by Gibbon's discussion of them at the end of chapter 30 of *The Decline and Fall of the Roman Empire*.

19. The date is suggested by E. H. Coleridge in *Complete Poetical Works*, 1097n.; that some such conversation took place at some time is confirmed by Scott in a letter of 1830; see *The Letters of Sir Walter Scott*, ed. H. J. C. Grierson, 12 vols. (London, 1932–37), 11:442.

20. Coleridge, *Sibylline Leaves*, 89–90.

21. Ibid., 89.

acknowledge his authorship of the poem. Coleridge did confess himself the author, but not before he had entered an elaborate defense of the eclogue, in which he acquitted himself, at least to his own satisfaction, of having incited Pitt's death, or of ever having entertained any malign sentiments toward him.

In the passage later adapted as part of his defense of Southey in the *Courier*, Coleridge claims that, had he himself just read the poem for the first time, he would have suspected the writer to have been "some man of warm feelings and active fancy," and the poem itself to be the product not of any firsthand knowledge of warfare, but simply of

> his own seething imagination, and therefore impregnated with that pleasurable exultation which is experienced in all energetic exertion of intellectual power; that in the same mood he had generalized the causes of the war, and then personified the abstract and christened it by the name which he had been accustomed to hear most often associated with its management and measures.

Above all, Coleridge tells us, he would have guessed that the minister was present to the poet's imagination only as a kind of poetic counter, without feelings and therefore incapable of suffering—never as "a real person of flesh and blood." Acknowledging at last that he is himself the author of the poem, he avers that, when writing it, he was "far . . . from imagining that the lines would be taken as more or less than a sport of fancy"; looking back now to that moment, he is perfectly sure that "there was never a moment in my existence in which I should have been more ready, had Mr. Pitt's person been in hazard, to interpose my own body, and defend his life at the risque of my own."[22]

But these defenses are a kind of epilogue to Coleridge's main attempt to justify the poem, which has involved mounting a defense at once far more and far less radical than this and arguing for a far more thorough dissociation between imagining in the sense of intending and *merely* imagining, in the sense of picturing in the mind or in language. His argument turns on the nature of figurative language and of the imagination that generates it. There is, he argues, a kind of joyousness involved in the invention and development of figurative utterances that is entirely at variance with the intensity of implacable hatred. Poetic imagery dissipates the intensity of the passions; it is, he suggests, something like a polite substitute for swearing, and he compares the "rapid flow" of imagery with "those outré and wildly combined execrations, which too often with our lower classes serve for escape-valves to carry off the excess of their passions, as so much

22. Ibid., 95–97.

superfluous steam that would endanger the vessel if it were retained."[23] Coleridge had earlier developed a similar argument about the Welsh habit, as he believed it to be, of name calling. In 1794, in an inn at Bala, he had provoked a furious argument by proposing a toast to George Washington. Soon, he wrote Southey, the names "Rogue, Villain, Traitor" were flying back and forth; but this, he explained, "is nothing in Wales—they *make calling one another Liars* &c— necessary vent-holes to the sulphureous Fumes of the Temper!"[24]

In the "Apologetic Preface" he invited the company to imagine a conversation more relevant to the fantasy of Pitt's death. Two sailors claim to harbor a desire to take revenge on one of their shipmates, who had done them some serious wrong. The first produces a highly figurative and foul-mouthed account of what he will do, imagining in detail how he will dismember his enemy and devote "every part of his adversary's body and soul to . . . horrid phantoms and fantastic places." The second is much more laconic and literal, as if taking a morbid pleasure in the contrast between the intensity of his desire for revenge and the matter-of-fact language in which it finds expression; for "all deep feelings of revenge," Coleridge assures us, "are commonly expressed in a few words, ironically tame and mild." "I'll tickle his pretty skin!" says the second sailor. "I won't hurt him! oh no! I'll only cut the ---- ---- to the liver!"[25] "I dare appeal to all present," Coleridge continues,

> which of the two they would regard as the least deceptive symptom of deliberate malignity? nay, whether it would surprise them to see the first fellow, an hour or two afterwards, cordially shaking hands with the very man the fractional parts of whose body and soul he had been so charitably disposing of; or even perhaps risking his life for him?[26]

In short, Coleridge is maintaining that the figurative language of "Fire, Famine, and Slaughter" is decisive evidence to establish that it does not mean what it says; that the very fact that he had imagined the death of Pitt in the figurative language of poetry proves that he had nourished no desire to see Pitt dead. "Could it be supposed, though for a moment," he argues, "that the author seriously wished what he had thus wildly imagined," the poem would be entirely indefensible. But surely "the mood of mind . . . in which a Poet produces . . . such

23. Ibid., 91–93.
24. *Collected Letters of Samuel Taylor Coleridge,* ed. Earl Leslie Griggs, 6 vols. (Oxford, 1956–71), 1:89.
25. Coleridge, *Sibylline Leaves,* 91–93.
26. Ibid., 93.

vivid and fantastic images" is most unlikely to coexist, is even incompatible with, "that gloomy and deliberate ferocity which a serious wish to *realize* them would pre-suppose." To desire or to intend the death of Pitt is so different an activity of mind from imagining his death, in the wildly figurative language of poetry, that to do either virtually precludes doing the other. "There is," wrote Burke in 1791, developing his favorite theme of regicide in his *Appeal from the New to the Old Whigs*, "a boundary to men's passions when they act from feeling; none when they are under the influence of imagination." Not so, Coleridge may be thought of as replying: men are dangerous only when they speak their cold desires without the aid of warm figures—exercising "a perpetual tautology of mind in thoughts and words, which admit of no adequate substitutes," and speaking with "that sort of calmness of tone which is to the ear what the paleness of anger is to the eye."[27]

In both the "Apologetic Preface" and the discussion of *Venus and Adonis* in *Biographia Literaria*, passion is the passive antagonist of the active fancy and imagination—and not much if anything in either place is staked on the difference between fancy and imagination, for the nature of both discussions requires that whatever is true of the fancy is true in spades of the imagination. Passion, Coleridge explains, is a state of restless inactivity that, "if not precluded . . . by a constitutional activity of fancy and association," will become morbid, brooding, threatening. By contrast, nothing very terrible need be apprehended from what we merely fancy, merely *imagine*. "These violent words," writes Coleridge, comparing his poem with passages by Jeremy Taylor and Shakespeare, are "mere bubbles," the productions of a "skipping spirit, whose thoughts and words reciprocally ran away with each other."[28] Indeed, the real burden of the "Apologetic Preface" is that Coleridge has nothing to apologize for. It is true, Coleridge says, that he had "wildly imagined" Pitt's death; but the wildness of that act of imagining was the wildness of the poet considered as the antithesis of the wildness of the political activist. The very process of imagining Pitt's death was the means of saving his life; for to imagine his death was at the same time to purge the poet of any malevolent imaginings against him. To read the poem, similarly, is to be dissuaded from any desire to kill him. Not only is what we imagine not what we intend; what we imagine becomes the opposite of what we intend, by the very process of imagining it.

In June 1795, however, in a lecture on the slave trade given a few months before "Fire, Famine, and Slaughter" may have first been conceived, Coleridge had

---

27. Ibid., 91–93; *The Works of the Right Honourable Edmund Burke*, new ed., 14 vols. (London, 1815–22), 6:239.
28. Coleridge, *Sibylline Leaves*, 91–95.

offered a very different account of the imagination. God has given us the faculty of imagination, he then wrote, to enable us to imagine a future better than the present, and to stimulate us to attain it. Imagination, by this account, is not itself a purposive, an intentional, faculty; but it does exist, as Coleridge puts it, to revivify "the dying motive within us"; it is what animates us to turn objects of aspiration into objects of intention.[29] If we were to interpret the imaginings in "Fire, Famine, and Slaughter" in terms of this version of the imagination, it would become a quite different poem from the one Coleridge later defended; not one that speaks the opposite of what we desire, or that magically removes the motive to realize our fantasies, but one that, by imagining an end to the war, stimulates us to take the murderous step—the assassination of Pitt—supposed to be necessary to achieve it.

The "Apologetic Preface," by contrast, is an attempt to take the politics out of the imagination by voiding the imagination of all connection with intention or desire, and so by making poetry, even poetry on political subjects, something that inhabits a quite other universe of discourse from politics itself, one characterized not by conflict but by harmony. As if to underline this, the preface goes on to recapitulate its implied comparison of Scott with Coleridge by a more elaborate discussion of Taylor and Milton. Opposites in politics, Scott and the Coleridge of 1798 are at one in the belief that the products of the imagination transcend the most violent political differences. Both Taylor and Milton imagined the elaborate torture of their political and religious enemies in hell, but because both (merely) imagined it, neither intended it; ideological opposites, as poets they too were at one. By 1817 and the *Wat Tyler* controversy, the separation of poetry from politics, so strenuously contended for earlier, had become for Coleridge so self-evident that it was absurd to question it. "Who in the Devil's Name," Coleridge asked the editor of the *Courier*, "ever thought of reading poetry for any political or practical purposes till these Devil's Times that *we* live in?"[30]

∿ ∾

Those reading Coleridge's impassioned self-defense in 1817, however—even more so those who first heard it, if we believe that his words in the "Apologetic Preface" are indeed "substantially the same" as in the spoken conversation—will certainly have heard in it the echo of the much more familiar, and thoroughly political, ar-

29. Coleridge, *Lectures 1795 on Politics and Religion*, in *CC*, vol. 1, ed. Lewis Patton and Peter Mann (1971), 235; for a similar early account of the imagination, see *CC* 2:131.

30. Coleridge, *Sibylline Leaves*, 94–95, 98–107; *Collected Letters*, 4:713, quoted in Leask, *Politics of Imagination*, 158.

gument whose language it was equally certainly alluding to.[31] The account of the imagination that Coleridge offers in his own defense can be seen as one that emerged directly out of the political crisis, and the crisis in the history of the imagination, that I began by describing. If the argument really was "substantially the same" as the original spoken defense, the "Apologetic Preface" may record his first thoroughgoing attempt to put the imagination at the service of a conservative politics by representing it as elevated above the merely political and as having nothing to do with desire and intention. I want to conclude, however, by proposing that this attempt is much more closely connected to the arguments of the mid-1790s than I have so far suggested; and that what was driving the attempt was more than a desire to disavow a fantasy of the death of the prime minister. The "Apologetic Preface" was also disavowing a fantasy of the death of the king. The clues are everywhere, in the poem itself and in Coleridge's contemporary political writings. I will discuss them in ascending order of persuasiveness, the weakest first.

1. The poem, like a few other poems of Coleridge's published about this time, is signed "Laberius." The Laberius he had in mind was no doubt Decimus Laberius, a Roman knight and writer of pantomime who owed his fame to one incident in his life. In 45 B.C. Julius Caesar, then dictator, compelled Laberius to perform one of his pieces on the public stage, though to do so would be to forfeit his rank. Laberius reluctantly complied, but used the occasion to protest against the loss of liberties under Caesar's rule, and apparently to predict Caesar's death: "Needs must he fear, who makes all else adread." Later that day he added:

> None the first place for ever can retain—
> But, ever as the topmost round you gain,
> Painful your station there and swift your fall.[32]

Radical and Opposition writers seem generally to have seen Sejanus as Pitt's Roman prototype, but their view of Pitt as dictator, anxious not to seem too anxious to get his hands on the Crown, fits the character of Caesar perfectly well. In a speech of December 1794, the radical orator John Gale Jones made the comparison a paragraph or two before accusing Pitt of being "the Prime Mover and instigator of the massacres of Paris, Toulon, and La Vendee,"[33] and it would not be surprising if many other examples could be found. But to the satirists

---

31. Coleridge, *Sibylline Leaves*, 91.
32. William Smith, *A Dictionary of Greek and Roman Biography and Mythology*, 3 vols. (London, 1880), 2:695.
33. John Gale Jones, *Sketch of a Speech delivered at the Westminster Forum, on the 9th, 16th, 23rd, and 30th Mar. 1795* (London, 1795), 41–42.

George III was Caesar too: to the old Etonian radical blackmailer Charles Pigott, for example; and to John Wolcot, who repeatedly satirized the sheer ordinariness of the king by hailing him, in large block capitals, as "CAESAR" or "GREAT CAESAR."[34]

2. The punishment Famine threatens against the four-letter villain includes seizing him "of his brood." We can take "brood" to mean no more than "kind" or "like," and read Famine as threatening to deprive Pitt of his ministers or other supporters. But if we take the more usual and more literal sense of the word, "progeny," the point of the threat appears to be that the multitude will lay violent hands on the villain's family, on his children; and this raises an intriguing question. Pitt had no children; but, more to the point, to suggest that he had, in radical and Opposition circles of the 1790s, would have been to suggest what was widely believed to be impossible. Pitt was famous for his apparent indifference to women and his total abstinence from sex: radical satirists in the mid-1790s remarked on his "maiden coyness"; described him as "Prettygirlibus indifferentissimus"; compared the childless minister with the philoprogenitive king; and linked all this to a presumed preference for masturbation.[35] His sexual abstinence, which his supporters represented as a virtue, was widely satirized by radicals as the result of a physiological deficiency: as well as having no chin and no bottom, Pitt, it was pretended, had no genitals. There is, for example, a political squib of 1795 that describes the imagined death of Pitt; the report on the autopsy notes that the marks of "sexual distinction . . . were not easily to be discerned."[36] The notion that Pitt had fathered a "brood" would have been like suggesting, as in the 1940s lyrics sung to the tune of *Colonel Bogey*, that Goebbels, who had no balls, had children of his own. The king, however (who could be accused as plausibly as Pitt of instigating the war with France), had fathered nine sons and six daughters; and in late 1795 Coleridge had drawn elaborate attention to the clause in the Treasonable Practices Bill that proposed to make it high treason to imagine the death not only of the king and the Prince of Wales but also of any of the king's heirs and successors.

34. [Charles Pigott], *The Jockey Club; or a Sketch of the Manners of the Age, part the Third,* 2d ed. (London, 1792), 19; "Peter Pindar" [John Wolcot], *Liberty's Last Squeak* (London, 1795), 9; *The Convention Bill, an Ode* (London, 1795), 7; and, preeminently, *The Royal Tour, and Weymouth Amusements* (London, 1795), where the appellation is scattered everywhere.

35. See *Mustapha's Adoration . . . Part II, No. II. More Wonderful Wonders!!!* ([London], [1794 or 1795]), first published in the *Courier,* 15 December 1794; and [Robert Merry], *Wonderful Exhibition!! Signior Gulielmo Pittachio* ([London], [1794]), first published in the *Courier,* November 28, 1794, where Pitt, a showman, in the absence of female performers, advertises that he "will indulge the Company with a Solo on the Viol d'Amour." See also the caricature *The Apotheosis of the Virgin in Breeches* (London, 8 June 1802); George 9872.

36. *A Faithful Narrative of the Last Illness, Death, and Interment of the Rt. Hon. William Pitt* (London, [1795]), 10.

3. Indeed, the whole issue addressed in the "Apologetic Preface"—what it means to "imagine" the death of Pitt—is brought forward at a time when the notion of "imagining" a death could not avoid recalling the arguments about imagining the king's death in the 1790s. But the point is more than a matter of general context. The structure of argument in the preface, by which Coleridge acknowledges that he has imagined Pitt's death but disavows "any serious wish to *realize*" it, evidently repeats that of the argument he had developed in his pamphlet *The Plot Discovered* of late 1795, where, attacking the provision of the Treasonable Practices Bill, he defends writers who, in recommending republican government, thereby imagine the deposition (and death, for in law it comes to the same thing) of one of the king's "distant successors," and denies that they ever dream of seeing it "realized," except under conditions that remove all guilt from the desire and its fulfillment.

4. Coleridge had first published his thoughts on the war with France and the revolt in La Vendée in an essay, "On the Present War," which had appeared in the pamphlet *Conciones*. The pamphlet begins with a prefatory "Letter from Liberty to her dear Friend Famine." The essay on the war has a double epigraph, two untranslated passages from Statius's epic poem the *Thebaid*, which describes the war that broke out between the two sons of Oedipus when Eteocles refused to honor the agreement he had made with his brother Polynices that each should reign for alternate years. The first epigraph is from a speech made to Eteocles by an ambassador sent to Thebes by his brother; it denounces the war Eteocles has let loose as "unholy," and it describes that war in terms that closely anticipate those used by Coleridge elsewhere in the essay to describe the civil war in La Vendée. The second epigraph is from a speech made by a former adherent of Eteocles, who has now deserted his cause. It warned the king, just as Coleridge would warn the instigator of the war with France in "Fire, Famine, and Slaughter," that he would deserve the same death as he had inflicted on his enemies and their families. In Statius, this sentence ends with an ironic address to the king, "bone rex," "worthy king"; in the epigraph, Coleridge omitted the last word, replacing it with three asterisks. It may be that the point of this omission was to leave room for the reader to squeeze the four letters of Pitt's name into the space vacated by the word "rex." But it may equally have been to avoid a charge of seditious libel, for had Coleridge included that word, he would have been imagining the king's death in what I have called the weak sense; and if it is for this reason that the king's name is unspeakable in *Conciones*, so it may be in the poem. But the effect of the omission in the epigraph is of course to call attention to what is omitted, and to invite the knowledgeable to discover, in this imagining of Eteocles's death, an imagining of the death of George III, and

in connection with the same events in France as are described in "Fire, Famine, and Slaughter."[37]

5. Finally, at the end of the same letter to the editor of the *Courier* in which he ridiculed the attempts of Southey's enemies to find politics in poetry, Coleridge suddenly found politics in Southey's own *Wat Tyler*. The poem, he suggested, "seems nothing but a string of servile plagiarisms from the Speeches of the *Opposition* Party from 1792 to the Peace of Amiens."[38] A similar plagiarism lies concealed in "Fire, Famine, and Slaughter." In the essay introduced by the epigraphs from Statius, Coleridge quotes a passage from a speech of January 1795 by the great dramatist and political orator Richard Brinsley Sheridan. It concerns the absurdity of supposing that the radical societies, with their tiny armory and war chest, could have launched an insurrection against "the armed Force and established Government of Great-Britain," and it appears to be quoted from the *Morning Chronicle*, which offered a far fuller version of Sheridan's speech than any other newspaper. The *Chronicle*, at this time Coleridge's preferred source of news, was in the process of publishing his "Sonnets on Eminent Characters," including the sonnet to Sheridan, which also appeared in January. In the *Chronicle* version of his speech, Sheridan goes on to argue that a love of liberty is not the same as republicanism and that it is perfectly possible to combine hatred of despotism with reverence for George III. "I am not to be misled by *names*," he declared; "I regard not that the *four letters* are the same which *form* the title of the Despot of Brandenburgh, and of the first Magistrate of this free country."[39] This sentence, in a speech Coleridge knew and admired, appears to be the origin of the four-letter conceit in "Fire, Famine, and Slaughter"; and in Sheridan's speech the "four letters" are *K, I, N, G*. They may still, in the poem, be intended to form the name "Pitt"; but if so, only by an act of erasure that, like the asterisks in the place of "rex," reveals what it pretends to conceal: that behind the fantasy of Pitt's death is a fantasy of regicide.

The conclusion seems to me irresistible. Coleridge may well have thought of "Fire, Famine, and Slaughter" as a poem in which the death that is imagined is Pitt's death, but somewhere in the penumbra of the poem, whether Coleridge recognized it or not, whether or not he knew he knew it, though it's hard to believe he did not, lies the imagined corpse of the king, too. In 1795 Coleridge described Burke's *Reflections* as a "magnificent Mausoleum, in which he has interred

37. Coleridge, *Conciones*, 4–6, 56; *Statius*, trans. J. H. Mozley, 2 vols. (London and Cambridge, Mass., 1928), 1:429, 455–57.
38. *Collected Letters*, 4:714.
39. Coleridge, *Conciones*, 50–51; *Morning Chronicle*, 6 January 1795.

his honest fame."[40] One point of elaborating, in the "Apologetic Preface," the
theory of imagination by which he denies having intended Pitt's death—denies
indeed any connection between poetry and politics—was to erect a tomb, inscribed with the name of the prime minister, beneath which could be interred,
in hugger mugger, the body of George III.

ᴠᴏ ᴄᴏ

The papers for the 1790s of the Treasury Solicitor in the Public Record Office in
London are full of reports of imaginings of the king's death or damnation (which
must be preceded by his death). These explosive outbursts, some perhaps more
or less faithfully reported, some certainly fabricated by false witnesses, have survived in the historical record as traces of the epidemic of disloyalty that true
Britons believed was rampaging through the nation. But their appearance in the
reports of legal proceedings, and among legal papers concerned with intended
prosecutions for "seditious words," is evidence also of an epidemic of loyalist
alarmism in those years, characterized by much the same symptom, a ready disposition to imagine the king's death, but vicariously, by imagining that others
were imagining it. The regicidal imaginings of loyalists were of course partly fac-
titious, as radical pamphleteers frequently pointed out; they were part of an attempt to silence demands for parliamentary reform by representing them as a
threat to the constitutional position of the king and therefore to his life. But the
regicidal outbursts of radicals were no doubt also in part provoked by the fact that
loyalists in the 1790s were apparently so sensitive to any apparent or imaginary
threat to the king's life. However calculated and calculating the phenomenon of
alarmism sometimes seems to be and sometimes certainly was, the tendency
of loyalists to make the king's safety so much the focus of their anxieties invited
both active reformers and the merely disaffected to recognize that here was their
most tender, their most vulnerable spot; that their sensitivity on this topic was
apparently so great because it was inseparable from a guilty knowledge that they
participated in—that it was impossible for them not to do so—the very imaginings they were so anxious to punish in others.

 "Damn the King and Country too!" cursed William Francis, an Essex
innkeeper, in May 1794; "if the French come I wonder who the Hell would not
join them?" "Damn the King and Queen!" cursed Edward Swift of Windsor a
fortnight later; "they ought to be put to Death the same as the King and Queen
of France were. . . . Damn and bugger the King and all that belong to him! . . .

---

40. Coleridge, *An Answer to "A Letter to Edward Long Fox, M.D."* (Bristol, [1795]), in *CC,* 1:332.

Damnation blast the King! I would as soon shoot the King as a Mad dog." The following month a wealthy Oxford Street coachmaker, Jonathan Panther, announced, in language more decorous but no less bloodthirsty, that he wished the heads of all the kings in Europe, and all the royal family, were cut off. "And if I had an opportunity of being their executioner," he continued, "and washing my hands in their blood, I would be contented to have my own hand cut off that instant." In February 1795, Peter Cox, a Cornish miner, drank Tom Paine's health and "perdition to all the Kings of the earth"; no sonner had he done so than "his jaw became locked, and he died on the spot, in the most excruciating torments. He left a pregnant wife, and four helpless infants behind him."[41]

"Fire, Famine, and Slaughter," I am arguing, is a polite and disguised descendant of these plebeian regicidal imaginings, these provocatives to alarmism, that so preoccupied the authorities in the mid-1790s. And the theory of imagination developed in the "Apologetic Preface," and even in the second volume of *Biographia Literaria*, by which Coleridge attempts to sever all connection between poetry and politics, between imagining and intending, must be seen as having in part originated as a disavowal of the poem's ancestry.

Centre for Eighteenth Century Studies
University of York, England

---

41. For Francis, see Public Record Office, London, *Treasury Solicitor's Papers*, 11\1071\3238; after a petition signed by his neighbors and the local vicar, Francis, who was known to be loyal and had spoken his words when drunk, was not prosecuted. For Swift, see *Treasury Solicitor's Papers*, 11\944\3433; Swift was imprisoned for a year (see Clive Emsley, "An Aspect of Pitt's 'Terror': Prosecutions for Sedition during the 1790s," in *Social History* [1981]: 179). For Panther, see *Caledonian Mercury*, 27 October 1794; the case was dismissed. For Cox, see *True Briton*, 2 March 1795.

Trading Words, Waging War: The Mystified Relationship between British Radicals and French *Révolutionnaires*

———————————— PHILIPPE ROGER

The question of interactions between British radicals and their French counterparts during the 1790s is complex when studied in terms of responses to the French Revolution in Britain, and answers are even more elusive when the opposite perspective is considered. This elusiveness is reflected in, as well as reinforced by, the paucity of historical studies from the French perspective, in sharp contrast to the rich bibliography on the British militant groups and their special relationship with revolutionary France. The enduring lack of interest in the topic among French historians can be traced back to the nineteenth century and might well be interpreted as a symptom of the prevailing "patriotic" reading of the French Revolution—although such an interpretation, however convincing in the case of Michelet, would be much less likely to explain, for instance, de Tocqueville's indifference not only to the British radicals but also to any form of British influence on the events in France. However, there is no avoiding another possibility—namely, that the lack of interest among historians simply mirrors or repeats a similar indifference on the part of the French revolutionaries toward their British counterparts and associates. Assessing the impact of British radical thought or experience on the French revolutionaries involves a frustrating attempt to give some historical shape to a slippery, deceptive episode; but here again, the frustration might well reflect the very nature of a relationship best described as a political and cultural *rendez-vous manqué*.

Over the span of only a few years, British radicals and French revolutionaries traded words—of encouragement, of praise, of affection. They also borrowed from each other phrases, slogans, and newly coined terms that they could brandish against their mutual ideological enemies. On the French side, particularly, the semantic and rhetorical aspects of the relationship appear to have been much more important than the political ones. It should be useful, then, to address the question of the French revolutionaries' attitude toward the British radicals in terms of language.

Historical lexicography, a discipline best illustrated in France by the monumental works of Ferdinand Brunot, published in the early twentieth century, has brought to light interesting data concerning the circulation of both political traditions and innovations. Historical lexicography is still a very active component of research on the eighteenth century and the French Revolution; and the work of Gunnar von Proschwitz, who has objected to Brunot's thesis that a "new French language" emerged virtually ex nihilo as a consequence of the Revolution, has been instrumental in renewing the lexicographical debate.[1]

The dating of first occurrences and the trajectory of semantic circulation have traditionally been the main axes of lexicographical work. It is a kind of game among lexicographers to unearth the earliest occurrence of a word—a determination that may be useful, or intriguing, or in some cases (when dissemination has not followed) merely quaint or picturesque. With political language, one has to be particularly careful: concept words (such as *constitution*) or words referring to particular national institutions (for example, *convention*) may be transferred from one language to another without carrying over their original political meaning. In such cases, imported terms may well document the authority and prestige accorded to a political culture identified as superior by the "borrowers"; but they are no proof of a semantically seminal transfer of the notion. Two examples will make the point more clearly.

Datations et Documents Lexicographiques provides us with an earlier date than previously recorded for the phrase *assemblée nationale*.[2] That date is 3 March 1774, when the *Gazette des Deux-Ponts,* a journal published with the encouragement of prince Maximillien-Joseph of Bavaria, reigning duke of Deux-Ponts, uses the expression in an article about American reactions to the Tea Act and the Coercive Acts: "permettra-t-on aux Américains, dans leurs assemblées nationales de se taxer eux-mêmes?" Such a finding raises numerous questions for the historian. What does the redactor mean by these colonial "assemblées nationales"? Could they be the "legislative assemblies" of the Colonies, which had just been disbanded by the British authorities but might be reconvened? Could they mean future "national

---

1. It fell to one of Brunot's foreign disciples, Frazer Mackenzie, a New Zealander, to turn his master's techniques to the study of lexical exchanges between French and English, with a special emphasis on the eighteenth century and the French Revolution. His dissertation, published by Droz in 1939, is entitled "Les relations de la France et de l'Angleterre d'après le vocabulaire," and the first volume was devoted to "Les infiltrations de la langue et de l'esprit anglais," while the second was concerned with reciprocal "infiltrations." The work opens with a long list of acknowledgments, starting with a dedication in Latin to Brunot, portrayed as a new Thomas Aquinas: "Nomen, Numen, Lumen." More sobering but no less significant in its resonance, however, the final dedication is to the "Entente Cordiale"—the Anglo-French diplomatic and military alliance that was at that moment (1939) being severely tested.

2. *Datations et Documents Lexicographiques,* vol. 42, ed. Bernard Quemada and Pierre Enckell (Paris, 1994), s.v. "assemblée nationale."

assemblies" of a still undecidable nature—especially for a European journalist writing roughly six months before the Continental Congress? Did he deliberately fashion a phrase that would titillate his European readers, not caring much about the local (that is, American) accuracy of the expression? And last but not least, who cares? Is it relevant to know what the anonymous redactor of the *Gazette des Deux-Ponts* had in mind? Is this precocious, isolated use of the phrase—in the plural, with an American referent, and in a gazette of limited circulation—meaningful enough to shed light on the semantic reworking of the term during the first months of the French Revolution?

Most lexicographers today are fully aware of the necessary precautions to be taken in handling the chronological information they bring to light. Not only do they warn researchers from other fields against the naive exploitation of linguistic data, but they also participate in the fine tuning of their own interpretative models, showing, for instance, how in some cases the national origin of a word can be misleading. A second example, bearing on the adjective *constitutionnel,* illustrates the problem of semantic circulation. A mock lexicon, published in France in January 1790, made fun of such circulation or "importation": "among [the English] imports to France, the constitutional words form an important article," wrote Nicolas-Antoine Chantreau in his *Dictionnaire national et anecdotique.*[3] Modern lexicographers, while confirming Chantreau's humorous remarks on Anglo-French trade (constitutional words in exchange for claret, as he characterized it), have tried to refine the analysis of semantic exchanges. In a volume published in 1988 in honor of Gunnar von Proschwitz, one can find a detailed study of the same word, *constitutionnel,* and its European destiny. To the question of whether *constitutionnel* is a French word or an anglicism, the lexicographer answers: "The term *constitutionnel,* like *confidentiel, officiel, populaire, popularité, motion* and others, is among those words of English inspiration [a strange lexicographical concept, let it be said in passing] that have settled in most Western languages, not through the intervention of the English Jacobins, but through the mediation of the French language, which was the language of enlightened Europe."[4] Evidence of that mediation, we are told, can be found in the accentuation of the word in such languages as Swedish, which reflects the French rather than the English pronunciation of the word. This conclusion is finally unsurprising—we have learned from historians that important works by

---

3. "Dans leurs [the British] objets d'importation en France, les mots constitutionnels forment un article considérable"; *Dictionnaire national et anecdotique pour servir à l'intelligence des mots dont notre langue s'est enrichie depuis la Révolution, et à la nouvelle signification qu'on reçue quelques anciens mots, par M. de l'Epithète* [Nicolas-Antoine Chantreau], *à Polticopolis, chez les marchands de nouveauté* (n.p., 1790), 13.

4. "'Constitutionnel': anglicisme ou mot français?" in *Idées et Mots au siècle des Lumières: Mélanges en l'honneur de Gunnar von Proschwitz* (Göteborg-Paris, 1988), 77.

English writers were read in French translation in many European countries. But here again, the important task must be to determine the reception of the word and the specific uses to which the newly minted words were put: like coins, such words (that is, *coinages*) do not circulate without suffering some alteration. Particularly in the realm of political culture, a literal translation never occurs. Transferred from one language (and ideological context) to another, a political term becomes a semantic mutant. Under the formal similitude (*constitutional* = *constitutionnel*), a new set of references, connotations, and implications is at work to forge a new meaning. The *constitutionnel* that circulated throughout Europe in French in the aftermath of the 1789 French constitutional debate was no longer the same word as the English *constitutional*. The various European derivations from the French adjective *constitutionnel* cannot be presumed to have conveyed the same meaning (nor to have evoked the same "accessory ideas," to speak like an eighteenth-century grammarian) that was put into circulation by the British reformers or radicals.

By thus refining their own methodology and pointing to the complexity of the world trade in words, lexicographers invite us not to stop at lexicography but rather to widen the semantic scope of the inquiry. In the case of the Franco-British radical relationship of the 1790s, the analysis of lexicographical data must be undertaken with great caution, and for two reasons. First, there is the unequal nature of the exchange, as I suggested above: while French revolutionary terminology occupies an important place in the British radicals' lexicon of the 1790s, the reciprocal movement is infrequent, slight, and hard to document. Second, the lexicographical studies themselves (those of Mackenzie in particular) have shown that it is prior to 1790 and outside of the context of British radicalism of the revolutionary years that the massive "infiltration" by a political and institutional English vocabulary took place into the French language.

❧ ❧

The British radicals are spectacularly absent from the French revolutionary stage —with the salient exception of Tom Paine. But who was Paine to the French? A hero of the American War; a French citizen; a deputy at the Convention by the sovereign choice of the electors of Calais; later on, after his eleven months in jail during the Terror, a lonesome and understandably embittered survivor; as for "un Anglais," that would have been the least likely description of Paine in Paris. The names of Price and Priestley (whose reputations were established much earlier, in the 1770s), although not unfamiliar to French patriots, never reached the heights of revolutionary fame. Those of other radical leaders such as Miller or Thelwall remained unknown to the French public.

Born in 1789 among unavoidable misperceptions, the fragile Anglo-Gallic radical relationship could only be further distorted as the French upheaval gathered momentum. Concurrently, the British movement suffered several setbacks, reaching a low point around 1793–94, and another in late 1795 when it "lay in pieces"—a state in which it would remain for a "full generation."[5] The very eagerness of the persecuted British radicals to become British "Jacobins," even calling themselves "sans-culottes" (as Thelwall did), did nothing to clarify perceptions from across the Channel. Not only did this deference put them under more pressure from a government that was preparing for and then waging war against France, but it also conveyed the idea that British radicals were to take lessons from the "Great Nation," having little to offer of their own in terms of either principles or resources. Even before the appropriation of Scottish and Irish radicalism as military sideshows, British radicals were seen in France in the very light their enemies were trying to cast upon them: as a carbon copy of their French counterparts, if not actually puppets of the *révolutionnaires*.

It is nonetheless true that in the first months of the French Revolution numerous exchanges took place between British societies, especially the London-based Revolution Society, and their French equivalents (or supposed equivalents): "Within the year, no fewer than seventy-seven French societies, most affiliated to the Jacobin society, had replied to the Revolution Society."[6] The London Revolution Society, after addressing its famous "November 4" resolution to the National Assembly, received in due time a congratulatory response. As a consequence, as Edward Royle and James Walvin have pointed out, "this small, obscure and politically insignificant London Society became more widely known in France than in Britain."[7] The exalted epistolary exchanges between French revolutionaries and English radical groups produced, in the early revolutionary years, some curious linguistic effects, especially in the periodicals and pamphlets that reported them to the public. These exchanges can be properly called "congratulation rituals," and were conducted by both British and French societies with elaborate rhetorical flourish. Such political rites raise interesting linguistic questions in terms of both rhetorical and reception theory. Hans-Ulrich Gumbrecht has described the radical rhetoric of the Montagnards as a performance consisting, for the orator, in "convincing those who think the same way you do," or "preaching to the choir," as English speakers might more figuratively

5.　Edward Royle and James Walvin, *English Radicals and Reformers, 1760–1848* (Brighton, England, 1982), 79.
6.　Ibid., 42; see also George Stead Veitch, *The Genesis of Parliamentary Reform* (London, 1913; reprint, [1965]), 130 n. 2.
7.　Royle and Walvin, *English Radicals and Reformers,* 79.

put it.[8] Paraphrasing Gumbrecht's definition, one is tempted to describe the cross-Channel exchanges as, at least for the French societies, so many exercises in convincing themselves that their interlocutors are the same as they are—a task made all the easier by the tendency of the British correspondents to imitate, more and more closely, the French Jacobins' rhetoric, their slogans, their politically coded pathos.

Consider the well-known case of congratulatory salutations between the radical Richard Price ("le fameux docteur Price," as he is called in the *Moniteur universel*) and the duc de La Rochefoucauld, who majestically answered Price's warm encouragements in the name of his colleagues in the National Assembly. It was this exchange, of course, that is known to most readers as the immediate cause of Edmund Burke's *Reflections on the Revolution in France* (1790). Burke was appalled by the interpretation of the English constitution offered up by Dr. Price, alarmed at possible contamination of English opinion, and offended by the idea that the French would take such opinions to be common in England. Indeed, the *Reflections* was begun, so Burke tells his readers in a preface, as a letter to a "young man in France" with the purpose of correcting false impressions in that country. Ever since Burke's polemical attack, Price's letter of friendship on behalf of the Revolution Society has been much quoted and commented upon; so, to a lesser extent, has La Rochefoucauld's answer. But no less interesting than the texts themselves is the way in which these first revolutionary (and at that point strictly epistolary) encounters were conveyed by journalists to the French public. There are, of course, major differences between the rhetoric of 1789, when the exchange between Price and La Rochefoucauld took place, and that of 1793. However, from the well-mannered politeness of a revolutionary, but definitely ducal, answer in November 1789 to the later, more brotherly and "virile" exchanges between "sans-culottes," as both parties referred to themselves, the rhetorical exercise as seen from the French side appears mostly a rite of self-assertion and self-promotion.

Before looking at these accounts in more detail, I want to note that Burke was only one, albeit the most famous, of quite a number of malevolent observers who made fun of these "congratulation rituals." An example of such a derisive view is provided in 1790 by a witty, nasty, and counterrevolutionary former Benedictine monk, Jean-Pierre Gallais, in his *Extrait d'un dictionnaire inutile*. Gallis's facetious lexicon is the richest (and most humorous) of a series of right-wing political pamphlets arranged in alphabetical format. In a style often reminiscent of Rivarol and the *Journal des Apôtres*, Gallais, a born wag, adopts a tongue-in-cheek

---

8.   Hans-Ulrich Gumbrecht, "Persuader ceux qui pensent comme vous: Les fonctions du discours épidictique sur la mort de Marat," *Poétique* 39 (1979): 362–84.

approach to revolutionary innovations. Read nowadays, his *Extrait* presents us with an extraordinary blend of post-Voltairian wit and pre-Celinian extravagance, particularly when he pictures an endless masquerade of foreign delegations peregrinating to the National Assembly. How delightful and gratifying, writes a sarcastic Gallais, to see "les Russes, les Tartares, les Chinois, les Mexicains, les Chiriguanes, les Cafres et les Anglais faire hommage à l'Assemblée, dans des discours bien arrangés."[9] Such orations, Gallais implies, are nothing but political histrionics. Placing the English at the end of a long list of unlikely visitors, Gallais conveys the sense of absurdity that surrounds these "unnatural" British demonstrations of solidarity with the French—an absurdity that, indeed, calls for a much simpler explanation: all these speeches are "arrangés," scripted in advance by the French revolutionaries themselves. It is not surprising that Gallais, an active Royalist (the Parisian printer Weber was to be guillotined for publishing another of his pamphlets in 1793, and Gallais himself was imprisoned during the Terror), should have derided the great parade of cosmopolitanism cherished by revolutionary audiences—at least in the first years of the Revolution.

More revealing than Gallais's screed, however, is the ironic style adopted by the *Moniteur universel* to convey the news of the gatherings of November and December 1789 at which Price and La Rochefoucauld exchanged compliments. A first piece appeared in the 26 December issue of the *Moniteur universel*, reporting on the dinner held in London on 4 November by the Revolution Society. Whether the redactor was a participant in the event is unclear, but his implied nationality is British: "The famous Dr. Price recently preached a sermon to commemorate the revolution that gained us [the British people] Freedom; he finished with the following words"—and here we find the most famous passage of Price's address—"Behold the light that you have struck out, after setting America free, reflected in France, and then kindled into a blaze that lays despotism in ashes," and so on. It was translated: "Voyez la lumière sortie de chez vous pour éclairer l'Amérique, se réfléchir sur la France et produire un feu qui réduit le despotisme en cendres." Such inaccuracy was common in this time of *belles infidèles*, but it is nonetheless interesting to note the significant loss incurred by the first phrase in the French version. "La lumière sortie de chez vous" is both a passive and an ambiguous image; "sortie de chez vous" suggests a departure, an exile, or, more accurately, a transfer: a *translatio lucis* modeled on the *translatio imperii* and *translatio studii*—the notion of the westward movement of empire and the concomitant movement of learning. While the English address praised

---

9.   [Dom Jean-Pierre Gallais], *Extrait d'un dictionnaire inutile, composé par une société en commandite et rédigé par un homme seul, à 500 lieues de l'Assemblée nationale* (n.p., 1790), 34. I have analyzed this mock dictionary in "Le Dictionnaire contre la Révolution," *Stanford French Review* 14 (1990): 65–83.

America and France as the latest conquests of a British-launched revolutionary light, the French translation leaves room for another understanding of the process as a dynamic in which 1688 is far less important than 1789; the French Revolution has now assumed the *flambeau de la révolution*. The discrepancies in the translation provided by the *Moniteur* discreetly reflect a completely different political *imaginaire*: revolution as a relay race, not a handing-down; and France as the new torch-bearing front-runner.

Two days later, on 28 December, the *Moniteur* devoted a second item to the Revolution Society, to its meeting of 16 December, which had culminated with the public reading of La Rochefoucauld's answer to Price. Written this time from a French perspective, the description of the proceedings is, to say the least, devoid of the expected solemnity:

> Le 16 de ce mois, la société des *Révolutionnaires* s'assembla à la taverne de Londres où, après avoir dîné et poré un grand nombre de *toasts*, on profita d'un court *interim* entre ces libations patriotiques pour faire lecture de la réponse du duc de La Rochefoucauld au docteur Price. Cette lettre fut très goûtée, et elle amena une liste de *toasts* constitutionnels anglo-galliques qui semblent annoncer que tôt ou tard il règnera une harmonie parfaite entre les deux nations. En attendant cet heureux moment, le champagne, le bourgogne et les flots de bordeaux en arrosèrent le germe.[10]

Clichés on English intemperance mingle with an abundant and mildly parodic use of political vocabulary, underscored by italicization. The ambiguous translation of "Revolution Society" as "société des *Révolutionnaires,*" a neologism, added an ironic touch to the description. Once again the commemorative purpose of the British Society and its reference to 1688 is ignored. Even though the piece as a whole does not have a malicious tone, it offers a strikingly light, offhand picture of the sympathetic Britons.

From 1789 to 1794, a road seemingly paved with good intentions would lead the French revolutionaries from an amiable levity to indifference, suspicion, and neglect for their allies and admirers from across the Channel, who would be understood and applauded only in direct proportion to their acquiescence to the

10. *Moniteur universel,* 28 December 1789, which may be translated as: "The 16th of this month the Revolution Society gathered at the London tavern, where, after having dined and offered a great many toasts, a short interim between these patriotic libations was allowed in order to read aloud the duc de la Rochefoucauld's response to Dr. Price. The letter was savored, and brought on a number of constitutional Anglo-Gallic toasts that seemed to forecast that sooner or later a perfect harmony will reign between these two nations. Until the arrival of such a happy day, champagne, Burgundy, and tides of Bordeaux watered its seed." Translations of French quotations are the author's.

French Jacobins' political agenda. Exiles fleeing Hanoverian tyranny would generally be given a warm welcome; but French militants and their leaders found themselves at odds with the more moderate tactical program of those among the British radicals who tried to stay and fight on in their own country: their cautious proposals for limited parliamentary reform, rather than the suppression of an institution deemed too corrupt for amendment, could hardly be understood, still less condoned or approved, by the French "clubistes" of 1792–94. The undeniable capacity for mobilization of the British movement in 1790–91 and, more importantly perhaps, the intoxicating rhetorical flourish of exchanged vows and promises had led the French patriots to hope for a prompt success by the radicals in England, at the very moment (autumn 1792) when the tide was turning and the image of revolutionary France deteriorating, even among staunch British reformers. The stereotypical nature of rhetorical exchanges between the French and the British, eerily disconnected from real events, is exemplified by a delegation of the Society for Constitutional Information to the Convention in the fall of 1792, led by John Frost. The delegates far exceeded their mandate, predicting with aplomb that "in a shorter time than we dare say, there will arrive from the continent addresses of solicitations to an English Convention."[11] The French could not do less than take for granted that it would indeed soon be so.

As the months passed (with the swiftness of revolutionary time), official exchanges became more and more disconnected from political realities—wishful statements from the British sympathizers eliciting automatic answers from the French, in an increasingly rigid duplication of the French revolutionary rhetoric.[12] The pragmatic, sometimes cynical, policy of the Directory—appropriating the organized sympathizers in Scotland and Ireland for the implementation of its military strategy—is, in fact, the logical consequence of an unbalanced relationship. When, shortly after the abortive expedition to Bantry Bay, the next French fleet sailed not toward Ireland, which was calling for help under brutal British repression, but toward Egypt, the unexpected destination not only heralded the rise of a new strongman drawing on a new political mythology; it also signaled the end of a worn-out illusion.

---

11.   Quoted in Veitch, *Parliamentary Reform*, 225–26.

12.   The exchange calls to mind the strictly codified communications orchestrated by the Soviet Communist Party between the center and the periphery of the Communist movement in the 1920s and 1930s. François Furet has suggested that the Jacobin party might well be considered the blueprint for modern political organizations as well as the distant ancestor of revolutionary parties such as the Bolsheviks. It would be interesting to explore the unequal relationship between British radical societies and the French "center" of revolutionary power in the early 1790s as anticipating a modern, Comintern-style world organization, devoted to the preservation of the "revolution in one country" but viewing the propagation of its ideas in foreign countries as the best weapon.

～　～

Testimony of the British radicals' presence remains, at best, scarce in the French radical politics of the 1790s. However dubious the task of explaining an absence or accounting for a *rendez-vous manqué*, I would like to explore briefly five of the possible reasons for the frustrations and ultimate failure surrounding these political and ideological exchanges.

I. War

The European war, declared by the French Assembly in 1792 against the emperor, king of Bohemia and Hungary, put the British radicals in a very difficult situation, placing severe constraints on both their travel and their expression. It gave the British cabinet a perfect opportunity to persecute activists. On the French side, the consequences were no less devastating. The discourse of "world citizenship" soon became hollow. During the Terror, the formerly celebrated cosmopolitanism was made into a downright political deviation by Robespierre. A foreigner such as the Prussian-born Anarcharsis Cloots, also known as "the orator of mankind," could not do less than offer to join the French armies to assert his patriotism. (Cloots presented the doubtful Convention with the idea of a "Légion Vandale" of his own conception, in which Prussian volunteers would enroll to fight Prussia; the Convention voted against it. Cloots was to be guillotined in 1794.) But being English was much worse than being Prussian. England became the absolute villain—a role it had assumed so often in the past that the recasting was easy. Sophie Wahnich has pointed out that, in the Terrorist discourse, "the English are, so to speak, the only explicit, concrete embodiment of generic foreignness."[13] The climactic moment in the demonization of the English was undoubtedly the decree passed on 26 May 1794 by the Convention ordering French troops "not to take prisoner any English or Hanoverian soldier." Unanimously approved by the Convention in the presence of Robespierre, who had come expressly to support it, the decree was too extreme to be applied in the field, in spite of repeated threats from the Committee of Public Safety. About a year before the decree was passed, Thomas Hardy and Maurice Margarot had drafted an "Address to the Nation from the London Corresponding Society." In that resolution, dated 8 July 1793, point 12, the shortest of all, reads: "That Great Britain is not Hanover!"[14] They could hardly have expected that their claim would be belied by a decree passed in the French Convention.

13.   Sophie Wahnich, "L'étranger dans la lutte des sections: Usage d'un mot dans une crise politique (5 nivôse an II–9 thermidor an II)," *Mots* 16 (1988): 116.
14.   I quote the address from Christopher Hampton, ed., *A Radical Reader* (Harmondsworth, England, 1984), 369.

Rather than dwelling on the obvious consequences of the European war and the hatred against everything English that it (re)kindled, I turn to a single, telling example of an enlightened pro-British revolutionary mind turned frantically anti-British over a ten-year span, the case of Louis Sébastien Mercier. In his pre-revolutionary *Tableau de Paris,* a best-selling book throughout Europe, chapter 888 in the penultimate volume, published in 1788, is entitled "Langue anglaise." Mercier attests to the progress made in France by both the English language and English political culture:

> Reading the English newspapers is as common in Paris today as it was rare forty-five years ago. This must have influenced our national ideas; literature, although constrained by the narrow taste of our academicians, has taken on an English flavor. Several political books that have been translated into our language have illuminated for us natural laws, as well as civil and political legislation, almost completely neglected by [French] writers of Louis XIV's day—all of them being completely ignorant of the English language.[15]

Let us turn now to his *Nouveau Paris* (1798), a powerful account of the changes that have taken place in the capital since the completion of the *Tableau de Paris* ten years earlier. It is also, and foremost, a powerful, impassioned, and partisan analysis of the major trends, prominent figures, and most crucial episodes of the French Revolution. As a member of the Legislative Assembly, Mercier was close to the Girondins, and he was among the seventy-three who protested when the Girondin leadership was outlawed in June 1793. It is remarkable, if not totally surprising at this point, that his six-hundred-page account of the Revolution from 1789 to the crushing of the Babeuf movement does not include a single reference to the British radicals—Paine included, even though Paine had sided with Mercier in refusing to vote for the king's death and shared the same harsh experience of imprisonment during the Terror. Mercier outdoes his archenemy Robespierre in his imprecations against England: "The bosom of that island nourished most of the calamities that have afflicted us over the course of several centuries."[16] Deep-rooted British hatred for France had recently blossomed in new crimes, among them, he claims, the demise of the Girondins through a secret alliance between Robespierre and the British government. "War," vows Mercier, "eternal war against the Britons until the time comes when they are

---

15.   Louis Sébastien Mercier, *Tableau de Paris* [1788], ed. Jean-Claude Bonnet (Paris, 1994), 1:1127. Mercier adds, ironically for the modern reader: "Lastly, that republican language is not extraneous to the king who governs us—and the better for us, my dear fellow citizens!"

16.   Louis Sébastien Mercier, *Nouveau Paris* [1798], ed. Jean-Claude Bonnet (Paris, 1996), 305.

forced to remain silent in our presence."[17] It is not without significance that this chapter ("Le cabinet britannique"), one of the longest in the *Nouveau Paris,* should close by mentioning the necessity of silencing the English in general. The only (implicit) presence of the British reformers in the chapter is a negative allusion to the antislavery movement (in which militants of the Society for Constitutional Information were instrumental), presented as a ploy on behalf of the British cabinet, a connivance with the reformers to unsettle the French colonies: "It has been proven that it is by diffusing ideas about the black and colored people that [the British cabinet] kindled the torch that set our colonies on fire."[18] A very different kind of light than the one "struck out" in Price's speech— or is it? Mercier's conspiracy theory about England and his global, violent rejection of everything British reflect a widespread French obsession with Pitt's war. And there is no denying the impact of that state of belligerence, nor underplaying the French resentment against "Pitt's agents," "Pitt's gold," and "Pitt's daggers" pointed against French republican bosoms. But war is only one element in a more complex picture. Returning now to the very first months of the French Revolution, I would like to show that, as early as 1789, references to British militant models were likely to fall on infertile soil.

II. Fashion

"Fashion" may appear to be a rather frivolous heading for a reality of far-reaching consequences, namely, the ill-timing of the French and English radicals' first encounters at the very moment that the prestige of the "British model" in France plummeted. A reference to de Tocqueville may be in order, so as to dispel any suspicion of levity. "La constitution anglaise passée de mode," de Tocqueville notes with typical swiftness and accuracy in one of only three fragments mentioning England in *L'Ancien Régime et la Revolution.* De Tocqueville's purpose is "to underscore the passing out of fashion of constitutionalism "à l'anglaise" among the French literati as a key factor in the constitutional debate of 1789. He calls as a witness Jean-Joseph Mounier, who was for a brief time a prominent member of the National Assembly and a good analyst of the events of the summer of 1789: "Only a little while ago, taking at their word a handful of [French] writers, we professed the most exaggerated admiration for England's constitution. Today, everybody pretends to despise it, on the word of some American author whose writings are filled with contradictions."[19] A passage in

17. Ibid., 307.
18. Ibid., 308.
19. "Il y a peu de temps que, sur la foi de quelques Ecrivains, on professait l'admiration la plus outrée pour la Constitution d'Angleterre. Aujourd'hui on affecte de la mépriser, d'après un auteur américain rempli de

Mounier's later, important speech on the *sanction royale* (to which de Tocqueville does not refer) is more explicit: "Less than a year ago, we spoke enviously of the Englishman's freedom, . . . and now we are hardy enough to look with disdain on the English constitution. We are hardy enough to say that the English are not free."[20] The decline of British constitutional values on the fast-moving ideological stock exchange played a crucial part in the radical stand taken by the overwhelming majority of the Constituents, as illustrated by the rejection of bicameralism on 10 September by 249 votes to 89, 122 deputies having apparently not heard the question. As de Tocqueville does not fail to point out, Mounier himself, while a theoretical champion of bicameralism, favored postponing the launching of the two-chamber system until after the separation of the Constituent Assembly—"as though," de Tocqueville comments, "the single chamber of which he so rightly highlights the dangers as a legislative body were not still more dangerous as a constituent body."[21] Keith Baker's analysis of these crucial months concurs with de Tocqueville's intuition: the admiration for the British constitution, or "British Freedom," was no longer a driving force among the French constituents. As early as mid-September 1789, Baker writes, "a first consequence" of the debate was "the triumph of a radical, Rousseauist definition of the constitution": the British constitution ceased to be the central reference, "the locus classicus of constitutional discussion" that it had been in France from Montesquieu on, through Delolme, Blackstone, and John Adams.[22] Another passage in de Tocqueville's manuscript has a marginal note summarizing the situation in one brilliant, paradoxical sentence: "One still lives in the midst of the old French regime with all of its abuses, while England's institutions already seem obsolete and insufficient."[23]

How swift was that shift, and could Mounier have been right in describing it as a sudden change? Looking closely at the National Assembly's proceedings during the summer and autumn of 1789, browsing the everyday exchanges of improvised arguments rather than the more carefully constructed speeches, one

contradictions"; Mounier, *Considérations sur les gouvernements et en particulier sur celui qui convient à la France*, quoted by de Tocqueville, *L'Ancien régime et la révolution: Fragments et notes inédites sur la révolution* (Paris, 1953), 2:209–10 n. 1. According to Mounier's own testimony, the *Considérations* were written on 7 or 8 August 1789. The "American author" is likely to have been John Adams, who had published a *Defense of the Constitutions of Government of the United States* to refute Mably's book on the same topic.

20. Mounier, "Sur la sanction royale," in *Orateurs de la Révolution française*, vol. 1, *Les Constituants*, Bibliothèque de la Pléiade (Paris, 1989), 904.

21. De Tocqueville, *L'Ancien régime et la révolution*, 2:209.

22. Keith Michael Baker, "Constitution," in F. Furet and M. Ozouf, eds., *Dictionnaire critique de la Révolution française* (Paris, 1988), 549.

23. De Tocqueville, *L'Ancien régime et la révolution*, 2:107, b., "On vit encore au milieu de tous les abus du vieux régime français que les institutions de l'Angleterre paraissent surannées et insuffisantes."

is struck by a return of the same dialogues and the same rhetorical scenes, repeated with regard to various topics: the legal definition of a Frenchman, the conditions to be met to cast a ballot, whether ministers should be allowed to sit in the Assembly. In each case, a deputy trying to bolster his argument by invoking the British example is immediately (and successfully) countered by one or several others rejecting a priori any reference to England. Citing the British example thus became the surest way not to carry the floor. There is perhaps no better testimony to the sudden loss of prestige suffered by the British model than these rebukes from deputies with backgrounds as different as those of Target, Lanjuinais, Noailles, the obscure Blin, or the notorious Mirabeau. No less striking is the wording of this brand new suspicion. Blin speaks of the "dépérissement de la constitution anglaise." Lanjuinais bluntly states that "it is not among the English that . . . models should be sought."[24] With typical flair, Mirabeau, who had not been averse to some British name dropping in the earlier debates, finally took the hint and denounced the English electoral system in a November speech: "some here rely on the English example; why base discussion on an absolutely different state of affairs, and why do so precisely on a point where you have unanimously recognized [the English organization] to be quintessentially wrong?"[25] Years before war tore the countries apart, the intellectual divide is obvious.

III. America

In the decline and fall of the "British reference," a major role was played by "American affairs," as they were called in Paris in the 1780s. The apex of Anglophilia (a strong current in France since Voltaire's *Lettres anglaises*) among French men of letters can be situated in the 1760s and 1770s—lexicographers and historians agree on that. But the interest, soon a passion, that was focused on the American events reversed the situation in a short while. French enthusiasm—the Parisian craze for the insurgents and everything American—was a decisive factor in unmaking the positive political image of Great Britain. In the complex triangulation of the political debate between England, America, and France, the disparaging arguments launched against British tyranny by the colonists or the British Whigs, once they were culturally as well as literally translated into French, proved disastrous for the political reputation of "marâtre" England—a wicked stepmother mistreating her children. That this new, damaging image of British politics was a polemic being shaped, to a significant degree, by British radicals, reformers, and pro-American Whigs, is a reality that was soon to be lost

24. *Moniteur universel,* 7 November 1789.
25. Ibid., 18 November 1789.

in translation. However, such an astonishing unanimity favoring British-bashing in the National Assembly raises the suspicion that two very different discourses had converged and temporarily reconciled: a "leftist" American criticism of Hanoverian despotism; and a much more conservative hostility toward British institutions, criticized as being stained by corruption and strained by violent convulsions and permanent unrest.

The French Revolution coincides with a disenchantment among the elites with the British political tradition: a disenchantment, accelerated and aggravated by the American crisis, that was eventually detrimental, in the French perception, even to those in England who fought along with the insurgents, verbally or otherwise. Made suspicious of "English liberties" by England's unfair treatment of its colonies; and disillusioned with radicals whose avowed goal was to mend, not destroy or replace, a corrupt parliamentary institution and a wicked monarchy, the French Jacobins of 1793, from the bottom on up, now have no qualms about reasserting a deep-rooted anti-English passion. In the *adresses* sent by provincial societies to the Convention, the English (although they did not fight during the first year of the war) are identified as the archenemies of revolutionary France more often than the Austrians or the Spaniards (who had invaded France's territory in 1792).[26] As Michel Vovelle comments, "This also reflects hopes turned sour: the English have recognized what liberty is, but they do not care to attain it; and the English people are enveloped in the global condemnation brought against their tainted government."[27]

In that bitter process, the part played by Burke's "defection" should not be underestimated. As early as November 1790, Burke gave a name and a face to dashed hopes, while casting a dark shadow upon British revolutionary dependability. The impact of Burke's *Reflections on the Revolution in France*, quickly translated in French and widely read, was all the more devastating owing to his great reputation. One of the very few well-known British radicals in France, he had been eulogized that same year, to the delight of the National Assembly, as a "fiery Republican" as well as an "unmoveable Whig" ("ce whig invariable")[28]—a most unfortunate description, in retrospect. His devastating attack against revolutionary France was a severe blow to the abashed French patriots; it also opened a serious confidence gap between them and their decidedly unpredictable British brothers.

26. See Sophie Wahnich, "La notion d'étranger en l'an II; les constructions d'un dialogue Paris-Province dans les *Archives parlementaires,*" *Annales historiques de la Révolution française* 62 (1990): 381–403.

27. Michel Vovelle, "Entre cosmopolitisme et xénophobie," in *Nations and Nationalisms: France, Britain, Ireland, and the Eighteenth-Century Context,* ed. Michael O'Dea and Kevin Whelan, *Studies on Voltaire and the Eighteenth Century,* no. 335 (Oxford, 1997).

28. *Moniteur universel,* 9 February 1790.

IV. Ill-fated Friends

With "ill-fated friends" (as opposed to *faux frère* Burke), I would like to draw attention to another aspect of Franco-British intellectual relations during the revolutionary decade. It would be interesting to look at the personalities and careers (both intellectual and political) of those French Anglophiles active during the period. A detailed mapping of such characters, a chart of their contacts, readings, and political agendas would be a useful counterpoint to the study of the highly codified official and collective exchanges between the radical societies and political bodies of the two nations. British political culture and ideas would probably appear to have been familiar mostly to a handful of French intellectuals who happened to withdraw soon or be withdrawn from the political stage. Let me mention two cases to support this assertion, those of Suard and Bonneville.

Jean-Baptiste-Antoine Suard was the editor of the *Journal de Paris.* He had been in personal contact with Walpole, Wilkes, Smith, Douglas, Stewart, Gibbon; and he was the proud owner of the best English-language library in France (an estimated two-thirds of his five to six thousand volumes were English books or books translated from English). As a political thinker associated with Malouet and the *monarchiens,* he attempted (unsuccessfully) in 1789 to reconcile rather than oppose the British and American models. It was his ambition to mesh the two political experiences into an anti-Rousseauist compendium—a task he never completed because of the Revolution, according to his account, but perhaps also because of its difficulty. After the downfall of the *monarchiens,* his situation became clearly isolated, shared only with his friend Morellet—a position he did not disclaim, calling his newspaper (which ceased publication in 1792) *Les Independans.* The case of Suard is illustrative of those few British-leaning French intellectuals who would quote Temple, Sidney, Bolingbroke, and (more rarely) John Adams, but who did not care for Paine; in his vast English culture, the most recent authors played a minor role; politically, he was a moderate and would later become moderately conservative.

Far from Suard, but far also from the political centers of revolutionary power, stands another good connoisseur and supporter of British reformist ideas, Nicolas Bonneville. His intellectual personality and political destiny make him a good example of another kind of marginalization. An *homme de lettres* interested in linguistics, political science, and the occult, he was a member of both the Cercle Social and the Amis de la Vérité, the latter a small but active group that preached, with a mystical accent, world revolution and political regeneration. Bonneville, a polyglot with a preference for English, had published David Williams's *Lettres sur la liberté publique* (in Brissot's translation)—the same David Williams who was to be granted French citizenship in August 1792. Bonneville had put his newspaper, *Le Tribun du Peuple,* under the moral patronage of his English predecessor Junius Brutus; and it does not come as a surprise that he corresponded with John Horne Tooke, mostly on linguistic matters. An Anglophile to the left of the political spectrum with a knowledge of and appreciation for English radical thought, Bonneville, always an original, would soon become no less marginal than the conservative Suard. He was never elected to office (he was defeated twice in the municipal elections, in 1790 and 1791). With the persecution of his Girondin friends and Brissot's doom, he was then beyond the political pale.

V. The Semiotic Creed and the Uniqueness of French Revolution

Finally, I would like to underscore that the semiotic creed, combined with the prevailing notion of the French event as something thoroughly new, "sans exemple," would logically convince French revolutionaries, as early as 1789, of the impossibility, indeed the impropriety, of any linguistic, semantic, or symbolic borrowing. Mirabeau's rejection of English precedents in November 1789 ("Why base discussion on an absolutely different state of affairs?") must be interpreted in the more general frame of the neological nature of French revolutionary politics. "Mirabeau a rendu la France néologue": such was the strange eulogy granted him by revolutionary grammarian Urbain Domergue in his *Journal de la langue française.*[29] Mirabeau imposed political neology as a decisive weapon against the old order; but neology was not only a tactical choice, it also reflected the deliberate attempt to shape a new political world, in fact and in words. And Mirabeau was only the first and most powerful of the numerous voices who would command French to recreate itself an act of both purification and foundation. The step was quickly taken from prerevolutionary infatuation with English as the language of politics (and economics) to the repudiation of all foreign models. The next step soon followed: after refusing the imports, the Revolution would encourage the exportation of the "language of the rights of man." Abbé Grégoire made it clear in 1794 in a strangely phrased maxim: "Il faut qu'on ne puisse apprendre notre langue sans pomper nos principes" [It must become impossible to learn our language (a desire apparently taken for granted by Grégoire) without swallowing our principles].[30]

29. *Journal de la langue française,* 8 October 1791.
30. Grégoire, "Rapport sur la nécessité et les moyens d'anéantir les patois et d'universaliser l'usage de la langue française (16 prairial an II)," in Michel de Certeau, Dominique Julia, and Jacques Revel, eds., *Une politique de la langue: La Révolution française et les patois* (Paris, 1975), 315.

～ ～

Another British radical tradition should not be left out of the story: that of clas-sical republicanism. It is not easily traceable through specific wording or explicit quotations in revolutionary texts or speeches, except for the occasional praise of Burke as a "fiery Republican." It has rarely been taken into account by scholars of the French Enlightenment and the Revolution, some of whom deny it any significant influence on French political thought. Here again I will side with Keith Baker, who argues that, far from being unknown to the French, the lan-guage of classical republicanism ran as an undercurrent from Rousseau and Mably to Marat. Such language was indeed, insists Baker, "a significant feature of French political culture on the eve of the French revolution."[31] Even though most his-torians have failed to recognize it, the discourse of classical republicanism did find its way through eighteenth-century French political theory to reemerge pub-licly with Marat, Robespierre, and Saint-Just. Hardly recognizable in its new French and Rousseauist clothes, that late French version of classical republican-ism radicalized the necessary suspicion toward all power and rewrote the narra-tive of the ancients' historical pessimism in terms of sublimity and sacrifice. Although the British reference, Baker suggests, was eliminated as early as 1789 in its constitutional version by the enlightened gentlemen of the Constituent Assembly—and was treated with condescension, suspicion, or indifference in its more radical, grass-roots versions—it would thus take a secret but spectacular revenge through the Maratist and Robespierrist reinterpretations of British clas-sical republicanism, which bypassed the less visible and barely intelligible British radicals of the 1790s. Marat would thus become one of the unlikely proponents of a radical British tradition—or maybe not so unlikely, if we recall his political debut, in England and in English, in the context of Wilkite agitation: his pub-lishing *The Chains of Slavery, A Work wherein the Clandestine and Villainous Attempts of Princes to Ruin Liberty are pointed out, and the Dreadful Scenes of Despotism disclosed, to which is Prefixed, An Address to the Electors of Great-Britain, in order to draw their Timely Attention to the Choice of Proper Representatives in the Next Parliament* (1774). Reprinting the same book in French, in late 1792, Marat insists in a footnote on its relevance to the French situation: his appeal to the English voters of 1774, he writes, "can very well be applied to the French voters" of 1792. On the one hand, Marat is trying to sell an obsolete book to a rather un-interested crowd, *L'Ami du Peuple* being at a low ebb at that moment. On the

31. Keith Baker, "Transformations of Classical Republicanism in Eighteenth-Century France," *Journal of Modern History* 73 (2001): 22–53.

other hand, the assertion has some durable truth to it. Harsh as it is, the comparison is grounded in Marat's central political conviction that revolutionary defiance is a perennial necessity that transcends all particular political circumstances. Suspicion and "surveillance" never fall out of fashion as political models do: they represent the core of every experience of confrontation with power as well as the primary, permanent duty of every individual fighting against any particular instance of that power. Politically marginal until 1792, Marat's special blend of violent republicanism "à l'antique," rephrased in a rhetoric that can be described as both populist and sublime, is an original rewriting, at one and the same time, of the English script and the ancient source. It would become, after his assassination, the prevailing or, more precisely, the last available discourse of the Robespierrist leadership.

Such are the delayed ways of cultural circulation, even in politics. It took the French many years to discover what Blake, Coleridge, and Wordsworth had been thinking and writing at the time of the Revolution. Meanwhile, it was certainly easier for revolutionary France to listen to the Maratist and Robespierrist echo of that older British tradition of republicanism than to hear what the British radicals of the 1790s had to say. Are not the British more understandable, anyway, when they speak in Latin?

Ecole des Hautes Etudes en Sciences Sociales et Centre d'étude de la langue et de la littérature françaises des XVIIe et XVIIIe siècles, Paris

The Loves of the Plants; or, the Cross-Fertilization of Science and Desire at the End of the Eighteenth Century

FREDRIKA J. TEUTE

The last decade of the eighteenth century was a period of intellectual ferment and social experimentation, as well as one of political innovation. In this revolutionary period, the transatlantic flow of radicalism included more than political opinions and the people who expressed them.[1] To take the most obvious example, print was not only a key medium of transmission but also an iconology in itself as a transformative force in the process of universal enlightenment.[2]

The preeminent arena in the search for transcendent laws governing nature and human society in the eighteenth century was science. The Enlightenment's course of scientific investigation and postulation of rationality left its tracks in the thinking of political renovators of the era.[3] An American generation born during the Revolution, bypassing politics, instead made the pursuit of objective knowledge their agenda for achieving the goals of human improvement and rational relations. For many young American intellectuals, among the published texts signaling the possibilities of a new age dawning were Erasmus Darwin's *The Botanic Garden* (1791) and Mary Wollstonecraft's *A Vindication of the Rights of*

I thank the participants at the Clark Library conference "British Radical Culture of the 1790s" for their comments on an earlier version of this article, particularly Peter Reill, director of the Center for 17th- and 18th-Century Studies, UCLA, and Robert Maniquis. Bruce Burgett, Joyce Chaplin, Lorna Clymer, Rachel Crawford, Michael Meranze, and Michael Warner have given me essential insights into the topic. Fellowships at the Huntington Library and American Antiquarian Society supported research for this article.

1. Robert R. Palmer, *The Age of the Democratic Revolution: A Political History of Europe and America, 1760–1800*, 2 vols. (Princeton, N.J., 1959, 1964), is the classic overview of the spread of democratic ferment at the end of the eighteenth century. The most recent work on transmission of radical politics between Great Britain and America is Michael Durey, *Transatlantic Radicals and the Early American Republic* (Lawrence, Kan., 1997).
2. Adrian Johns, *The Nature of the Book: Print and Knowledge in the Making* (Chicago, 1998), esp. 444–542.
3. Gordon S. Wood, *The Radicalism of the American Revolution* (New York, 1992), 361–64. For the impact of science on the new American nation's founders, see John C. Greene, *American Science in the Age of Jefferson* (Ames, Iowa, 1984); Silvio A. Bedini, *Thomas Jefferson: Statesman of Science* (New York, 1990); I. Bernard Cohen, *Science and the Founding Fathers: Science in the Political Thought of Jefferson, Franklin, Adams, and Madison* (New York, 1995); and Robert Ferguson, *The American Enlightenment, 1750–1820* (1994; Cambridge, Mass., 1997).

Woman (1792). Embedded in each was a clarion call for social progress, linking scientific knowledge with institutional critique and sexual freedom. Attempts to propound a new order of personal relations founded on innate, universal characteristics paralleled the scientific quest to classify the natural world.

In New York City, Dr. Elihu Hubbard Smith (1771–98) was at the center of a circle of aspiring men and women who enacted Enlightenment ideals of intellectual, political, and social inquiry. The Friendly Club, a weekly gathering of young male professionals organized under Smith's auspices, provided a structure for both homosocial intercourse and a wide-ranging interrogation of history, political economy, philosophy, and science as well as contemporary issues of great moment. In their outlook, they tended toward freethinking, deism, antislavery, and elite republicanism. This fraternity included, besides Smith, dramatist William Dunlap, novelist Charles Brockden Brown, Presbyterian divine the Reverend Samuel Miller, physician Dr. Edward Miller, jurist William Johnson, lawyer Anthony Bleecker, and physician-senator Dr. Samuel Latham Mitchill. Surrounding these men and intervening in their homosociality in ways essential to their sense of self-completion was a group of young women. Besides the wives of their friends, Johnson, Mitchill, Edward Miller, and Smith frequently sought the company of Margaretta Mason, Maria Nicholson, Maria Templeton, and Margaret Bayard. They shared with the men ideals of personal fulfillment, intellectual achievement, and commitment to human progress through reading, critical discussion, writing, and conversation. This mixed company constituted a larger association of friends whose social interactions completed the Friendly Club's agenda of individual and social improvement.[4]

The Friendly Club circle's activities encompassed medical practice, publishing enterprises, dramatic productions, antislavery activities, conversation-making, diary-keeping, and letter-writing. In this diverse set of practices, Smith and his friends, male and female, sought to cultivate improved selves in a com-

---

4.   See *The Diary of Elihu Hubbard Smith (1771–1798)*, ed. James E. Cronin (Philadelphia, 1973), 45–46, 392, 448, 449, 459, passim, on Smith's, the Friendly Club's, and associated women's activities; 28 February 1799, March–April 1800, 8 July 1800, Commonplace Book, 1799–1803; 27 March 1827, Commonplace Book, 1809–1829, Margaret Bayard Smith Papers, Library of Congress (hereafter MBS Papers, DLC). These women came from prominent families; Mason's, Nicholson's, and Bayard's fathers were leaders in the Revolutionary War. The women themselves would participate in the public life of the new nation. Margaretta Mason in 1799 married Senator John Brown of Kentucky. Maria Nicholson's sister Hannah married Albert Gallatin. In 1800 Margaret Bayard married Samuel Harrison Smith, the Jeffersonian editor of the *National Intelligencer*, and they moved to the new capital in the District of Columbia. Maria Templeton became the wife of a member of the Friendly Club, William Johnson, in 1809. See entries for C. B. Brown, John Brown, John Bayard, Albert Gallatin, and James Nicholson in the *Dictionary of American Biography*.

munity of interest and affection. Among them, science was a crucial collabora-
tive medium for intellectual and social exchange. The women botanized together; the men instructed the women in Lavoisier's chemical principles.
Scientific conversation became a vehicle for experiencing sociability and sharing sensibility; heterosexual company made rational discourse affective. Smith
promoted the social virtues of science to Americans through his various publishing ventures. With two of the men, Drs. Miller and Mitchill, Smith inaugurated the first successful medical journal, the *Medical Repository,* in 1797. A
year later, Smith brought out the first American edition of Erasmus Darwin's
*The Botanic Garden. A Poem in Two Parts. Part I. Containing The Economy of
Vegetation. Part II. The Loves of the Plants. With Philosophical Notes* (1798). At the
same time, Smith also edited and published his friend Charles Brockden Brown's
first novels and published his own opera, *Edwin and Angelina* (1797). From publications and personal reflections emerged an ideology of friendship that strove
for objective relations bonded by subjective sympathy. Natural science, with its
methodologies of observation and classification and descriptions of an organic
world, provided both model and metaphor for a new system of social relations
built upon both affinity and distinction. Intellectual inquiry and individual aspirations merged in a quest for complete human fulfillment.

To these men and women in New York, Mary Wollstonecraft's promulgation
of social intercourse based on equitable rights signified the ideal. She exemplified
the Enlightenment, questioning conventions and seeking rational principles. She
cultivated the social "sciences," "gratifying her friends" by her publications. Her
death in 1798 was "an incalculable loss for intellect & truth." The news caused
"to most of our circle . . . so severe a pang" that the "loss of 50,000 french" soldiers in their resistance to counterrevolutionary forces would have been less
wrenching. Joined in Wollstonecraft's life were the causes of reason, science, print
dissemination, social revolution, and love.[5] She organized her personal life based
on her political beliefs in individual freedom. Reason, however, contained its
own undoing. Her pursuit of self-realization unleashed sexual desires that undermined control of her own fate. William Godwin's *Memoirs* of his wife exposed
the fault line in nature's mix of self and other. The intellectual, political, and personal experiments of the 1790s imploded from the combustible mix of reason
and desire embedded in the taxonomic hierarchies projected on plant and animal life.

---

5.   21 October 1797, Elihu Hubbard Smith to Idea Strong; 5 November 1797 entry; 7 November 1797, Smith
to Samuel Miles Hopkins (*Diary,* ed. Cronin, 382, 386, 389).

Modern science was rooted in an ideology of reason that was meant to subordinate human passions but instead ultimately unleashed them. Reason and passion are inextricably entwined. Prefixed to rationality is its opposite, for the impulse to design the world with rationality was fundamentally irrational. The polarization of order and chaos involved both an ideal of reason and a fantasy of unreason. Eighteenth-century skeptics and freethinkers intended to dismantle hierarchies; as they did so, they inevitably installed others. The attempt to demystify secular and religious authority involved another sort of mystification, nature's rationality. Ordering nature naturalized order, establishing categories that erected hierarchies and systematized difference. Complexity of form and sexual function became distinguishing characteristics informing rational principles for analyzing the social organization of life. In the arrangements of nature, scientific observation posited metaphors for human relations, and humans found license in scientific laws to experiment in heterodox political and social ideas.[6] Cross-fertilization of reason and feeling in the late Enlightenment produced a radical sensibility that spawned a multiplicity of models for social relations.[7]

~ ~

In 1789 English physician and poet-naturalist Erasmus Darwin (1731–1802; grandfather of Charles Darwin) published a didactic poem, *The Loves of the Plants*, printed in Lichfield and sold in London by radical publisher and bookseller Joseph Johnson. In 1791 Darwin added a part 1, *Containing the Economy of Vegetation,* to *Loves of the Plants,* and the whole work was entitled *The Botanic Garden,* also published by Johnson in London. Darwin's purpose was

> to inlist Imagination under the banner of Science; and to lead her votaries from the looser analogies, which dress out the imagery of poetry, to the stricter ones, which form the ratiocination of philosophy. While their particular design is to induce the ingenious to cultivate the knowledge of Botany, by introducing them to the vestibule of that delightful science, and recommending to their at-

---

6. Janet Browne, "Botany in the Boudoir and Garden: The Banksian Context," in David Philip Miller and Peter Hanns Reill, eds., *Visions of Empire: Voyages, Botany, and Representations of Nature* (Cambridge, 1996), 159–65; and Alan Bewell, "'On the Banks of the South Sea': Botany and Sexual Controversy in the Late Eighteenth Century," in ibid., 173–93.

7. Chris Jones, *Radical Sensibility: Literature and Ideas in the 1790s* (London and New York, 1993), viii, 1–4, 10–17, 85–107, passim; and Jerome McGann, *The Poetics of Sensibility: A Revolution in Literary Style* (Oxford and New York, 1996), 5–8, 13–18.

tention the immortal works of the celebrated Swedish Naturalist, Linnæus.[8]

Darwin, whose works were published in the mid- to late eighteenth century, was one of several English botanists who promulgated to a general readership Carl Linnæus's taxonomy of plants. In adopting the poetic genre, Darwin explicitly sought to convey the rigors of scientific knowledge through the pleasures of fancy. The phrase "that delightful science" indicated both that botany specifically conjoined sensory and intellectual stimulation and that imagination and rationality were conceptually linked, even interdependent, entities. "In the first Poem, or Economy of Vegetation," Darwin put forward "the physiology of Plants . . . ; and the operation of the Elements, as far as they may be supposed to affect the growth of Vegetables." In the second part, *Loves of the Plants* (published first, as noted above), "the Sexual System of Linnæus is explained, with the remarkable properties of many particular plants."[9]

There Darwin's imagination took erotic flight. Propagating the Linnæan sexual system for classifying plants, Darwin let sexual relations multiply and proliferate on the page. His verse teemed with a full panoply of male-female and same-sex permutations and variations.[10] In *Loves of the Plants* Darwin simultaneously attributed humanality to plants and naturalized sex in humans. Beneath his seeming anthropomorphization of the vegetable kingdom was his belief that plants feel.[11] Assigning gender roles to male and female, he declared,

> What Beaux and Beauties crowd the gaudy groves,
> And woo and win their vegetable Loves.
>
> (2.1, 9–10)

Taking off on the heterogeneity of vegetation's reproductive systems, Darwin ramified the multiple combinations of stamens (males) and pistils (females). The resulting plethora of alternative sexual liaisons smothered any normative heterosexual, monogamous model. His poem promoted an organic vision of all of life

---

8. [Erasmus Darwin], *The Botanic Garden. A Poem in Two Parts. Part I. Containing the Economy of Vegetation. Part II. The Loves of the Plants. With Philosophical Notes* ([London: J. Johnson, 1791 (pt. 2 first published, Lichfield: J. Jackson, 1789)]; 1st American ed. from 3d [pt. 1] and 4th [pt. 2] London eds.; New York: T. and J. Swords, 1798), ed. Elihu Hubbard Smith, "Advertisement to the London Edition," unnumbered page. Unless otherwise noted, all quotations are from this edition, cited henceforward in the text by part, canto, and line.

9. Ibid.; Ann B. Shteir, *Cultivating Women, Cultivating Science: Flora's Daughters and Botany in England, 1760 to 1860* (Baltimore, 1996), 17–26.

10. Londa Schiebinger, *Nature's Body: Gender in the Making of Modern Science* (Boston, 1993), 30–32.

11. Desmond King-Hele, *Doctor of Revolution: The Life and Genius of Erasmus Darwin* (London, 1977), 190–97; and Maureen McNeil, *Under the Banner of Science: Erasmus Darwin and His Age* (Manchester, 1987), 87–89.

responding to impulses unmediated by conventional institutions. Populating the poem are passionate women,

> The freckled Iris owns a fiercer flame,
> And *three* unjealous husbands wed the dame.
>
> (2.I, 71–72);

five sister nymphs,

> Each wanton beauty, trick'd in all her grace,
> Shakes the bright dew-drops from her blushing face;
> In gay undress displays her rival charms,
> And calls her wondering lovers to her arms.
>
> (2.I, 113–16);

vamps,

> The fell Silene, and her sisters fair,
> Skill'd in destruction, spread the viscous snare.
> The harlot-band *ten* lofty bravoes screen,
> And, frowning, guard the magic nets unseen.
>
> (2.I, 139–42);

and potent males,

> *Four* of the giant brood with Ilex stand,
> Each grasps a thousand arrows in his hand;
> A thousand steely points on every scale
> Form the bright terrors of his bristly mail.—
>
> (2.I, 161–64)

Darwin consigned his scientific information to extensive notes in small type at the foot of the page, thereby subordinating scholarly annotation to poetic license.

Following Linnæus's classification, Darwin described flowers in his poem by the classes of male reproductive organs (stamens) and orders of female pistils found in each. The first classes contained both sexes and were arranged according to the number of males in the blossom; XII had twenty males; XIII, "*Polyandria*," had "Many Males." The next classes depended on the "Powers," that is, the different heights, of the stamens. The ways in which males adhered in "their union" to the females determined succeeding classes: "One Brotherhood," "Two Brotherhoods," "Many Brotherhoods," "Confederate Males," and "Feminine Males." Two classes of plants had flowers containing only one sex, "One House" and "Two Houses"; in "Polygamy," there was a mixture of single-sex and both-sex flowers. Finally, in "Clandestine Marriages," flowers were not discernible in the plants.[12]

With this last, he evoked images of autoeroticism or secret orgies, for

> The fair Osmunda seeks the silent dell,
> The ivy canopy, and dripping cell;
> There, hid in shades, *clandestine* rites approves,
> Till the green progeny betrays her loves.
>
> (2.1, 93–96)

Fertilization between parent-plant and offspring provided imagery of incest in a Gothic brew of passion and transfixed horror at its outcome:

> So, in her wane of beauty, Ninon won
> With fatal smiles her gay unconscious son.—
> Clasp'd in his arms, she own'd a mother's name,—
> "Desist, rash youth! restrain your impious flame,
> "First on that bed your infant-form was press'd,
> "Born by my throes, and nurtur'd at my breast."—
> Back as from death he sprung, with wild amaze
> Fierce on the fair he fix'd his ardent gaze;
> Dropp'd on one knee, his frantic arms outspread,
> And stole a guilty glance toward the bed;
> Then breath'd from quivering lips a whisper'd vow,
> And bent on heaven his pale repentant brow;
> "Thus, thus!" he cried, and plung'd the furious dart,
> And life and love gush'd, mingled, from his heart.
>
> (2.1, 125–38)

Darwin rather gleefully suggested at the outset the naughtiness and illicit pleasures offered in his poetic vision, especially for female readers. In his "Proem" to part 2, the naturalist-poet evoked the aura of a peep show. Summoning the "Gentle Reader," he offered "a Camera Obscura . . . to thy view, in which are lights and shades dancing on a whited canvas, and magnified into apparent life!— If thou art perfectly at leisure for such trivial amusement, walk in, and view the wonders of my Inchanted Garden." Reversing Ovid, who "did, by art poetic, transmute Men, Women, and even Gods and Goddesses, into Trees and Flowers; I have undertaken, by similar art, to restore some of them to their original animality, after having remained prisoners so long in their respective vegetable mansions; and have here exhibited them before thee. Which thou may'st contemplate

---

12. [Darwin], *The Botanic Garden*, pt. 2, pp. iii–iv.

as diverse little pictures, suspended over the chimney of a Lady's dressing room, *connected only by a slight festoon of ribbons.*"[13] The poet exulted in a titillating riot of possibilities; anything goes, Darwin seemed to say. Including for women. The poem exuded the joy of love for both sexes:

> Oh! stay, bright habitant of air, alight,
> Ambitious Visca, from thy angel-flight!—
> —Scorning the sordid soil, aloft she springs,
> Shakes her white plume, and claps her golden wings;
> High o'er the fields of boundless ether roves,
> And seeks amid the clouds her soaring loves!
>
> (2.I, 257–62)

The last canto ended with the polyandrous plant Adonis in which

> A *hundred* virgins join a *hundred* swains,
> And fond Adonis leads the sprightly trains;
>
> . . . .
>
> —Thick, as they pass, exulting Cupids fling
> Promiscuous arrows from the sounding string;
> On wings of gossamer soft Whispers fly,
> And the sly Glance steals side-long from the eye.
> —As round his shrine the gaudy circles bow,
> And seal with muttering lips the faithless vow,
> Licentious Hymen joins their mingled hands,
> And loosely twines the meretricious bands.—
> Thus where pleased Venus, in the southern main,
> Sheds all her smiles on Otaheite's plain,
> Wide o'er the isle her silken net she draws,
> And the Loves laugh at all but Nature's laws.
>
> (2.IV, 489–90, 497–508)

With this celebration of a promiscuous Tahitian marriage ceremony, Darwin signaled rejection of church-sanctioned rituals of monogamous marriage and endorsement of free love. The sexual diversity of plant life had its corollary in human cultures. Botany proved to be a medium for the exploration of heterogeneous sexuality and a conduit for politicized social commentary.

Darwin's evocation of Tahiti suggested both nature, innocent of civilization's restrictions, and male scientific exploration, suffused with sexual libertinism. Although he treated with a light touch promiscuity, incest, and pornography, by

---

13. Ibid., ix–x.

the end of the century these themes resonated with more tolerant sexual practices and carried radical political and social connotations. Analogized to the penis, the mimosa, the famous sensitive plant, figured in pornography of the period. Satirists made use of it to lampoon Joseph Banks's corruption by his exposure to Tahitian women and exotic flowers on James Cook's first voyage to the South Seas.[14] By exoticizing its erotic sensitivity to touch, Darwin played off the plant's pornographic associations:

> Weak with nice sense, the chaste Mimosa stands,
> From each rude touch withdraws her timid hands;
>
> . . . .
>
> Veil'd, with gay decency and modest pride,
> Slow to the mosque she moves an eastern bride;
> There her soft vows unceasing love record,
> Queen of the bright seraglio of her Lord.—
> So sinks or rises with the changeful hour
> The liquid silver in its glassy tower.
> So turns the needle to the pole it loves,
> With fine librations quivering as it moves.
>
> (2.I, 299–300, 307–14)

However prurient the male perspective was in *Loves of the Plants*, that the personified female flowers averred desires and enjoyed sexual gratification empowered women to think and act on their own behalf. The poem contained a double appeal for women. It provided both a language and models for critiquing sexual mores and social institutions. Darwin's provocative personifications invited women to attend to scientific understanding and to enter into imaginative identification with the subject, "though thou may'st not be acquainted with the originals, [they] may amuse thee by the beauty of their persons, their graceful attitudes, or the brilliancy of their dress." The poem engaged intellect and legitimated individual desire: it activated sensibility. This was the radicalism of the late Enlightenment's message to women, whether the purveyors of the message

---

14. Cook's voyages to the South Pacific in the 1760s and 1770s exposed Englishmen to a wealth of information that opened to question and eroded European standards of normative social behavior. Banks accompanied Cook on the first voyage (1768–71) as a scientific explorer and became a subject of controversy as knowledge of his sexual adventures in conjunction with his collecting expeditions on shore became known in the 1770s. See David Philip Miller, introduction to Miller and Reill, eds., *Visions of Empire*, 1–18; Browne, "Botany in the Boudoir and Garden," 160–61; Bewell, "'On the Banks of the South Sea,'" 174, 176–85; Schiebinger, *Nature's Body*, 33; Roy Porter, "Mixed Feelings: The Enlightenment and Sexuality in Eighteenth-Century Britain," in Paul-Gabriel Boucé, ed., *Sexuality in Eighteenth-Century Britain* (Manchester, 1982), 1–27; and Robert M. Maniquis, "The Puzzling Mimosa: Sensitivity and Plant Symbols in Romanticism," *Studies in Romanticism* 8 (1969): 129–55.

always intended females to pursue its full implications or not. The exuberance of intellectual and social experimentation was contagious.[15]

By portraying all of life's forms as organized around sexual reproduction, Darwin imagined plants and animals along with humans, as partaking of common instincts, emotions, and manners arising from their sexual impulses. His organicism celebrated the social affections and sensory pleasures found in nature. He shifted the basic principle of natural existence away from Lockean notions of sentient intellect to sexuality. This concept, of an organism's qualities existing or predicated with regard to sex, first arose from Darwin's *Loves of the Plants*. William Cowper remarked in 1800, "It is on their sexuality that he has built his poem." With the introduction of this notion, sexual characteristics as biological "facts" were naturalized, and socially determined gender attributes could be disassociated from sexual distinctions. In nature, all shared equal capacities for feeling and thinking. The immediate effect was liberating, freeing individuals' behavior from social norms.[16]

This is not to say that Darwin and Linnæus before him did not erect sexual and class hierarchies, gender-inflected, male-dominated, and rank-biased. Linnæus's project to establish a systematic classification of natural life was part of an Enlightenment restructuring that imposed a human intellectual order on a nature that increasingly had been construed as disorderly. The Western Hemisphere's cornucopia of environmental information and of variegated plant and animal life both prodded the pursuit of and posed problems to taxonomic systems. The world's variety undermined universal laws even as it provoked the search for them. Indeed, over the course of the eighteenth century, scientific knowledge did not progress in a straight line. Naturalist-scientists diverged in their paths of investigation and conclusions. Most famously, Georges-Louis Leclerc, comte de Buffon, rejected the basis of Linnæan nomenclature as artificial and employed an environmental, comparative approach that led to his typifying many American species as having degenerated in the New World environs

15. [Darwin], *Botanic Garden*, pt. 2, p. x (quotation); Browne, "Botany in the Boudoir and Garden," 159–61; and Bewell, "'On the Banks of the South Sea,'" 175–77. I place more importance on this empowering aspect of Darwin's poem than does Shteir (*Cultivating Women, Cultivating Science*, 27). However conventional in its virgin- or vamp-like imagery, *Loves of the Plants* places women in control. See G. J. Barker-Benfield, *The Culture of Sensibility: Sex and Society in Eighteenth-Century Britain* (Chicago, 1992), 351–95. On the eroticism of the poem and the interaction of mental analysis and emotional sensation, see McGann, *Poetics of Sensibility*, 131–35.

16. McNeil, *Under the Banner of Science*, 87–89. See "sexuality," *OED*; Thomas Laqueur, *Making Sex: Body and Gender from the Greeks to Freud* (Cambridge, Mass., 1990), 154–57, 171–75. See William Godwin, *Enquiry concerning Political Justice and Its Influence on Modern Morals and Happiness* (1793), ed. Isaac Kramnick (1976; Harmondsworth, England, and New York; reprint ed., 1985), 16–24, on an emerging anti-Lockean perspective at the end of the eighteenth century that emphasizes individual diversity and empirical judgment.

from Eastern-Hemisphere archetypes. Linnæus's and Darwin's publications, then, were part of an ongoing debate over the nature of nature's structure.[17]

❧ ❧

Choosing to issue Darwin's *Botanic Garden* in a "first American Edition" in 1798, Elihu Hubbard Smith indicated the agenda of his cohort of Enlightenment enthusiasts. Protagonists of America as the outpost of human progress and universalist potential would have found Darwin's perspective more compatible with their vision than Buffon's. By publishing, and publicizing, Darwin, Smith was implicitly rejecting Buffon's denigration of American specimens and environment and endorsing the Linnæan-Darwinian view of nature. In *Zoonomia* Darwin propounded an evolutionary theory of life forms' adaptations to their desires and needs that was more consonant with ideals of American perfectibility than Buffon's theory. In his attempt to classify animal orders, Darwin emphasized primal desires (lust, hunger, and security) as the stimuli of transformation. Focusing on the power of senses as prime movers in human improvement, he connected sensory reactions to a theory of diseases. Smith deemed *Zoonomia* "the most masterly performance ever given to the world on the subject of Medicine." His colleagues published this work almost as soon as it appeared in print in England. Dr. Samuel L. Mitchill edited part 1, and the printers to the Columbia College medical school published it in 1796. The following year part 2 appeared in print in Philadelphia.[18]

17. Schiebinger, *Nature's Body*, 28–31, 37–39, 79–80; and Shteir, *Cultivating Women, Cultivating Science*, 16–17. Joyce E. Chaplin develops the theme of eighteenth-century openness in views of nature, resisting the teleology of scientific objectivity. The naturalist-artist Mark Catesby, for instance, working with New World specimens at the same time as Linnæus developed his taxonomy, ignored or rejected the Linnæan system and described a far more ecologically grounded and functionally determinative natural history. His incipient theory of nature appears to be ruled by disorder and destructive forces ("Mark Catesby: A Skeptical Newtonian in America," in Amy R. W. Meyers and Margaret Beck Pritchard, eds., *Empire's Nature: Mark Catesby's New World Vision* [Chapel Hill, N.C., 1998], 34–43).

18. Erasmus Darwin, *Zoonomia; or, The Laws of Organic Life*, 2 vols. (London: J. Johnson, 1794–96), esp. chap. 39; Erasmus Darwin, *Zoonomia; or, The Laws of Organic Life*, vol. 1 (New York: T. and J. Swords, 1796). The Swords brothers published other works of the Friendly Club in the 1790s, including Smith's edition of *Botanic Garden*. Charles Caldwell edited part 2 of *Zoonomia*; Erasmus Darwin, *Zoonomia; or, The Laws of Organic Life*, pt. 2, 2 vols. (Philadelphia: Thomas Dobson, 1797). Darwin also laid out his theory of the origins and evolution of life in his poem *The Temple of Nature; or, The Origins of Society. A Poem, with Philosophical Notes* (London: J. Johnson, 1803), published in America a year later by T. and J. Swords (New York, 1804) and Bonsal & Niles (Baltimore, 1804). See King-Hele, *Doctor of Revolution*, 238–46, 288–97; McNeil, *Under the Banner of Science*, 92–98; and 19 October 1796, Smith to William Buel (*Diary*, ed. Cronin, 236).

Darwin's goal of systematizing knowledge about animal forms and diseases influenced Smith's determination in 1796 to initiate a quarterly periodical, the *Medical Repository*. By collecting and publishing accounts from every region of the United States, he intended to produce a comprehensive "History of the Diseases of America." Smith signed up friends for subscriptions to all three publishing ventures (*Zoonomia, Botanic Garden,* and the *Medical Repository*), forwarded copies of the works to them, and solicited in return useful material for the journal. In his cultivation of a network of collaborators, Smith purposefully established circuits for transmitting scientific information and publications among his fellow Americans.[19]

On this side of the Atlantic, a rising generation emerged after the Revolution carrying forward a faith in human reason and stamping it with a distinctively American mark. They believed in the preeminent power of mind over physical circumstances. The desire to dispel human misery, superstition, and ignorance by dispensing scientific knowledge prompted Smith to make Darwin's work available to an American audience of "readers of Poetry" and "students of Nature" in an affordable and convenient volume. The London edition of *Botanic Garden* was a deluxe, quarto two-volume set selling at twelve dollars or more in America, which placed it beyond the reach of most of its likely readers. Indeed, commented Smith, it was "more adapted for a library than for daily use." In England, the high price presumptively made *Botanic Garden* the preserve of an exclusive, upper-middle-class and aristocratic readership—also immunizing it from government censorship on the assumption that costly books contained no dangerous content. In this case, the price reserved to a relatively safe elite class the consumption of the text's underlying radical ideas of sexual license and social critique. Smith's intention, on the other hand, was to disseminate Darwin's work to "a large & respectable portion of the human race," thereby extending the welfare of mankind. In the intellectual investigations that were beaming truth into human darkness, "the prism of Darwin illuminated & beautified the dazzling reflection, with the primitive radiance of reason, & the rainbow hues of fancy."[20]

19. 11 August 1796, 19 October 1796, Smith to William Buel; 17 August 1796 entry, "(Circular) To the Physicians, of the United States"; 16–30 June 1798 entries (*Diary*, ed. Cronin, 201, 236, 204–6, 449–53, passim). On a trip home in June 1798 at the same time that he was soliciting subscriptions to his forthcoming edition of *Botanic Garden*, Smith spent time botanizing, assiduously following the Linnæan system. Interestingly, he had difficulty determining the class of a plant based on the number of stamens. Linnæus's sexual classification was ultimately abandoned in the nineteenth century. See Catherine O. Kaplan, "Six Degrees of Elihu Hubbard Smith: A Cultural Network of the Early Republic, 1795–1798" (paper presented at the Omohundro Institute of Early American History and Culture Colloquium, 3 May 2000, Williamsburg, Va.), for an argument about the creation of cultural capital and its circulation among Smith and his confreres.

20. [Darwin], *Botanic Garden*, "Advertisement to the American Edition"; 10 August 1798, Smith to Darwin; 17 October 1795 entry (*Diary*, ed. Cronin, 461, 74); Browne, "Botany in the Boudoir and Garden," 153–58.

The American edition was in itself designed to further this agenda. The volume stood as an exemplar of the state of American printing arts and an example of American utilitarianism. The publishers had sought "to attain convenience and cheapness, without any censurable sacrifice of correctness and elegance." The London edition was too expensive, and the Dublin octavo edition most commonly circulating in America was shoddy goods, according to Smith, full of mistakes and inaccurate illustrations. Comparing size, paper, and type, Smith proclaimed the single-volume American edition of "commodious form," superior to the Irish and not inferior to the English. The plates were "executed in the best manner the state of the arts" in New York City would allow. He and the publishers had made "all suitable exertions to give it to the world in a dress worthy of the American press."[21]

Smith took his projection of American arts and letters one step further. He inserted himself into the volume. In one bold stroke, he both brought himself to the attention of Darwin and his circle in England and deployed his own local cultural credit on behalf of the book. Smith prefaced the American edition with his poetic "Epistle / To the Author of the Botanic Garden."[22] He thus invited comparison with the likes of English poets William Cowper, William Hayley, and Richard Polwhele, whose odes to Darwin were included at the front of *Botanic Garden*. But he outstripped their polite encomiums with an ambitious, six-page hortatory poem celebrating and exemplifying the rise of human intellect. "Fond Science" presided over the spread of knowledge as progressive developments in communicative forms culminated in type and the printing press. With this triumph, Science overcame barbaric ignorance and tyrannical power. "Genius and Taste," once only for "lords" and "monks," was now available for

> . . . old and young, the humble and the poor.
> Hence, wide diffused, increasing knowledge flies,
> And error's shades forsake the jaundiced eyes;
> Man knows himself for man, and sees, elate,
> The kinder promise of his future fate;
> Nations, ashamed, their ancient hate forego,
> And find a brother, where they found a foe.

Proof of the equalizing and universalizing effects of print and science lay in the circulation and lasting impact of the "Botanic Song" throughout the world. Not

---

21. [Darwin], *Botanic Garden*, "Advertisement to the American Edition"; unnumbered page, 10 August 1798, Smith to Darwin (*Diary*, ed. Cronin, 461).
22. [Darwin], *Botanic Garden*; poem follows advertisement, unnumbered pages; 10 August 1798, Smith to Darwin (*Diary*, ed. Cronin, 461).

only did it improve readers then; it would also incite "the prying mind" to further investigate the nature of "each differing clime":

> Till one vast brotherhood mankind unite
> In equal bands of knowledge and of right.

With ignorance defeated, "loud proclaim . . . immortal, Darwin's name." By composing and including this didactic poem, Smith too became a participant in the enlightened prospect of illuminating human minds with scientific knowledge through the egalitarian medium of print. By printing an American edition, he proved his own point about the efficacy of print. In promulgating Darwin, he publicized himself, American arts and letters, and rational principles.

As Smith said in the advertisement to his edition, Darwin's work needed no introduction to an American audience. *Botanic Garden* was a huge success in the 1790s on both sides of the Atlantic, going into a fourth London edition by the end of the decade, as well as three Irish editions and the American one. Knowledge of and demand for the book spread quickly. The original version of *Loves of the Plants* appeared in print in April 1789; by the fall a copy had reached Greenfield, Connecticut, where Smith had "first perusal of it, at my friend and former instructor, Dr. [Timothy] Dwight's." The contents inspired in Smith at the time a desire to bring out an American edition. It met a ready audience. By 1799, John Hartwell Cocke, then a student at the College of William and Mary, later a southern planter with enlightened social views concerning slavery and a correspondent with the Transcendentalists, owned a copy, apparently for use in his study of natural philosophy under the tutelage of Bishop James Madison. *Zoonomia* and *Botanic Garden* were essentials in doctors' medical libraries. Smith's circle in New York read regularly in both. One of the women, Margaret Bayard, noted "Darwin" in her commonplace book in relation to books on natural history for children. By 1807, the intention of Smith and his colleagues to provide "their countrymen" the opportunity "of possessing a book so pleasing in its manner, and so fruitful of instruction" had been greeted with enough enthusiasm to warrant a second edition of *Botanic Garden*.[23]

---

23. King-Hele, *Doctor of Revolution*, 190; and 10 August 1798, Smith to Darwin (*Diary*, ed. Cronin, 461). Cocke's copy of *Botanic Garden* (1st Am. ed., 1798), is inscribed on the flyleaf: "John H Cocke / Wm. & Mary / College / 1799"; Rare Books, Earl Gregg Swem Library, College of William and Mary. See [5 October 1798] Timothy Pierce, New York, to James Pierce (Elizabeth C. Barney Buel, ed., *Chronicles of a Pioneer School from 1792 to 1833, Being the History of Miss Sarah Pierce and Her Litchfield School* [Cambridge, Mass., 1903], 369); and *Diary*, ed. Cronin, 201–461, passim. Bayard's notation is inside back cover, Commonplace Book, 1799–1803, MBS Papers, DLC. See also [Erasmus Darwin], *The Botanic Garden. A Poem, In Two Parts. Part I. Containing The Economy of Vegetation. Part II. The Loves of the Plants. With Philosophical Notes*, 2d Am. ed. (New York: T. & J. Swords, 1807), iii. Darwin's works contin-

∿ ∾

Natural history offered approaches to understanding both human and natural spheres. Scientific knowledge led to technological improvement and human progress. Botanizing was a popular pastime in polite circles in the eighteenth century, and botany an approved field of scientific inquiry for women. But these givens do not entirely account for Darwin's "hit." There were other sources on the Linnæan system; and there were alternative natural histories. *Loves of the Plants* became a sensation because of the teeming life, heterodox sexuality, and vision of unbounded possibilities presented in the volume.[24] The sexual-social fantasy was not just the provenance of men; women partook of liberation, too. The terms *pleasure* and *joy* repeatedly described the study of botany in this period; and they were evoked in Darwin's text. In his prefatory poem Smith depicted its effect similarly:

> *Here*, read with rapture, studied with delight,
> Long shall it charm the taste, the thought excite;
> And youths and maids, the parent and the child,
> Their minds illumined, and their griefs beguiled,
> By all of fancy, all of reason, moved,
> Rise from the Work invigor'd and improved.

The study of organic nature, encompassing human society, excited mental pleasure and forged sociability. Rapture and delight were necessary for human improvement; fancy *and* reason liberated people. Darwin believed that feeling was organic and reason inductive; nature was a state of universal sympathy in which plants and animals alike partook. In science's sensibility, feeling excited thinking—the two worked together to release human energy.

The political implications were present in the lives and poems of Darwin and Smith. Both were physicians with grand projects to organize and broadcast

---

ued to circulate into the nineteenth century in America among women as well as men. An erudite young woman, Sarah Alden Bradford, attended with her father in 1813 a series of public lectures on botany in Boston. Fascinated herself, she declared there was "hereabouts a kind of Botanic mania." To further her studies, her father recommended her reading *The Botanic Garden*. The analogies, including sexual reproduction, between plant and animal kingdoms stimulated her curiosity and reinforced her Unitarian belief in an organized universe under the superintendence of a Creator. Eight years later she was reading Darwin's *Zoonomia* (Joan W. Goodwin, *The Remarkable Mrs. Ripley: The Life of Sarah Alden Bradford Ripley* [Boston, 1998], 49–52, 95). That *The Botanic Garden* was acceptable to an orthodox Congregationalist minister, a student of an Episcopalian bishop, and a Unitarian young woman suggests that Darwin's benevolent views of organic naturalism were compatible with a wide range of theological positions under normal, nonpoliticized circumstances.

24. Shteir, *Cultivating Women, Cultivating Science*, 2, 17–21, 30, 35–36; and Schiebinger, *Nature's Body*, 28–32.

medical knowledge. The young man from Litchfield, Connecticut, with poetic ambitions for publicizing American talents wanted to impress the bard of Lichfield. The affinity felt by Smith for Darwin was more, though, than mutual interest in botany and poetry. Just as Smith was part of an intellectual circle of professional men centered around the Friendly Club, Darwin had belonged to the Lunar Society of Birmingham. Between the mid-1760s and 1791, when antirevolutionary riots forced them to disband, an informal association of men met periodically to discuss politics, philosophy, literature, and art and to apply science to technological advances. Members included Matthew Boulton and James Watt, whose steam engines drove the industrial revolution; Josiah Wedgwood, who utilized his pottery-works' production (the cameo of an enchained African with the logo, "Am I Not a Man and a Brother") to promote abolition of the slave trade; and Joseph Priestley, whose rationalist ideas extended beyond chemistry to radical politics and theology.[25]

In both groups, scientific interests were linked to unorthodox positions in society, religion, and politics: abolition of the slave trade and slavery; deism or freethinking; sympathy with the French Revolution; the causes of human progress and social justice. Yet, members did not allow diverse opinions to factionalize their gatherings. For both societies of men the paramount ideal was philosophical investigation of the terms of human progress, executed through friendly criticism and conversation. Scientific exchange, not partisan polemics, was the medium in which friendship was grounded. As scientists, these men sought to create a public culture separate from politics, in which they played central roles as disseminators of information, monitors of society's welfare, and critics of entrenched authority.[26] Both Smith and Darwin imagined in their poems an international community of humankind organized around universal principles of liberty and brotherhood. In publicizing Darwin, Smith applauded and promulgated the intellectual, political, and social values entwined in *Botanic Garden*'s verses.

In the *Economy of Vegetation* (part 1 of *Botanic Garden*), Darwin connected scientific insight with political inspiration. Repeatedly celebrating Benjamin Franklin for his experiments with electricity (1.I, 383–88; 1.II, 355–56), Darwin credited him with spotting the spread of tyranny:

25. McNeil, *Under the Banner of Science*, 2–3, 10–13, 27–28, 64–85; Hugh Honour, *Neo-Classicism* (Harmondsworth, England, 1968), 94; Erasmus Darwin, *The Botanic Garden, 1791: The Botanic Garden; A Poem, in Two Parts. Part I. Containing The Economy of Vegetation. Part II. The Loves of the Plants. With Philosophical Notes* (London: J. Johnson, 1791; facsimile reprint ed., Menston, England, 1973), ed. Desmond King-Hele, iii–iv; pt. 1, canto 2:, lines 303–16.
26. Jan Golinski, *Science as Public Culture: Chemistry and Enlightenment in Britain, 1760–1820* (Cambridge, 1992), 1–10, 56–59, 65–69.

> "So, borne on sounding pinions to the *West*,
> "When Tyrant-Power had built his eagle nest;
>
> .   .   .   .
>
> "Immortal Franklin watch'd the callow crew,
> "And stabb'd the struggling Vampires, ere they flew.
> "—The patriot-flame with quick contagion ran,
> "Hill lighted hill, and man electrified man;
> "Her heroes slain, awhile Columbia mourn'd,
> "And, crown'd with laurels, Liberty return'd."
>
> (1.II, 361–62, 365–70)

As Franklin had apprehended the secrets of lightning, so his powers of observation had penetrated political machinations. Like circuits of electricity, currents of liberty ran through America; coursing its way to Ireland, "'The Warrior, Liberty, with bending sails / Helm'd his bold course to fair Hibernia's vales,'" where it sparked truth and virtue's radiance over superstition (1.II, 371–76). Then was liberty roused in France; "'Touch'd by the patriot-flame, he rent, amazed, / The flimsy bonds'" of priests and kings and spread the call around the world (1.II, 377–94). For Darwin the spread of revolution meant that reason and equity vanquished political tyranny and religious superstition.

In extending his critique to the imperial project, he exposed the crux between science and human advancement. First, Darwin excoriated Spain's desecration of the Western Hemisphere, decrying "'the crimes of modern days.'" Then he pointed to Britain's perfidy underneath the record of civilized advancement. New forms of repression went hand in hand with progress. He retailed the crimes,

> "When Avarice, shrouded in Religion's robe,
> "Sail'd to the West, and slaughter'd half the globe;
> "While Superstition, stalking by his side,
> "Mock'd the loud groan, and lap'd the bloody tide;
> "For sacred truths announced her frenzied dreams,
> "And turn'd to night the sun's meridian beams.—
> "Hear, Oh Britannia! potent Queen of isles,
> "On whom fair Art, and meek Religion smiles,
> "Now Afric's coasts thy craftier sons invade,
> "And Theft and Murder take the garb of Trade!
> "—The *Slave*, in chains, on supplicating knee,
> "Spreads his wide arms, and lifts his eyes to Thee;
> "With hunger pale, with wounds and toil oppress'd,

> *"Are we not Brethren?'* sorrow chokes the rest;
> "—*Air*! bear to heaven upon thy azure flood
> "Their innocent cries!—*Earth!* cover not their blood!"
>
> (1.II, 414–30)

Behind England's liberal, tolerant empire, along with Spain's ancien régime, lay coercive exploitation. Arts and commerce could liberate human potential—or assert corrosive dominion. The expansion of Enlightenment inquiry over the course of the eighteenth century disassembled inherited hierarchies but also replaced them with new scales of valuation and difference. The impetus to dissect involved differentiation. Reason in the new order's service thus could rationalize equally invidious distinctions.

Tensions between inherent equivalence and "natural" differences marked antislavery discourses delivered to the New-York Manumission Society by two members of the Friendly Club in 1797 and 1798. Both the Reverend Samuel Miller and Smith called for gradual emancipation; both appealed to white benevolence to ameliorate the condition of enslaved African Americans. Miller's lecture revealed how the argument of sympathy cut both ways. Miller claimed to spare his fellow Americans' "feelings" by passing "over in silence the unnumbered cruelties, and the violations of every natural and social tie, which mark the African trade, and which attend the injured captives in dragging them from their native shores, and from all the attachments of life." Miller thus invoked Americans' imaginative identification with Africans' suffering, only to insert contractual rights and reasons of justice as "more immediately applicable to ourselves." By positing social contract principles, Miller elevated his fellow citizens and distanced them from the state of nature that was Africa, that "unhappy, ill-fated region" already under "torments" assigned by "nature's God," even as he castigated "civilized man" for adding "rapine and violence, captivity and slavery," to Africans' burdens.[27]

Smith's condemnation of enslaving Africans revealed a late Enlightenment equivocality over reason's efficacy. His reading of history made clear that the rise of Western civilization in itself did not guarantee the triumph of reason over force. Gunpowder, "by equalizing the powers of men," was more effective than the invention of letters or printing in dismantling man's exploitation of man. Most important to undermining "this savage constitution of society" was the Reformation, after which authoritarianism could not withstand "the keen spirit

---

27. Samuel Miller, A.M., *A Discourse, Delivered April 12, 1797, at the Request of and before the New-York Society for Promoting the Manumission of Slaves, and Protecting Such of Them as Have Been or May be Liberated* (New York: T. and J. Swords, 1797), 10–12, 28–29.

of investigation." Smith countered proslavery arguments on the basis of justice, humanity, and policy. He rejected civic humanism and republicanism's bases of power and created a transcendent universalism founded on human capacity. Africans' oppressors

> forgot . . . that whatever might be the will of the Deity, in respect to any particular race of men, nothing could justify another for inflicting unprovoked injury upon them. . . . They forgot that the differences in the talents and erudition of men arose simply from external circumstances; that the same course of species of events which now elevated the inhabitants of Europe and their descendants to the summit of political pre-eminence, formerly as much distinguished the progenitors of their unhappy slaves from the rest of mankind; that the cradle of the sciences was in Africa, and their first nurslings, and their earliest fathers, Africans.[28]

In his attack on Western imperialism's enslavement of Africans, Smith confronted a contradiction in the Enlightenment teleology of human progress. By the end of the century, studies of species and peoples from around the globe had contributed to a fluid understanding of differences among cultures due to climate and environment. The impulse to schematize could also turn characteristics into valorized rankings.[29] The notion of improvement implied a less desirable state, not just temporally; in projecting their own advancement, these thinkers degraded the status of others. The proposition that organisms and societies developed from crude to complex naturalized a hierarchy consigning the simple to the lower rungs of the system. The proliferation of systems of value during the eighteenth century left uncertain the trajectory for the course of mankind's improvement. Before he could further influence the cause to which he had devoted so much effort, he died in New York during the 1798 yellow fever epidemic while ministering medical care to one of its victims.

The multivalence of the late Enlightenment found chaotic expression in the French Revolution. When the reaction set in, anti-Jacobins made explicit the connection between scientific investigation and social experimentation, and sexual license became the vehicle for attacking radical politics. George Canning and John Frere published in the *Anti-Jacobin* "Loves of the Triangles," parodying Darwin and his poem. They turned his playful eroticism into lewd lasciviousness

28. Elihu Hubbard Smith, *A Discourse, Delivered April 11, 1798, at the Request of and before the New-York Society for Promoting the Manumission of Slaves, and Protecting Such of Them as Have Been or May Be Liberated* (New York: T. & J. Swords, 1798), 10, 14–15.
29. Golinski, *Science as Public Culture*, 20–21.

and his scientific depictions into derogatory nonsense, all in the context of the French Revolution and free love.[30] Darwin was a freethinker; he practiced free love between two marriages, producing two illegitimate daughters, and he advocated female education grounded in science and a wider academic curriculum.[31] The consonance of his personal life, scientific perspective, and political outlook with Mary Wollstonecraft's did not go unnoticed.

Richard Polwhele, who had contributed one of the odes to Darwin in Smith's 1792 edition, thought better of his enthusiasm for "all the vivid plants with passion glow" by 1798. What seemed enlightened philosophy in Darwin's science of nature turned to licentious disorder in the light of Mary Wollstonecraft's sexual economy. In Polwhele's attack on her and all female freethinkers in *The Unsex'd Females*, he made botany the metaphor and the agent of illicit sexual coupling, charging that the practice of botany led to lascivious behavior in girls who

> With bliss botanic as their bosoms heave,
> Still pluck forbidden fruit, with mother Eve,
> For puberty in sighing florets pant,
> Or point the prostitution of a plant;
> Dissect its organ of unhallow'd lust,
> And fondly gaze the titillating dust.[32]

Even the illustrations in *Botanic Garden* provided visual evidence of the linkage between sensuality and science. William Blake's plate of the "Fertilization of Egypt" was a graphic representation of virility, and Henry Fuseli's depiction of a sinuous "Flora attired by the Elements" was provocative in its sexual allusiveness.[33] As a one-time lover of Wollstonecraft's, Fuseli became fodder for Polwhele's attack on her. On this side of the Atlantic William Cobbett brought out Polwhele's poem in an American edition in 1800. These anti-Jacobin publicists pinpointed the cross-pollination between the exercise of reason and the enactment of personal desires. Scientific materialism led to deism and skepticism, to throwing off the social constraints of political authority and organized religion. Individuals living by their own intellectual lights ended up acting on their own emotions and passions. In the conservative critics' view, reason led to unreason, undermining social order and releasing monstrous appetites, with catastrophic results. Wollstonecraft's life and the French Revolution stood as proofs.[34]

30. *The Anti-Jacobin; or, Weekly Examiner*, 16 April, 23 April, 7 May 1798, 180–82, 188–89, 204–6.
31. Shteir, *Cultivating Women, Cultivating Science*, 22–24, 26–27; and Schiebinger, *Nature's Body*, 32–33, 34–35.
32. *The Unsex'd Females; A Poem* (1798; New York, 1800), 8–9; quoted in Shteir, *Cultivating Women, Cultivating Science*, 28.
33. Darwin, *Botanic Garden*, 1791, ed. King-Hele, part 1, canto 3, line 136; and frontispiece.
34. Schiebinger, *Nature's Body*, 33–35; and Shteir, *Cultivating Women, Cultivating Science*, 27–29.

❦ ❧

The late Enlightenment held reason and desire in dynamic tension as it opened multifarious opportunities for individual expression. Botany in particular had become a field in which men and women explored the diversity of the natural world and of themselves, and during the 1790s botanical examples and language offered means for critiquing and subverting social conventions. Wollstonecraft, for one, used botanical metaphors to denounce woman's sexual subordination and to posit alternatives. Beyond a full array of sexual options, Darwin's *Loves of the Plants* offered images of fraternal, sororal, and heterosexual bonds of social affection. In the 1790s, friendship stood as a radical option to marriage. Eschewing marriage symbolized a broad imaginative leap, as men and women sought different relationships and achievements outside established civil and religious prescriptions. Botanizing was a primary site for humans to commune with nature and with each other, exchanging sexual and social knowledge about the organic world and themselves.[35]

This social converse, engendered by intellectual investigation and shared experience, was what appeared so alarming to conservative polemicists and so inspiring to its participants. Margaret Bayard Smith (1778–1844) was part of that liberating conversation. As a young woman at the end of the 1790s, she was full of intellectual aspirations and emotional longings for completeness. As part of the heterosexual circle around the Friendly Club, she engaged in their intellectual exploration, social heterodoxy, and political idealism.

Two events permanently marked her life in 1800. She entered into print for the first time with two pieces, an essay and a poem, in her friends' periodical, the *Monthly Magazine*, edited by Charles Brockden Brown. And she married Samuel Harrison Smith, editor of the Jefferson administration's newspaper the *National Intelligencer*, moving with her husband to Washington, D.C. The volatility of the late Enlightenment's potent mix of values percolated in both events.

She entitled the essay, written on the eve of her wedding, "The Evils of Reserve in Marriage." She intended it to propound conjugal friendship grounded in "candour" and unbounded confidence. Instead, it revealed the slippage between rational and irrational when shared ideas and feelings produced a "sensibility" that was too "exquisite." Her essay captured the paradoxical potential of

35. Mary Wollstonecraft, *A Vindication of the Rights of Woman, With Strictures on Political and Moral Subjects*, ed. Carol H. Poston, 2d ed. (1792); (New York, 1988), 29–31, 35, 52–53 and n., 164, 168; and Bewell, "'On the Banks of the South Sea,'" 175–76, 185, 190–91. See also Clare A. Lyons, "'Sex Among the Rabble': Gender Transitions in the Age of Revolution, Philadelphia, 1750–1830" (Ph.D. diss., Yale University, 1996), for an analysis of sexual freedom in Philadelphia at the turn of the century.

sympathy for social identification as well as individual self-absorption. The very bonds that brought husband and wife together ultimately became a source of alienation. These themes adumbrated the changing social world into which she was moving in the early nineteenth century.[36]

In her poem, she memorialized her heterosexual friendships of the 1790s. This elegiac poem celebrated an outing to the Passaic Falls taken in May 1800 by Templeton, Bayard (Smith), Bleecker, Brown, and two other men, most likely Johnson and Miller. Years later Bayard Smith republished the poem in Godey's *Lady's Book* along with a memoir that focused on Brown and Bleecker, both by then deceased. Bayard Smith emphasized and carefully elucidated the meaning of friendship for the six, who were "friends in the truest and fullest sense of that too often abused word." They "were attached friends, living in habits of the most familiar and intimate intercourse—as brothers live with sisters—and the whole of this little company seemed as if they had but one soul between them." The "identity of taste, of thought, of feeling" was so close that the sights and sounds about them evoked "similar emotions . . . and simultaneous expressions of delight." Individually and collectively they "were given to intellectual pursuits, and loved nature with an enthusiasm that, in the estimation of the worldly minded, was deemed the excess of romance."[37] Bayard Smith endowed the term *friend* with a mutuality of idea and sensation that reverberated in the nature around them.

Wandering through the woods and viewing the falls, the six friends "beguiled the long summer's day in converse sweet, or in alternate recitations from the poets, with whom all were familiar." Losing track of time, they were caught by dusk and stayed overnight at an inn, where the group delegated to Bayard (Smith) the task of celebrating their excursion in a visitors' album.[38] There she inscribed "Lines By a Young Lady. Written at the Falls of Passaick, July 1800." She evoked the sublimity of a setting where nature's torrent and unrestrained feelings echoed each other. These friends were

> Prone to admire the ever changeful scene,
> Which Nature opens to the observant eye,

---

36. "The Evils of Reserve in Marriage," signed "N." (presumably, a typographical error, meant to be "M.," as the next piece was signed), *Monthly Magazine, and American Review* 2, no. 6 (June 1800): 409–11. This essay and its ramifications for companionate marriage are further analyzed in Fredrika J. Teute, "The Uses of Writing in Margaret Bayard Smith's New Nation," in Philip Gould and Dale M. Bauer, eds., *Cambridge Companion to Nineteenth-Century American Women's Writing* (Cambridge, 2001), 203–20.

37. Mrs. Harrison Smith, "The Falls of Passaic," [Godey's] *Lady's Book and Magazine of Belle Lettres, Fashions, Music &c* 14 (1837): 266.

38. Ibid., 265–68.

> To tread, delighted, the enamell'd green,
> And gaze, with rapture, on the starry sky.

As they approached the falls, their ardent feelings merged with nature's force.

> Hark! the loud tumult of the water's roar!
> Behold yon foaming stream's impetuous tide!
> See headlong dash'd upon the rocky shore,
> The oak, all shatter'd, once the forest's pride!
>
> . . . .
>
> For ages shall these roaring waters glide,
> These rocks succeeding ages shall remain;
> While a few years shall stop the purple tide,
> That now with ardour swells the youthful vein.

Awed by the scene, nature both intimated human mortality and inspired hope of immortality.[39]

Forty years later, when Bayard Smith published her reminiscence, she revised the poem slightly, toning down the passion,

> While a few years shall chill the fervent glow,
> Whose ardour animates the youthful vein.

She also covered over the fact that the six stayed overnight together when neither woman was engaged to any of the men. She asserted that "the ladies were the betrothed brides" of two of the men. With this claim, she elided the liberating quality of this group's interrelationships in the 1790s and replaced it with the circumscribed conventions of the nineteenth century. She concluded the piece, "The next morning after their return to the city, this happy party dispersed to their several homes, never again to be re-united in one circle. They were sundered by time—space and circumstance."[40] In poem and reminiscence, Bayard Smith recorded both the transcendent potential of the 1790s and the retreat from this precipice.

The Jeffersonian accession to power in 1800 was part of the conservative backlash against the radical possibilities envisioned in the 1790s, especially for white women and African Americans.[41] Bayard Smith experienced in her personal

---

39. "Lines By a young Lady. *Written at the Falls of Passaick, July,* 1800," signed "M.," *Monthly Magazine, and American Review* 3, no. 5 (November 1800): 399.

40. Harrison Smith, "The Falls of Passaic," 265–66, 268.

41. Seth Cotlar, "In Paine's Absence: The Trans-Atlantic Dynamics of American Popular Political Thought, 1787–1803" (Ph.D. diss., Northwestern University, 2000), argues that a popular cosmopolitanism penetrated America from Europe in the era of the French Revolution and that the Jeffersonian election of 1800 constituted a counterrevolution against this radical democratic movement.

situation the larger political and social shifts in the Anglo-American transatlantic world. The themes of her essay and poem foreshadowed impending loss. For the next twenty years, she channeled her energies into family responsibilities and the construction of a national political culture in the federal capital. The consolidation of republican orthodoxy, in which she participated, constrained the ambitions of individual fulfillment she imagined in the 1790s.[42]

Although radical freethinking did not disappear after the turn of the century, heterodox views receded from print, especially in America, where ideology focused on creating a cohesive national political consciousness. Darwin's works continued to circulate, and in England the interpenetration of science and radicalism wove through the thinking of the Romantic poets, especially Shelley.[43] But after new printings in America and Great Britain in the first decade of the nineteenth century, Darwin's books were not reprinted until the 1820s,[44] when the dissolution of the Republican ascendancy's power at the hands of the Jacksonian Democrats seemed to reopen society and the press to heterodox views. Wollstonecraft's *Vindication*, which had appeared in a third edition by 1796 and in multiple reprintings on both sides of the Atlantic, did not resurface in print until 1833 in New York City. The Free Enquirer, the workingmen's press owned by Frances Wright and Robert Dale Owen, was the publisher, and they appended a frank biography approving her love life along with her social views.[45] A year later, Harriet Martineau, the English journalist of radical universalist bent known for her political economy tracts and her feminist and antislavery sympathies, began her tour of the United States. In the winter of 1834–35 she arrived in Washington, and she was entertained at a salon presided over by Bayard Smith.

Though she had resumed publishing her writings in the 1820s, Bayard Smith made critical interventions in current policy issues only obliquely. She was an astute observer of American society's power hierarchies and social inequities, but she addressed them through a rhetoric of indirection. The counterattacks of anti-Jacobin polemicists wielding vicious gendered pens may have taught her early on

42. Fredrika J. Teute, "Roman Matron on the Banks of Tiber Creek: Margaret Bayard Smith and the Politicization of Spheres in the Nation's Capital," in Donald R. Kennon, ed., *A Republic for the Ages: The United States Capitol and the Political Culture of the Early Republic* (Charlottesville, Va., 1999), 89–121.

43. See, for a compendium of all possible links, Desmond King-Hele, *Erasmus Darwin and the Romantic Poets* (New York, 1986), esp. 187–226, 277–80; and Carl H. Grabo, *A Newton among Poets: Shelley's Use of Science in Prometheus Unbound* (Chapel Hill, N.C., 1930).

44. New printings of *The Botanic Garden* included: London: J. Johnson, 1804–5; New York: T. & J. Swords, 1807; London: Jones & Company, 1824; London: Jones & Company, 1825. *Zoonomia*: London: J. Johnson, 1801; Dublin: B. Dugdale, 1801; Boston: Thomas & Andrews, 1803; Boston, Thomas & Andrews, 1809; Philadelphia: E. Earle, 1818.

45. Mary Wollstonecraft, *A Vindication of the Rights of Woman, with Strictures on Political and Moral Subjects. With a Biographical Sketch of the Author* (New York, 1833).

to keep her cover. Genteel moral prescriptions of woman's duty within the home had confined her spirit. She kept her discontent with domesticity and her universalist views mostly to herself. She was not shy of politics, however, and was a vehement anti-Jackson partisan. Martineau's visit provided Bayard Smith with an opportunity to celebrate the celebrity and through her elevate the principles of intellectual investigation and social justice, pointedly underscoring the short-comings of the current era. Bayard Smith, in lauding Martineau, reinscribed Enlightenment categories of appraisal onto nineteenth-century ameliorative endeavors. She focused on Martineau's scientific expertise in addressing social ills and her universalist values in promoting the general, not sectarian, good. In her evocation of Martineau, she recalled the transatlantic ideals circulating in the 1790s. Just faintly can be heard the echo of the manifestoes of that age.

First, Bayard Smith appealed to a cosmopolitan humanism that rose above national rivalries, as she declared,

> We greet thee, stranger, from Britannia's land,
> With cordial welcome, and with clasping hand.
> And said I *stranger*? Say the word no more,
> Since Martineau's a stranger on no shore.
> Her warm benev'lence—her expanded mind,
> Embrace as kindred all of human kind.

Invoking a common Anglo-American culture, Bayard Smith bestowed on Martineau friendly and familial affections (while alluding to her status as a single woman) and empowered her to critique American progress:

> Then welcome, friend and sister! since you come
> From our forefathers' transatlantic home.
> Differing in forms, not principles—our aim,
> Our laws, our customs, language, still the same;
> Then, while with philosophic eye you trace
> The various powers develop'd in our race;
> Be rival interests, prejudice, and pride,
> And ev'ry hostile feeling laid aside.

By reminding Martineau of America's incomplete attainments, Bayard Smith pointed them out herself. Jacksonian Democrats could be particularly criticized for subscribing to egalitarian principles of the Revolution without bringing about the reality of legal equality for white women and African Americans.

> Remember, 'tis the *infant*—not the man,
> Whose strength you measure, and whose pow'rs you scan;

> An *infant Nation*, who maintains the cause
> Of *general suffrage*, and of equal laws;
> By whom the grand experiment is tried,
> For which her sages toil'd—her heroes died.
> And with a generous sympathy survey
> The dangers which assail, or errors which betray.

Like another woman before her, Martineau applied her intellectual abilities and a scientific approach to social problems. Bayard Smith referred to the *Vindication of the Rights of Woman* and to the French Revolution. She suggested that this time a woman's pen would succeed in women's rights and antislavery causes.

> Extend to us the philanthropic zeal,
> That warms your bosom for your country's weal:
> With the strong powers of your unfettered mind,
> Assert the social rights of all mankind—
> No longer now the power to *man* confined,
> To vindicate these rights, by heaven assigned,
> The *pen*, not *bayonet*, now their force maintain,
> Nor woman's pen is now employed in vain,
> Since you O! Martineau, embrace the cause,
> Of social happiness and equal laws.

Martineau directed her "genius" not to the pleasures of literary imagination

> But the deep tracts of science to explore,
> To simplify its rules, and teach the poor
> Their real interests. This the task designed
> By all the labors of thy powerful mind.

In prescribing for the working classes "their real interests" of conforming to middle-class values, Martineau, and Bayard Smith in praising her, revealed the crux of the Enlightenment. Rankings of valuation structured intellectual investigation, and progress was relative to the moral order imposed. Nevertheless, through her ode to Martineau, Bayard Smith took on the category of differentiation most deeply embedded in scientific systems of the eighteenth century, sexual difference. She set up a triad of female pens, comparing Martineau to Hannah More and Maria Edgeworth, and privileged Martineau's mental powers, nonsectarian views, and social activism over More's Christian charity and Edgeworth's moral didacticism. Better than More's "*Christian virtue*,"

> *Thy* kindred spirit, Martineau, essays
> Of life to smooth the rough and thorny ways,

> With stronger genius, and as high an aim,
> Thy bosom burning with as pure a flame.

Edgeworth, on the other hand, lacked this purity of motive; her preoccupation with worldly fame tainted her endeavors.

> Thy moral system wants the vital power
> To live through strong temptation's trying hour;
> Wants the exalting, the inspiring glow,
> Which hopes immortal only can bestow.

Most importantly, Bayard Smith's emphasis on Martineau's "unfettered mind" implicitly endorsed Martineau's and Wollstonecraft's belief in female intellectual equality with men, a position More and Edgeworth had attacked with the anti-Jacobins in the 1790s. Bayard Smith ended the poem with a challenge:

> And Patriots warmly feel, and gladly then
> Confess the influence of a female pen.[46]

Through her own pen, in elevating Martineau, Bayard Smith revived the 1790s ideals of Wollstonecraft—and of her own Friendly Club circle. Yoking reason to feeling, Bayard Smith employed her intellect to summon present-day "patriots" to respond to the universalist Enlightenment goals of the revolutionary era and to recognize the equality of women. In her recourse to scientific investigation, she recalled the exciting potential for human improvement and social experimentation opened up by natural science at the end of the eighteenth century. Yet, imprinted in those goals more deeply still was a hierarchy of values that would force conformity to the benevolent standards of those in charge of human progress.

Omohundro Institute of Early American History and Culture

---

46. *Daily National Intelligencer* (Washington, D.C.), 7 February 1835.

Irish Republicans and Gothic Eleutherarchs: Pacific Utopias in the Writings of Theobald Wolfe Tone and Charles Brockden Brown

— Nigel Leask

Utopianism and the French Revolution

In Book XI of *The Prelude* Wordsworth famously hailed the relocation of political virtue in the modern age of revolutions:

> Not in Utopia,—subterranean fields,—
> Or some secreted island, Heaven knows where!
> But in the very world, which is the world
> Of all of us,—the place where, in the end,
> We find our happiness, or not at all!
>
> (11.724–28)

Repudiating Montesquieu's and Rousseau's contention that the virtuous republic was an impossibility in the complex commercial states of modern Europe, the French revolutionaries sought to fuse utopianism with constitutional politics. The statist utopias of twentieth-century totalitarian regimes that (arguably) built on that foundation have given utopianism a bad name in our epoch. In this essay I want to examine Gregory Claeys's argument that the French Revolution dissipated the enthusiasm of some writers for utopias just at the moment when others cultivated serious hope for their realization, though situated more and more frequently in distant, exotic places.[1]

In the 1790s Atlantic republican tradition that this essay addresses—briefly, in relation to S. T. Coleridge and Robert Southey, subsequently, in more sustained fashion, in regard to the writings of Irish revolutionary Theobald Wolfe Tone and American novelist Charles Brockden Brown—the French revolutionary failure resulted in the return of utopia to the "secreted island" where Sir Thomas More's Raphael Hythloday had first discovered it in 1516. More had described how, when the founder of Utopia civilized the barbaric aboriginal inhabitants of Abraxus, "he promptly cut a channel 15 miles wide where the land

---

1. Gregory Claeys, "Utopianism, Property, and the French Revolution Debate in Britain," in Krishnan Kumar and Stephen Bann, eds., *Utopias and the Millennium* (London, 1993), 50.

joined the continent, and thus caused the sea to flow around the country."[2] The late-eighteenth-century Atlantic imagination was thoroughly seduced by the utopian promise of a Pacific *Terra Australis*— above all of Tahiti, Bougainville's "heureuse isle de Cythere, . . . la veritable Eutopie"[3]—which facilitated the insularism of many postrevolutionary utopias. A moving instance of this sentiment as a response to revolutionary disillusionment is conveyed in a letter written by the Dantonist leader Camilles Desmoulins to his wife on the eve of his execution by guillotine in 1793: "O ma chère Lucile! j'étois né pour faire des vers, pour défendre les malheureux, pour te rendre heureuse, pour composer, avec ta mère et ton père, et quelques personnes selon notre coeur, un Otaïti. J'avois rêvé une république que tout le monde eût adorée."[4]

Of course, there was another possible setting for republican utopia in the late eighteenth century, namely, the recently independent United States of America. Coleridge's "Book of Pantisocracy" is not among the ten or so positive utopias of the 1790s described by Claeys, not least because, like so many Coleridgean projects, the book was never actually written; but its fate illustrates some of the difficulties facing American utopias in the later 1790s. If the Harringtonian Jewish commonwealth extolled by Coleridge in 1795 in his Bristol *Lectures on Revealed Religion* provided the political theory of pantisocracy, the Quaker State of Pennsylvania, free of slavery and with a Jubilee principle inscribed in the thirty-sixth article of its constitution, seemed to offer an appropriate geographical locale. But even if, as I have elsewhere argued, the politics of pantisocracy continued to influence Coleridge's thinking for many years after his move away from political radicalism, the ideological transformations of America during the 1790s had rapidly proved a stumbling block to the original scheme.[5] There is a startling discrepancy between Coleridge's eulogizing of American liberty in his 1795 lectures or the "Monody on the Death of Chatterton" and his openly critical attitude in *The Watchman* of 1796, where he wrote, "the Americans are lovers of freedom because their ledgers furnish irrefragable arguments in favour of it; but the vital spirit and high internal feelings of liberty they appear not to possess."[6] The commercial, Federalist America of John Adams and the Jay-Grenville Treaty of 1795,

2. Sir Thomas More, *Utopia*, ed. George Logan and Robert Adams (Cambridge, 1975), 43.

3. Bougainville's *Journal*, cited in Neil Rennie, *Far-Fetched Facts: The Literature of Travel and the Idea of the South Seas* (Oxford, 1995), 89.

4. Ibid., 140. "Oh, my dear Lucile! I was born to write poetry, to defend the unfortunate, to make you happy, and to share, with your mother and your father, along with a few others who share our sentiments, another Tahiti. I dreamed of a republic that everyone would have adored" (editor's translation).

5. See Nigel Leask, "Pantisocracy and the Politics of the 'Preface' to *Lyrical Ballads*," in Alison Yarrington and Kelvin Everest, eds., *Representations of Revolution* (London and New York, 1993), 39–58.

6. *The Watchman, The Collected Works of Samuel Taylor Coleridge,* vol. 2, ed. Lewis Patton (Princeton, N.J., and London, 1970), 212.

which realigned the United States with counterrevolutionary Britain rather than revolutionary France, seemed to have eclipsed the Jeffersonian republic idealized in the writings of Crevecouer and Brissot.

Claeys indicates that in the eighteenth century the term "utopia" often carried a technical meaning of communal or strictly egalitarian property-holding opposed to commerce and the accumulation of private wealth.[7] The post-1793 notion that this ideal could best be realized in small, isolated societies was one that would influence the communitarian experiments of Robert Owen and others: divested of their economic primitivism, such experiments played a crucial role in the development of nineteenth-century socialist thought. A more problematic but equally characteristic development of the idea in Britain was the location of utopias in colonial space remote from Europe, often based on the travel accounts from the second age of discovery, just as More's *Utopia* had been on accounts from the first. James Burgh's Cessares (1764), Thomas Spence's Crusonia (1782), Carl Wadstrom's Sierra Leone (1787), Wolfe Tone's Hawaii (1790), Thomas Northmore's Makar (1795), and Robert Southey's Caermadoc (1799)[8] were all utopias established in isolated regions of Africa, the Caribbean, South America, or the Pacific. The moral legitimacy of colonizing someone else's land rarely seems to have given pause to European settlers, who regarded themselves as progressive Prosperos to aboriginal Calibans, although many such utopias contained an inbuilt critique of mercantilism and "speculation commerce." Even the "unrespectable" radical and land redistributionist Thomas Spence—in one of the many eighteenth-century utopias inspired by Defoe's *Robinson Crusoe*—imagined the lawgivers of the island of Crusonia "naming the Continent, which they have colonised, *Fridinea*, from [their founder Robinson Crusoe's] Man *Friday*, because it was his country."[9]

The colonial inflection of insular utopias often bridged the divide that separated "respectable" from "unrespectable" radicalism in the 1790s, to borrow Iain McCalman's useful distinction.[10] In the decade following the abandonment of the "respectable" radicalism of the Pantisocracy scheme, its two major promoters both enlisted in the service of the British empire: in 1801 Robert Southey was appointed secretary to the new Irish chancellor of the exchequer Isaac Cony,[11]

7.   Gregory Claeys, ed., *Utopias of the British Enlightenment* (Cambridge, 1994), xxv.

8.   The utopian Caermadoc appears in the manuscript version of *Madoc* completed in 1799 and survives in the extensively revised published version of 1805 as the name of a Welsh colony in America.

9.   Thomas Spence, *A Supplement to the History of Robinson Crusoe, being the History of Crusonia* (1782), in *Essays in Honour of William Gallacher* (Berlin, 1966), 292–308, 306.

10. Iain McCalman, *Radical Underworld: Prophets, Revolutionaries, and Pornographers in London, 1795–1840* (Cambridge, 1988), 31–49.

11. Mark Storey, *Robert Southey: A Life* (Oxford, 1997), 146–47

while in 1804 Coleridge filled a similar post under Sir Alexander Ball, high commissioner of Britain's new Mediterranean colony of Malta. In a letter of 1801 to William Taylor, Southey sardonically commented on "the nationalization of liberty politics. . . . shall we not see the Mackintoshes archimages of Hindoostan [the erstwhile radical James Mackintosh had taken a job in the Bombay judiciary] and the admirers of Babeuf chancellors of the Exchequer?"[12] The recent historiography of British imperialism has heavily emphasized the importance of "proconsular despotism" and a revival of aristocratic pomp in colonial government around 1800.[13] To men such as Southey, Mackintosh, or later James Mill, however, Britain's colonies provided a laboratory where many of the social experiments and utopian ideas that seemed to have failed in the revolutionary moment of European metropolitan states could be tried again.

WOLFE TONE'S "SANDWICH ISLANDS MEMORANDUM"

One of the most remarkable overlaps between republican and colonial utopianism in the period was Theobald Wolfe Tone's "Sandwich Islands Memorandum," although as we will see, Tone's ideological trajectory ran in an opposite direction from that of the English pantisocrats. In 1788 Tone, a Protestant lawyer from Dublin, embarked upon a literary career to earn some money while studying at the Middle Temple in London. His antisentimental roman à clef *Belmont Castle, or Suffering Sensibility*, was published in Dublin in 1790, and he also contributed a spate of literary reviews to the *European Magazine*, including a piece on Andrew Kippis's *Life of Captain James Cook*. Kippis's book played an important part in Tone's next project. In August 1788 Tone sent a detailed memorandum to Prime Minister William Pitt proposing the establishment of a British military colony on the recently discovered Sandwich Islands (Hawaii), where Cook had been killed a decade earlier, and which, Tone argued, might serve as a base to harry Spanish shipping in the eastern Pacific. The plan was developed in collaboration with his brother William, an officer in the East India Company artillery, and was later hailed by its author as "my first essay in what I may call politics."[14] It was apparently a scheme that Tone cherished long after his conversion to revolutionary republicanism, and of which he remained proud up until

---

12. *Memoirs of William Taylor of Norwich*, ed. J. W. Robbards, 2 vols. (London, 1844), 1:383.
13. See, for example, C. A. Bayly's important *Imperial Meridian: The British Empire and the World, 1780–1830* (London, 1989).
14. *Life of Theobald Wolfe Tone, compiled and arranged by William Wolfe Tone (1826),* expanded ed., ed. Thomas Bartlett, 2 vols. (Dublin, 1998), 1:27; hereafter cited in the text as *Life*. William Tone had an active career in the service of the East India Company and wrote a classic study of the Marathas of western India. Cf. Bayly, *Imperial Meridian*, 127.

his suicide in a Dublin jail ten years later, on the eve of his execution for rebellion against the British state. Pitt's total silence in 1788 had been a bitter blow to Tone's political ambitions; nevertheless, undeterred, he rejigged the original Sandwich Islands plan two years later in Belfast, with the help of Thomas Russell (future cofounder of the United Irishmen) and American republican veteran Thomas Digges. The new plan was written at the height of the Nootka Sound incident of 1790, when Britain's dispute with Spain over trading rights on the northwest coast of Canada brought the two powers to the brink of war. It was addressed initially to the duke of Richmond and later to the foreign secretary, William Grenville, and developed the original plan by proposing to promote a republican war of liberation in Spanish America.

Wolfe Tone's plan needs to be seen in the context of the numerous projects for British colonial expansion in the wake of Cook's voyages in the Pacific, but it also partakes of the utopian mood of the late Enlightenment. In 1783 James Matra had proposed a distinctly dystopian convict settlement in New South Wales as a means of clearing out England's overcrowded prison hulks after American independence had closed down England's previous penal dumping ground. Matra's plan was reluctantly accepted by Pitt in 1784, and the first fleet sailed with 160,000 convicts to Botany Bay three years later.[15] But the Nootka Sound incident revived Britain's sense of the desirability of a strategic base in the Pacific, and Botany Bay was on the wrong side of the ocean. In February 1790 the exiled Venezuelan liberator Francisco Miranda met with Pitt and solicited British military assistance to free America from Spanish colonial power. Given Pitt's opposition to outright territorial conquest and his pragmatic sense of the difficulty of employing Protestant arms to liberate Catholic colonies, he was more interested in using Miranda to gain access to the intelligence networks of exiled Mexican and Peruvian Jesuits in Italy, a body that might supply Catholic leaders for a future bid to oust Spain from its American colonies.[16] This revolutionary Jesuit network would reappear in quite a different ideological guise in the paranoiac conspiracy theories of the later 1790s, as we will see below. Neither Tone's nor Miranda's plan came to anything: Britain's commercial and colonial rivalry with Spain was rapidly stalled by mutual fears of the darkening clouds of the French Revolution, which forced new alliances between former antagonists. Miranda, betrayed by perfidious Albion for a trade treaty with Spain, crossed to revolutionary France to solicit assistance for the liberation of his native land, a voyage that anticipated Wolfe Tone's journey to Paris in 1796, via the United States of America.

15.   Robert Hughes, *The Fatal Shore* (London, 1987), 62–67.
16.   Guadalupe Jimenez Codinach, *La Gran Bretagna y la independenzia de Mexico, 1808–1821* (Mexico City, 1991), 102.

Apart from representing a timely intervention in British strategy, Tone's plan for a Hawaiian military colony was partly based on a classical republican model resembling in some of its features James Burgh's Harringtonian utopia of the Cessares (1764).[17] The choice of Hawaii, renowned for its fierce natives who had murdered Cook in 1779, may have been prompted by more than its strategic proximity to the American continent. It also underlines Tone's conscious rejection of the sensuous and epicurean paradise of Tahiti, celebrated by Diderot in his *Supplement to Bougainville's Voyage*. Tone admitted that the plan was inspired by the military colonies of ancient Rome, but it is also redolent of the spirit of the Protestant Irish Volunteer movement, which had provided the basis for Grattan's successful bid to secure legislative independence for the Irish Parliament in 1782. In an unpublished essay of 1790 Tone, alluding to Robert Burns's poem "The Cotter's Saturday Night," described the "self-appointed, self-arrayed, self-disciplined" patriot army as "a wall of fire" "encompassing the island" (*Life*, 2:1778).[18] (The Irish Volunteer movement was itself partly inspired by the citizen militias of the rebellious American colonists.) "The idea," wrote Tone,

> is to construct a settlement on somewhat of feudal principles, to reward military attendance and exertion by donative lands, to train the rising generation to arms and danger, to create a small but impenetrable nation of soldiers, where every man should have a property, and arms and spirit to defend it, to temper the ferocity of the natives by the arts of European culture, and to call forth from the tomb, where for a century it has slept, the invincible daring of the old bucaniers, uncontaminated by their disgraceful debaucheries in peace, and their still more infamous barbarities in war. (*Life*, 1:524)

Tone admitted the difficulties of providing incentives for colonists to settle in the remote Sandwich Islands, which justified his military policy, "as it may first be necessary to coerce the colonists a little for their own future good, which cannot be so well done on any other plan" (*Life*, 1:524). He extolled the virtues of a "strong military principle, that principle which has held the rock of Malta for ages against the Turkish empire" (*Life*, 1:5367) as an alternative to the political impostures and "pious frauds" employed by some classical and biblical lawgivers. Tone's principle of donative land and the sort of masculinist military

17. James Burgh, *An Account of the First Settlement, Laws, Form of Government, and Police, of the Cessares, A People of South America* in Claeys, ed., *Utopias of the British Enlightenment*, 71–136.
18. Burns's lines read, "A *virtuous Populace* may rise the while, / And stand a wall of fire, around their much-lov'd ISLE," "The Cotter's Saturday Night," 11.179–180, *Poems and Songs*, ed. James Kinsley (Oxford, 1969), 121.

freemasonry associated with the buccaneers or the medieval Knights of St. John has more in common with a primitivist Robespierrist despotism of liberty than with the liberal commercial societies imagined by "modernist" republicans such as Paine, Wollstonecraft, or Condorcet. But it is not difficult to see in it a model for the secret society of United Irishmen that Wolfe Tone and Thomas Russell co-founded the following year among other radicalized members of the Protestant Volunteer movement in Belfast. In their revolutionary manifesto, the conspirators urged "our countrymen in general to follow our example, and form similar societies . . . for the promotion of constitutional knowledge, the abolition of bigotry in religion and politics, and the equal distribution of the rights of man through all sects and denominations of Irishmen."[19] The paradox of conspiracy—the cultivation of secrecy to win revolutionary enlightenment—was one that loomed large in the distorting mirror of anti-Jacobin conspiracy theory, as we will see in the next section in relation to Brown's novels.

Tone's utopian colony, unlike Northmore's 1795 Godwinian Makaria (also set on a Pacific island), was predatory rather than isolationist. In this respect it resembled Sir Thomas More's original utopia, whose citizens, despite holding property in common, waged war on their neighbors and hired assassins to eliminate political opponents. Tone's 1790 memorandum envisaged the Sandwich Islands as "a huge magazine arsenal" that would provide a base for "the utter subversion of [the Spanish] empire in South America" (*Life*, 1:530). Citing the numerous Mexican rebellions of the previous half century, he envisaged his colony as being "open to receive all the discontented spirits" from the Spanish colonies (*Life*, 1:531] and an ideal launching pad for military expeditions against the western seaboard from Panama south to Chile. Briefed by Thomas Digges, an expert on Spanish American affairs, Tone insisted on the importance of winning over the Catholic priests and populace, a solicitude that may have contributed to his own pioneering efforts to overcome the sectarian divide splitting the Irish radical movement.[20] Like most of the utopian Pacific colonies that I have mentioned here (in contrast to Matra's dystopian plan for New South Wales),

19. Quoted in Marianne Elliot, *Partners in Revolution: The United Irishmen and France* (New Haven, Conn., and London, 1982), 23. For an account of the recent historiography of the United Irishman, see the special issue of *Eighteenth-Century Life* 22, n.s., 3, (1998), "Ireland, 1798–1998: From Revolt to Revisionism and Beyond"; and Kevin Whelan, *The Tree of Liberty: Radicalism, Catholicism, and the Constitution of Irish Identity, 1760–1830.* (London, 1996).

20. See his influential pamphlet of 1791, *An Argument on behalf of the Catholics of Ireland.* Tone's anti-Spanish aggression in the "Sandwich Islands Memorandum" is perhaps surprising given that his pamphlet *Spanish War! An Enquiry into How Far Ireland is Bound of Right to Embark in the Impending Contest on the Side of Great Britain*, published in 1790 in reaction to the Nootka Sound incident, had insisted on Ireland's right to abstain from hostilities with a valuable trading partner. Tone was still wearing two political hats, one of them a "colonial utopian" hat suggesting service to the British Empire, the other a nationalist hat supporting the liberation of his own island community from colonial despotism.

Tone's was never realized, but paradoxically it seems to have inspired the development of his republican nationalism over the next few years. One cannot help being struck by the geopolitical analogies between Tone's offshore island colony as a base for encouraging republican revolution against Spanish despotism on the South American mainland and his plan, presented to the French Directory six years later in 1796, advocating the employment of a liberated Ireland as a base for inducing republican insurrection and *chouannerie* in mainland Britain.

The exposure and trial of the French spy William Jackson in Dublin in 1795 implicated Wolfe Tone and other United Irish leaders in treasonable conspiracy against the British government. At the same time, the conversion of a secret society into a mass movement in the wake of the Fitzwilliam crisis (which Marianne Elliott describes as "the crucial turning point in Ireland's drift towards revolution")[21] forced Tone to flee with his family to America in the summer of 1795. The Irish émigrés whom Tone joined in Philadelphia (including fellow United men Dr. James Reynolds, Archibald Hamilton Rowan, and later James Napper Tandy) were mainly middle-class Protestant and Dissenting radicals, often from Ulster, in contrast to the plebeian Catholic immigrants from Ireland of the following century.[22] Their background of political activism injected new energy into the American anti-Federalist party. Once established in Philadelphia, Tone devoured the newspapers (notably, the democratic republican *Aurora*), haunted the bookshops, and mastered the distinctive idiom of American political rhetoric.

But Tone the utopian projector found nothing to praise in the young American republic, the principles of which deviated so greatly from those of his imagined Pacific colony. Elliott indicates that "of the group of Irish exiles gathered in Philadelphia, Tone was alone in his unwavering desire to return to Ireland."[23] His high-minded republicanism was offended (echoing Coleridge's remarks in *The Watchman*) by what he considered "a selfish, churlish, unsocial race, totally absorbed in making money, . . . half English, half Dutch, with the worst qualities of both countries."[24] Even his attempt to become a Crevecourian American farmer in Princeton, New Jersey, was short-lived; he could not put down roots in American soil. By early January 1796, responsive to a coded message from

---

21. Marianne Elliot, *Wolfe Tone: Prophet of Irish Independence* (New Haven, Conn., and London, 1989), 250.
22. In 1783–1814, between 100,000 and 150,000 Irish emigrated to America, two-thirds of whom were Ulster Presbyterians of Scots ancestry, although in the wake of 1798 large numbers of Catholics sought refuge in America from Orange persecution. In 1815–45, by comparison, between 800,000 and 1,000,000 Irish sailed across the Atlantic, a large majority of whom were Catholics from the southern counties, particularly in the 1838–44 period. See K. A. Miller, *Emigrants and Exiles: Ireland and the Irish Exodus to North America* (New York, 1985).
23. Elliot, *Wolfe Tone*, 266.
24. Ibid., 266.

John Keogh, a fellow United Irishman in Ireland, Tone was on board a ship bound for France, where he would successfully solicit military assistance from the French Directory for an invasion of Ireland. Most other Atlantic republicans, with the lesson of 1793 before them, had come to believe that utopia was achievable only in small, isolated communities, not by revolutionizing modern European states. Exile from his native Ireland seems to have led Tone's thinking in an opposite direction. The ideal commonwealth that he had initially projected in the Sandwich Islands was now relocated back to his own national community, the "very world which is the world of all of us, or not at all."

IRISH CONSPIRATORS IN BROWN'S "CARWIN THE BILOQUIST"

I want to turn now to the critical role of utopias and the representation of Irish republican émigrés in the writings of America's first professional novelist, Charles Brockden Brown. Having given up his legal career after reading Godwin's *Political Justice* and *Caleb Williams* (the latter the model for the seven novels Brown published between 1798 and 1803), in 1795 he was teaching in a Quaker school in Philadelphia and mixing in the city's radical anti-Federalist circles and debating clubs. Wollstonecraft's *Vindication of the Rights of Woman* inspired his first literary work, a philosophical dialogue entitled *Alcuin or the Rights of Woman*, the initial part of which was published in 1798.[25] The utopian second part, "The Paradise of Women," was not actually published until 1815, but its account of a feminist agrarian island commonwealth is typical of the utopian enthusiasm that gripped Brown in the mid-nineties, when it was written. David Clark describes Brown's early journals as containing "plans for utopias, including part of an original alphabet [and] a system of shorthand he is known to have invented,"[26] and the link between utopias and language reform is germane to his later novels. As far as I know Brown never met Wolfe Tone in Philadelphia, although it is not an impossibility, given that both were habitués of the city's bookshops and republican networks in late 1795. "Tone," as we shall see, may figure more as a pun than a historical presence, despite the marked similarities between his Pacific utopia and that of Brown's most memorable Irish revolutionary conspirator.

Brown's move to New York in 1797 to begin a new career in journalism brought him into the ambit of the influential circle of Federalist intellectuals known as the Friendly Club, which included Charles Adams (son of President John Adams), Timothy Dwight, Samuel Miller, and Elihu Hubbard Smith.

25. My account is based on David Lee Clark's *Charles Brockden Brown: Pioneer Voice of America* (Durham, N.C., 1952), 114.
26. Ibid., 41.

Brown's new circle seems to have exerted a brake on his radicalism although, as I will suggest, it would be a mistake to read the novels written in 1798 and 1799 as simple recantations of his earlier politics. In any case, ideological ambivalence seems a characteristic of the group as a whole, as Fredrika Teute argues in her essay in this volume. Catherine Kaplan has drawn attention to Elihu Hubbard Smith's agrarian utopia (composed in 1796 and 1797 after his reading of Brown's *Alcuin*), pointing out the paradox that "this young, Federalist city-dweller fashioned a republic whose sturdy yeomen independence and purity would have delighted Thomas Jefferson or James Madison, not Alexander Hamilton."[27] Nevertheless, there are considerable differences between Smith's rule-bound utopia, established in an undisclosed location "nearly equidistant from the Atlantic and the Mississippi," and Wolfe Tone's or Brown's Pacific utopias, the latter to be discussed below.

One of the recent publications from Britain being eagerly discussed by the Friendly Club in 1798 was John Robison's *Proofs of a Conspiracy*, a gothicized conspiracy theory that attributed the French Revolution to an international plot of Freemasons, Jesuits, and Illuminati based at Ingolstadt in Bavaria, who, Robison argued, had "divided Europe into colonies" in order to undermine the ancien régime.[28] To divert attention from their heinous crimes against society, Robison imagined the Illuminati propagating "a beautiful scene of Utopian happiness—and they rock us asleep by the eternal lullaby of morality and universal philanthropy."[29] Like Edmund Burke, he interpreted Jacobins as advanced Enlightenment skeptics who had incongruously embraced economic and political primitivism; "determined to have the elegance and grandeur of a palace without the prince . . . [they] would keep the philosophers, the poets, the artists, but not the Maecenases."[30] The Massachusetts minister Jedediah Morse, praised by Brown in the *Monthly Magazine* for August 1799, feared that the Bavarian Illuminati had already established several lodges in the United States, while Timothy Dwight lamented that the daughters of America were in danger of becoming "disciples of Voltaire" and "the concubines of the Illuminati."[31]

27. Catherine Kaplan provided me with a draft of her unpublished paper "'The Institutions of the Republic of Utopia' Or, The World According to Elihu Hubbard Smith" and a copy of Smith's utopian plan; I am grateful to her and to Fredrika Teute for putting us in touch.

28. John Robison, *Proofs of a Conspiracy against all the Religions and Governments of Europe, carried on in the Secret Meetings of Free Masons, Illuminati, and Reading Societies*, 5th ed., corrected (Dublin, 1798), 418. Brown's friend Dunlap noted in his diary for 14 September 1798, "Read C. B. Brown's beginning for the life of Carwin, as far as he has gone he has done well, he has taken up the scheme of the Illuminati" (Clark, *Pioneer Voice*, 190).

29. Ibid., 451.

30. Ibid., 444.

It is not, however, Robison's Bavaria but Ireland that features as the nerve center of global revolution in Brown's unfinished *Memoirs of Carwin the Biloquist* (composed in 1798 although not published until 1803–5, when it appeared serially in the *Literary Magazine*).[32] Brown wrote *Carwin* as a sequel to his first published novel, *Wieland, or the Transformation: An American Tale* (1798), in which he had followed technique used in *Caleb Williams* (as the novel's subtitle makes clear) of "making the picture of a single family a model from which to sketch the condition of a nation."[33] Brown's fiction characteristically works backward, progressively uncovering mysteries that appear to be complex involutes of deception, psychological trauma, and political conspiracy. In *Wieland*, the solution of the mystery of the voices that shatter the domestic idyll of the Wieland and Pleyel families begs a whole new series of questions about the background and motivation of the shadowy ventriloquist Carwin. To underline the utopian theme, which has only a subliminal presence in the 1798 novel, I will have to do violence to Brown's powerful fictional technique of narrative retrospection, first discussing Carwin's career as narrated in the *Memoirs* and then proceeding to the chronologically prior *Wieland*.

Both novel and fragment are set in the North Atlantic colonial world between the end of the Seven Years' War and the American War of Independence, although they are charged with the ideological preoccupations of North America in the 1790s. In the *Memoirs* we learn that Carwin, despite his apparent Irish identity in *Wieland*, is in fact the son of a poor Pennsylvanian farmer, possessing an extraordinary talent for ventriloquism, which he has taught himself. Moving to Philadelphia, Carwin comes under the spell of a mysterious Irishman called Mr. Ludloe, who, it appears—from his insistence on rational sincerity, benevolence, and antimatrimonialism—is a dedicated follower of certain tenets of William Godwin's *Political Justice*. Brown names the shadowy Ludloe after the historical Edmund Ludlow (1617–92), the English Parlimentarian, Commonwealthman, and regicide who had been Cromwell's commander in chief in Ireland in 1651–52 and who had gone underground after the Restoration as a revolutionary plotter against the Stuart monarchy.[34] In one episode Ludloe is a member of the audience at an open-air recital of Shakespeare's *Tempest*, when Ariel's

---

31. Ruth Bloch, *Visionary Republic: Millennial Themes in American Thought, 1756–1800* (Cambridge, 1985), 211.

32. Clark, *Pioneer Voice*, 126.

33. I am indebted to Pamela Clemit's illuminating chapter on Brown in *The Godwinian Novel: The Rational Fictions of Godwin, Brockden Brown, Mary Shelley* (Oxford, 1993), 109.

34. Brown here follows Godwin's example in *Caleb Williams* of naming his central character after Lucius Cary, Viscount Falkland, a Royalist hero of the Civil War, only reversing the ideological affiliation from Royalist to republican.

song is mysteriously sung from midair, and he rightly suspects (although, it turns out, he is never able to confirm his suspicion) that Carwin is the author of the biloquistic deception. Ludloe rapidly offers himself as Prospero to Carwin's Ariel, although Godwin's account of Ferdinando Falkland's tutelage, and eventual persecution, of Caleb Williams provides Brown's immediate fictional model.

In contrast to Godwin's Burkean Falkland, however, Ludloe turns out to be a conspirator, a kind of revolutionary eleutherarch straight out of the pages of Robison's *Proofs of a Conspiracy*. Excitedly contemplating the potential of Carwin's biloquism as a technique of political imposture, he exclaims: "no more powerful engine . . . could be conceived, by which the ignorant and credulous might be moulded to our purpose. . . . A voice coming from a quarter where no attendant form could be seen would, in most cases, be ascribed to supernal agency, and a command imposed on them, in this manner, would be obeyed with religious scrupulousness."[35] This is of course an extremely un-Godwinian argument, explicitly attacked in book 5, chapter 15, of *Political Justice* ("Of Political Imposture"), where it is associated with Rousseau's *Social Contract*.[36] But Ludloe is still enough of a Godwinian to invite Carwin back to Ireland, pay his transatlantic passage, and accommodate him in his house in Dublin while grooming him for membership of the Illuminati.

Brown's anti-Jacobin exploration of the paradox of conspiracy lies at the heart of his account of Carwin's education by Ludloe. The latter's Godwinian insistence upon treating all alike by "one inflexible standard" of sincerity is compromised by his love of logical paradox and his casuistical defense of "political imposture": "since men in their actual state are infirm and deceitful, a just estimate of consequences may sometimes make dissimulation my duty" (*WCB*, 312). Ludloe fashions Carwin as an instrument for unfettering the minds of men from their prejudices and sends him on a trial mission to despotic and superstitious Spain. After his metamorphosis into a Spanish Catholic, he sets about subverting religious faith and encouraging skepticism, as well as, like Maturin's *Melmoth the Wanderer* (another mysterious Irish Protestant agitator in the gothic tradition), "annihilating the scruples of a tender female, or facilitating my access to the bosoms of courtiers or monks" (*WCB*, 314). Meanwhile, Ludloe secretly corresponds with his agent, furthering his political education by exposing "the absurd and unequal distribution of power and property, . . . the source of luxury and crimes" (*WCB*, 315).

---

35. Charles Brockden Brown, *Wieland and Memoirs of Carwin the Biloquist*, ed. Jay Fliegelman, (Harmondsworth, England, 1991), 300, hereafter cited in the text as *WCB*.

36. A recent application of Rousseau's doctrine was Robespierre's 1794 "Cult of the Supreme Being," designed to forge what the Jacobin leader called "a rapid moral instinct . . . without the slow assistance of reason-

True to Robison's account of the Illuminati, Brown describes how Ludloe delineates "schemes of Utopian felicity where the empire of reason should supplant that of force" to nurture Carwin's political idealism. Oddly enough for one dedicated to subverting the European ancien régime, Ludloe believes that the ideal republic is not achievable in corrupt Europe. Carwin, recollecting the utopian origins of his native America, the Puritan "City on a Hill," suggests to his instructor that "a few, sufficiently enlightened and disinterested, [might] take up their abode in some unvisited region" of America to establish a pantisocratic community (*WCB*, 317). Bidding his promising young initiate back to Dublin, Ludlow darkly hints to him that such a utopian society does in fact already exist, but not in America. "Resting on the two props of fidelity and zeal," he urges, "an association might exist for ages in the heart of Europe, whose influence might be felt, and might be boundless, in some region of the southern hemisphere; and by whom, a moral and political structure might be raised, the growth of pure wisdom, and totally unlike those fragments of Roman and Gothic barbarism, which cover the face of what are called the civilised nations" (*WCB*, 319).

This "colonial" utopian plan (quite unlike anything in the conspiracy theories of Robison or Abbé Barruel, who confine their Illuminist "colonies" to Europe) confirms Carwin's suspicions "that such a scheme had actually been prosecuted, and that Ludloe was a coadjutator" (*WCB*, 319). While unveiling the existence of a de facto Pacific utopia, Ludlow hints at the "arduous probation" that a prospective initiate into such a society must endure, enjoining a total secrecy on pain of death, an unswerving fidelity to the cause of perfectibility, and an incessant confession of one's inner secrets to one's instructor. Ludloe's utopia serves as the final reward for this grueling vocation, and Carwin is promised that "in a few years you will be permitted to withdraw to a land of sages, and the remainder of your life will glide away in the enjoyments of beneficence and wisdom" in the aforementioned "new model of society, in some unsuspected corner of the world" (*WCB*, 323).

Carwin's skeptical training understandably leads him to suspect that Ludloe's "imaginary colony" (*WCB*, 324) might be no more than a high-level "pious fraud"—a secular version of the Christian heaven—to encourage his dupes in the commission of acts of political subversion and assassination. His doubts seem to be checked, however, when Caleb Williams–like he sneaks into Ludloe's library and rifles through his collection of sixteenth- and seventeenth-century travel accounts, as well as his heavily annotated copies of the "political romances of Sir Thomas Moore, Harrington and Hume." In a hand-drawn atlas Carwin

ing" among the citizens of the Republic. See Gregory Dart, *Rousseau, Robespierre, and English Romanticism* (Cambridge, 1999), 100.

discovers Ludloe's "geographical secret," a map of the Pacific "representing two islands, which bore some faint resemblance, in their relative proportions, at least, to Great Britain and Ireland" (*WCB*, 342). (The analogy is rapidly qualified, however, by the information that "none of the larger islands in our globe resembled the one before me"; *WCB*, 342). On perusing another map of the unknown Pacific regions between the south pole and the equator, he notes that "nothing was to be seen . . . but water, except in that spot where the transverse parallels of the southern tropic and the 150th degree east longitude intersect each other" (*WCB*, 342). Were Ludloe's islands situated on the transverse parallel of 150 degrees and the northern tropic, they would appear on the map near Wolfe Tone's Hawaii; their intersection on the southern tropic, however, locates them nearer the epicurean Tahiti.

Because Brown's narrative is set in the 1760s, before the Pacific voyages of Wallis, Bougainville, or Cook, he obviously cannot name these islands without risking anachronism. Instead he imagines Carwin wondering upon what authority Ludloe had fixed "habitable land" in a spot as yet unvisited by any European traveler. The 1798 reader of course knows better, in the aftermath of the tremendous wave of interest in Tahiti generated by the publication of the accounts of the voyages of Bougainville and Cook. Another of Brown's unfinished fragments, the *Narrative of Signior Adini* (probably written about the same time), casts some more light on this shadowy Pacific utopia. Like Ludloe, the reclusive European immigrant Adini is obsessed by a "geographical secret," but his enigmatic references to a certain "Socratic land" lead his friends to doubt his sanity.[37] One day Adini discovers Raphael Ellen, the narrator's son (named, it transpires, after none other than Sir Thomas More's Raphael Hythloday), studying a map of Cook's Pacific discoveries. Pointing to the Pacific, Adini excitedly exclaims: "to thee this . . . is nothing but a waste of waters. Alas! how fond and blind are thy deceivers. To thee it is a realm of barren and inhospitable turbulence, populous only in the mute and scaly kind. To the better informed it is a world of in-

---

37. Apart from projecting utopias, Adini's other main preoccupation seems to be perfecting a short-hand writing system to "equal the flight of the most vehement oratory" and "expedite the mode of communicating thoughts, . . . no inconsiderable step to the goal of happiness and wisdom." (This obsession with creating a system of phonocentric writing of course links Adini with the interests of Elibu Hubbard Smith and Brown's other friends in the Friendly Club; in relation to his other fictions, it connects with Ludloe's quest for control of Carwin's disembodied voice as an instrument of "pious fraud" in the cause of revolutionary liberation.) See "The Narrative of Signior Adini," in Paul Allen, *The Life of Charles Brockden Brown*, facsimile reprint ed., introd. Charles E. Bennett (Delmar, N.Y., 1975), 359–387, 369. The fragment is not included in the abridged English edition of the *Memoirs of Charles Brockden Brown* by William Dunlap (London, 1822), although it is included in the two-volume Philadelphia edition of Dunlap's *Life* (1815), which I have not been able to see.

tellectual beings, whose majesty is faintly reflected on the diminutive stage, by the pigmy actors of Europe."[38]

Echoing the tutelary relationship between Ludloe and Carwin, Adini evidently wishes to train the boy Raphael to fulfill a noble revolutionary destiny: "perhaps a second Raphael [Hythloday] might witness an equally unpleasant and surprising revolution in the system of Eutopia."[39] The extravagance of this conjecture, however, leads Mr. Ellen to wonder whether to Adini's disturbed mind Sir Thomas More's "Raphael . . . [was] a real voyager, a precursor of himself to that miraculous land; or was his imagination filled with phantoms, that might with sufficient aptness be designated by the appellation of Eutopian?"[40] Like other political projectors, Adini has been mistaken in "paint[ing] as real what is only desirable or possible," thereby mistaking imaginary utopias for reality.[41] As Brown had earlier written in his *Journal*, "the idea of a perfect commonwealth is not the same extravagant thing in education as in politics."[42] (Neither this nor Brown's implied critique of Adini's idealism reveals much sympathy for radical politics; nor, however, do they represent a rejection of utopianism *tout court*, being more concerned with warning of the dangers of crudely applying theory to practice.)

Returning now to *Carwin the Biloquist*, the reader is never exactly clear whether or not Ludloe had intended Carwin to discover his "geographical secret"; whatever his intention, however, Carwin now rests convinced that his mentor's "plans of civilization had been carried into practice in some unvisited corner of the world" (*WCB*, 344–45). Ludloe's utopia appears to Carwin not just as a political fiction but also as a reality in the as-yet unexplored waters of the Pacific Ocean. Whether it is fact or fiction (the analogy with the Adini fragment suggests Brown preferred the latter), Carwin's discovery of Ludloe's "geographical secret" fans his revolutionary enthusiasm: "[it kept] up my zeal to prosecute the journey I had commenced under [Ludloe's] auspices" (*WCB*, 345). Despite this declared enthusiasm, however, Carwin's deceitful withholding of the secret of his biloquism from Ludloe (despite the latter's strong suspicions) reveals nothing less than his own refusal of the total confessional transparency enjoined upon the political neophyte, hinting at the breakout that we infer must follow in the *Memoirs*' unwritten conclusion. A certain symbolic equivalence is perhaps evident

38.   Allen, *Charles Brockden Brown*, 380.
39.   Ibid., 382.
40.   Ibid., 383.
41.   Ibid., 383.
42.   Clark, *Pioneer Voice*, 44.

between Ludloe's "geographical secret" and Carwin's undeclared gift of biloquism, suggesting Brown's critical notion of the revolutionary employment of utopian discourse in the 1790s. Both are anti-Godwinian technologies for coercing the wills of individuals by seducing the imagination rather than convincing the reason, analogous to the cat-and-mouse game played out between Caleb and his master Falkland in Godwin's 1794 novel.[43]

"WIELAND" AND THE FAILURE OF THE AMERICAN UTOPIA

I want to conclude by turning back to Brown's *Wieland* and considering Carwin's role in shattering the American utopia of the Wieland family after he has escaped from Ludloe's tutelage in Ireland. Jay Fliegelman has convincingly located Brown's novel in relation to a crisis affecting notions of representation and voice in the new American republic. In the act of declaring independence, Jeffersonian publicists defined political authority in rhetorical terms as "the ability to secure consent. . . . increasingly it signified an oratorical ability not merely to persuade but to excite, animate, motivate, and impress" (*WCB*, xxix). Tonal and gestural inflections—that is, body language (known in rhetorical theory as "pronunciato")—rather than logical argument assumed central importance in political oratory. James Burgh's influential *Art of Speaking* (1764) had argued that in a republic "true eloquence" translated the "sceptre of the monarch" into "the tongue of the orator."[44]

The utopian transparency of a "discourse of nature"—the republican faith in the formula *vox populi, vox dei*—lies at the heart of the pantisocratic community in rural Pennsylvania established by the Wieland and Pleyel siblings after the death of their parents in the novel's first section. Theodore Wieland—son of a German religious enthusiast who has retreated into the American wilderness

43. As Mrs. Carter, the skeptical interlocutor of Brown's 1798 philosophical dialogue *Alcuin* puts it, in response to Alcuin's description of the utopian "paradise of women" "a class of reasoners has lately arisen, who aim at the deepest foundation of civil society. . . . it was necessary to subdue our incredulity, as to the effects of their new maxims, by exhibiting those effects in detail, and winning our assent to their truth by engrossing the fancy and charming the affections. The journey that you have lately made, I merely regard as an excursion into their visionary world" (*Alcuin: A Dialogue*, ed. Lee R. Edwards [New York, 1971], 68). The dialogic context of this must qualify Mrs. Carter's remarks, but we can take Brown's overall treatment of utopia here to suggest that, in the words of Lee Edwards, "the function of utopias is not so much to provide exact models but to jog the mind into channels or perception which are permanently blocked by its ordinary procedures" (p. 103).

44. See Jay Fliegelrnan's *Declaring Independence: Jefferson, Natural Language, and the Culture of Performance* (Stanford, Calif., 1993), 31. The Scottish Commonwealthman Burgh, we might recall, was also the author of the utopian *Account of the Cessares*, as well as the *Political Disquisitions* of 1774, a defense of the American colonies against monarchical oppression.

(only to spontaneously combust in his dome-roofed temple of nature during a fit of devotional zeal) transforms his father's temple into a school of eloquence dominated by a bust of Cicero: "His favourite occupation consisted in embellishing his rhetoric with all the proprieties of gesticulation and utterance" (*WCB*, 27). There is a marked ideological difference between Wieland and his skeptical brother-in-law Henry Pleyel, allegorizing the blend of Puritan enthusiasm and enlightened rationalism constitutive of American identity.[45] Nevertheless, the harmonious transparency that marks the intercourse between Theodore, Pleyel, and their two sisters Clara and Catherine establishes an ideal logocentric community free of any external restraints, a polity marked by pure representation. As Clara affirms, "we were left to the guidance of our own understandings, and the casual impressions which society might make upon us" (*WCB*, 24).[46]

Into the heart of this American utopia—in conformity with the standard 1790s anti-Jacobin plot—drops the mysterious (apparently English or Irish) Carwin, whose homely rustic garb nevertheless identifies him with a Jeffersonian ideal of agrarian virtue combined with "wisdom and eloquence." What instantly strikes Clara is Carwin's "tone" of speaking (the word "tone" itself—in relation to Carwin—is reiterated four times in chapters 6 and 7); his words are remarkable not so much for their meaning but for "the tone that accompanied them . . . the voice was not only mellifluent and clear, but the emphasis was so just, and the modulation so impassioned, that it seemed as if an heart of stone could not fail to be moved by it" (*WCB*, 59). Around the same time, mysterious disembodied voices begin to plague members of both families, sowing seeds of disharmony between them. At first the voices seem benevolent, but they soon begin to expose the psychological flaws and ideological fissures that compromise and divide all the main characters. Wieland, still hag-ridden by his father's bizarre death, has no hesitation in interpreting them literally as evidence of "celestial interference." Pleyel, despite his skeptical temper, is equally credulous in an empiricist rather than enthusiastical register: "he scrupled not to deny faith to any testimony but that of his senses, and allowed the facts which had lately been supported by this testimony, not to mould his belief, but to give birth to doubts" (*WCB*, 86).

45. As Brown's "unreliable" narrator Clara Wieland insists, "Moral necessity, and calvinistic inspiration, were the props on which my brother thought proper to repose. Pleyel was the champion of intellectual liberty, and rejected all guidance but that of his reason" (p. 28).

46. Brown has turned Godwin's political allegory in *Caleb Williams* inside out; as Clemit indicates, "in opposition to Godwin's exploration of the intrusion of government into private life, Brown is preoccupied with how people might behave in a world without institutional restraints, . . . which forces characters into a dangerous self-reliance" (p. 109).

Pushed to an extreme, both Wieland's blind faith and Pleyel's skepticism are shown to be equally malleable by the unknown will that controls the voices. Meanwhile, Carwin (whom we can only guess, if we haven't yet read *Carwin the Biloquist*, is their true author) even takes pains openly to suggest that the voices are really artful deceptions designed to manipulate and seduce the individuals who hear them: "Mysterious voices had always a share in producing the catastrophe, but they were always to be explained by some known principles, either as reflected in to a focus, or communicated through a tube" (*WCB*, 85). Perhaps because they are more interested in the "tone" of Carwin's voice than in what he actually says, neither the usually perspicuous Clara Wieland nor any of the other characters are able to apply Carwin's lesson to the solution of the present mystery, with ultimately tragic results.[47]

The familial and affective bonds uniting the group are quickly disrupted by Carwin's ventriloquism. Clara overhears her brother's voice plotting to murder her, Pleyel (who is emotionally involved with the virtuous and chaste Clara) overhears her flirting with a mysterious lover in the summerhouse and breaks off his engagement, and, in the novel's most tragic and climactic "transformation," Wieland obeys what he believes to be the voice of God and brutally murders his wife and children to prove his religious zeal. Clara Wieland's insight that "if the sense be depraved, it is impossible to calculate the evils that may flow from the consequent deductions of the understanding" (*WCB*, 39) suggests that Brown's real polemical target is the disaggregated and immature political culture of 1790s America rather than the "jacobinical" figure of Carwin. Like the plague that sweeps through Philadelphia in Brown's novel *Arthur Mervyn*, transmitted by fugitives from revolutionary Saint Domingue, the American republic has no immunity against the revolutionary ideologies imported to its shores in the 1790s.

At a climactic moment in the novel, Pleyel discovers a newspaper story reprinted from the British papers that identifies Francis Carwin as a fugitive Irishman who has escaped from Newgate Prison in Dublin after murdering a certain Lady Jane Conway and robbing "the honorable Mr Ludloe" (147). After the novel's sanguinary climax, Carwin confesses the truth of his ventriloquism to Clara but denies the murder imputed to him in Ireland or his responsibility for Wieland's insane actions.[48] Brown was completing work on *Wieland* during the

---

47. Carwin's double bluff is intended by Brown to reveal the hold of psychological and ideological predispositions—the power of early associations—over reason, thereby confounding the brittle and purely rhetorical consensus upon which the American republic is constructed.

48. Because Brown never completed the *Memoirs of Carwin*, we cannot know the truth of Carwin's disavowal, but on analogy with the case of Clithero Edny, another mysterious fugitive Irishman at the center of Brown's 1799 novel *Edgar Huntly*, Carwin's denial seems believable. The somnabulistic and guilt-besotted Clithero believes he has murdered his virtuous Irish benefactress Mrs Lorimer and her villainous brother

summer months of 1798 that saw the United Irish rebellion and its bloody suppression, and imagines Carwin as (allegedly) escaping from the very prison in which Wolfe Tone was to be executed in November 1798, when Brown was working on the sequel, *The Memoirs of Carwin*. The link with Irish radicalism is not unique in Brown's writings of this period. Clithero Edny, Irish villain of his later novel *Edgar Huntly*, hails from Armagh, the center of the 1795 troubles. The year 1798 was also the year of the Alien and Sedition Acts, which reflected the Federalist government's fears of Jacobin conspiracy by foreign (and largely Irish) émigrés. As Michael Durey has indicated, at least seventy-four of the known immigrants to the United States in the 1790s had been members of popular radical movements in Britain and Ireland, and of these, one-half were Irish; of the remainder three-fifths were English and two-thirds Scots.[49] Quasi-masonic Irish societies abounded, such as the Hibernian Society in Philadelphia, the Friendly Sons of St. Patrick in New York, and the Republican Greens militia. From a Federalist point of view, Jeffersonian republicanism seemed to have undergone a terrifying transformation in the crucible of British and especially Irish Jacobin conspiracy, represented in Brown's political allegory by Carwin's American nativity, his Jeffersonian rustic garb, and his seductive eloquence.

As Fliegelman points out, in contrast to the villains of many eighteenth-century novels, Carwin (despite his attraction to Clara) is less the seducer of women than of opinion (*WCB*, ix). Carwin actually sheds no blood, and at the novel's climax appears pathetic in comparison with the monstrously tragic figure of Theodore Wieland, transformed by the voices into a homicidal maniac. It seems plausible to read Carwin's biloquism as a metaphor for the disembodied and manipulative voice of the new print-born energy of public opinion. Brown here anticipates William Hazlitt's account of public opinion as *vox et praeterea nihil*, nevertheless possessing the "confident circulation and irresistible force"[50] to

Wiatt. In fact he has killed the latter, but only in self-defense, and has tried but failed to kill the former from mistaken motives of benevolence: he only imagines his culpability, but in the end he is driven to destructive madness in America, where he has taken refuge. The petty motives underlying Carwin's ventriloquistic experiments on the Wieland community are out of all proportion to their tragic consequences. A more positive Irish allusion in *Edgar Huntly* is the novel's hero Sarsfield, named after the seventeenth-century Irish Catholic leader Patrick Sarsfield. Sarsfield was a maternal ancestor of William Duane (1760–1835; see below), editor of the Philadelphia *Aurora*, upon whom Brown appears to model his character. Like his fictional counterpart, the Irish-educated Duane had served in British Bengal, from whence he was deported in 1795 for criticizing East India Company policy in his radical newspapers *The Bengal Journal* and *The Indian World*, and settled in Philadelphia. For the full story, see P. Thankappan Nair, *A History of the Calcutta Press* (Calcutta, 1987), 202–12.

49. Michael Durey, "Tom Paine's Apostles: Radical Emigrés, and the Triumph of Jeffersonian Republicanism," *William and Mary Quarterly*, 3d ser., 44 (1987): 666.

50. William Hazlitt, "On Public Opinion" (1828), in *Selected Writings*, ed. Jon Cook (Oxford, 1991), 144–45.

wreak havoc with the fiction of representation devised in the early 1780s by what Fliegelman calls "a small group of privileged white men who . . . had described themselves as 'We the People'" (*WCB*, xi). Joyce Appleby has indicated that only in the 1790s did American democratic republicanism "find a national voice where in the past [its] strength had been local," owing in large part to the establishment of more than 450 newspapers and 75 magazines between 1783 and 1800.[51] Although by no means all of these were anti-Federalist (Brown's own *Monthly Magazine* and *Literary Magazine* were certainly not), newsprint was nevertheless "the circulating medium that brought Republicans together under Jefferson's banner," playing a decisive role in the republican electoral victory of 1800.

The professional background of British and Irish immigrants in this decade is exemplified by the fact that eighteen of them edited no fewer than forty-nine newspapers and magazines, mostly in the politically sensitive middle states, but also in Philadelphia, where, for example, the Irish former London Corresponding Society member William Duane edited the republican *Aurora*.[52] The Federalist publicist Ames lamented that "the newspapers are an overmatch for the government. They will first overcome and then usurp it. This has been done; and the Jacobins owe their triumph to the unceasing use of this engine."[53] Through the new media of print culture, and particularly the ideologically partisan newspapers, the old wounds of primitive enthusiasm appear to have reopened in the political conflict of party that plagued America in the 1790s. Maybe this explains why Brown sent a copy of his novel to Thomas Jefferson in 1798, to highlight the havoc wrought by the uncontrolled abuse of what Ludloe had described as Carwin's "powerful engine, . . . by which the credulous and ignorant might be moulded to our purpose."[54] From the Federalist perspective, the Jacobin controllers of the news press, with their appeal to the disembodied voice of public opinion, were mobilizing an ultramodern technology of representation in order to disseminate a primitivistic political ideology.[55]

---

51. Durey, "Tom Paine's Apostles," 681–82.
52. Ibid., 683.
53. Ibid., 684.
54. Clark, *Pioneer Voice,* 163.
55. Jay Fliegelman takes a slightly different tack in arguing that "Brown's master trope of ventriloquism" evokes the specter of the novelist speaking out "not physically in person but through the multiplicity of other voices and the depersonalized authority of print." He notes in this connection Brown's moving mimicry of the female voice of Clara Wieland (like Carwin) and the absence of the author's name from the title page of the first edition (*Wieland,* xxxix). Brown was doubtless aware of the analogies between the art of his fiction and the seductive power of Carwin's biloquism. But there is a difference; whereas Carwin's formidable "engine" is mystificatory, Brown's is intended to demystify—rather in the Radcliffean counter-gothic tradition. Both his polyphonic play of voices and his development of the Godwinian technique of the unreliable narrator leads him to "the solution of appearances" in which readers can

In conclusion, it is perhaps ironic that the first published novel by a professional American writer should turn out to be so apparently anti-utopian, albeit in the mold of subsequent American classics such as Hawthorne's *Blythedale Romance* and James's *The Bostonians*. Yet this point needs some qualification; we should recall that the Carwin who arrives in America from Ireland has thrown off the regulative ideal of Ludloe's island utopia and employs his "powerful engine" for obscure personal, rather than political, motives, unlike the protagonist of Godwin's *St. Leon*, published the following year, in 1799. But similar to Rousseau's magical ring of Gyges in the sixth *Reverie of a Solitary Walker*, which has the power of making its wearer invisible, Carwin's biloquism carries with it a constant temptation to seek personal gratification rather than public benefit: "the man whose power sets him above humanity must himself be above all human weaknesses, or this excess of power will only serve to sink him lower than his fellows."[56] Carwin's abuse of his power has the unintended effect of showing up the tragic weaknesses of a flawed utopia, as realized in the American fiction of representation. I have speculated that Theobald Wolfe Tone's "Sandwich Islands Memoir" may lie somewhere in the background of Brown's imagining of a Pacific utopia (it is much more pertinent than his friend Elihu Hubbard Smith's contemporaneous utopian scheme) and that the ideological ramifications of Irish republican immigration to the United States fanned the flames of his political anxieties. But in the end, Brown's two novels, taken together and considered alongside the fascination with utopianism manifest in his immediate intellectual circle, may not be as anti-utopian as they seem at first glance. Rather, they might be taken to urge the necessity of utopia as a regulative ideal that is always just beyond the horizon of its realization in any particular political state.[57]

Queens College, Cambridge

examine the nature of their own susceptibility to fictions. As he put it in his apology for the novel in his letter to Jefferson, "I am . . . obliged to hope that an artful display of incidents, the powerful delineation of characters and the train of eloquent and judicious reasoning which may be combined in a fictitious work, will be regarded by Thomas Jefferson with as much respect as they are regarded by me" (Clark, *Pioneer Voice*, 163).

56.   J. J. Rousseau, *Reveries of a Solitary Walker*, trans. Peter France (Harmondsworth, England, 1979), 103.

57.   In this respect my reading of *Wieland* differs from Clemit's, because he fails to account for Carwin's break from Ludloe, and thereby identifies Carwin with St. Leon and Mary Shelley's Victor Frankenstein; see *Godwinian Novel*, 135.

Filling Up and Emptying Out the Sublime: Terror in British Radical Culture

On Bastille Day 14 July 1989, the bicentennial of the French Revolution inspired the greatest party Paris had given since its liberation from Nazi occupation. Pageantry continued long into the night. American musicians, Chinese acrobats, African dancers, and other costumed guests merged with an enormous crowd that danced down the alleys of the Champs Elysées through public gardens and into side streets. Television viewers around the world watched these scenes and listened to the speeches delivered to President Mitterrand. President Gorbachev brought praise from the USSR. President Bush brought along the iron key to the Bastille that, two centuries before, Lafayette had given to Tom Paine to deliver to George Washington. Among thousands of smiling foreign dignitaries, however, one guest cast a dark cloud over the party—Prime Minister Margaret Thatcher, who, wherever she appeared in Paris, was booed. For Madam Thatcher had voiced on French soil the hallowed Victorian notion that the French were claiming for themselves what the Magna Charta began in 1215 and the Glorious Revolution fulfilled in 1688. French newspapers, radio, and television carried stories about these remarks and magnified national insult with outraged or sarcastic commentaries. Back in London the *Times* wondered what, besides Mrs. Thatcher's distaste for revolutions and socialists, lay behind her provocative bad manners. One of the reasons for her sour mood may be found in an interview she had given years earlier, in which she alluded to her reading of *A Tale of Two Cities*. Its tumbrels carrying victims to the guillotine amid shouts of bloodthirsty crowds had apparently never stopped rumbling in her mind. It is unlikely that the prime minister—even from the back rows of spectators where she had been seated by the offended French—could have heard the passing fanfare without remembering the novelist's famous descriptions of the Terror.[1]

---

1.   See Philip Jacobson, "Politicians Stay away from Big Parade," London *Times,* 12 July 1989, p. 9; and Robert Kilroy-Silk, "It Was the Best of Thatcher, It Was the Worst," London *Times,* 14 July 1989, p. 16. Kilroy-Silk does not invoke the common Whiggish idea of English revolutionary priority, best known from Macaulay's essays. Perhaps he was unfamiliar with them—or perhaps he could not imagine that Madam Thatcher would have known them.

If the prime minister was, indeed, haunted that day by scenes of terror from *A Tale of Two Cities*, she would not have been thinking uncommon English thoughts. A popular school text with many theatrical, film, radio, and television treatments, the novel dominates English-speaking memory of the French Revolution, not to mention the many other stories about the French Revolution it has inspired—such as Baroness d'Orczy's *The Scarlet Pimpernel* (1905)—stories devoid even of Dickens's sympathy for the oppressed French poor and his mockery of aristocrats. The success of such works attests to the survival of what began in the 1790s—the portrayal of the Revolution as diseased Reason that weakened religion, glorified systemization, and caused evil to spring forth as the Terror. The events that constitute the Terror and their legendary elaborations in European culture have long played a role in the manipulations of historical memory; and, although the question of whether to assign originary violence to revolutionaries or to reactionaries is still raised among historians and French politicians alike, reactionary shock largely prevails even two hundred years later. Many seem to take modern political terror as French at its root, and otherwise prudent scholars often speak indiscriminately of the French Revolution's, the Chinese Cultural revolution's, or Hitler's or Stalin's "reign of terror." Dickens permanently coded the way intellectuals had long read and still commonly read the Revolution, magnified by the last century's forms of revolutionary violence.

In the 1790s much dispute over causes of the Terror was, of course, no more complicated than many a postwar discussion over who fired the first shot. Many English radicals, like their French counterparts, simply found the cause of the Terror in the ancien régime and in the reactionary politics of such figures as William Pitt. William Godwin, for example, availed himself of this radical commonplace. In his preface to *Caleb Williams*, a novel about repression, including class, familial, and judicial varieties, he describes himself as writing "under terror," as if no one would misunderstand that he was referring to the British regime of the 1790s. Coleridge, as a young radical in the 1790s, asserted that all French terror arose only in response to reactionary terror against the Revolution. There were also grand philosophical gestures seeking to put the Terror "in perspective," as we would say today. Kant, for instance, with never an interruption in his daily routine in Konigsberg, calmly contemplated the French Revolution's violence as a necessary part of political change.[2]

---

2. William Godwin, *Caleb Williams*, ed. David McCracken (New York, 1970), 2. For Coleridge's most direct characterization of the Pitt terror, see "On the Present War," in *Conciones Ad Populum, Or Addresses to the People*, in *Lectures 1795: On Politics and Religion, The Collected Works of Samuel Taylor Coleridge*, vol. 1, ed. Lewis Patton and Peter Mann (Princeton, N.J., 1971), 72 (hereafter cited as *CC* in the text). On Kant's response to the Revolution, see Immanuel Kant, *The Conflict of the Faculties (Der Streit der Fakultäten)*,

During the 1790s, the Terror had also inevitably been seen, both in Paris and by foreign sympathizers, as violence simply replicating previous political and religious massacres; and, in proportion to these, it was deemed numerically insignificant. Nor was the social and political philosophizing of terror new in and of itself. One of the best-known justifications for terror was established in the sixteenth and seventeenth centuries in the accommodations of Calvin's *Institutes of the Christian Religion*. Calvin clearly separates spiritual and earthly fear, but he insists on civil repression as a reminder of godly wrath. Forgetting to fear God, so Calvin and many others argued, lies at the heart of original sin.[3] Nor would radicals in the 1790s have forgotten Hobbes's *Leviathan* and its exchange of terror in a state of nature for the protective tyranny of the sovereign. In seizing authority for terror, Jacobins seized what was already claimed by all authoritarian thinkers as a necessity for civil happiness. Terror was then logically authorized as all the more necessary for revolutionary success.

But however much the Revolution's Terror was consonant with ingrained theological and political ideas, few writers in England of any stripe could comfortably associate it with the terrorist concepts of Calvin or Hobbes; and it did far more than replace the Black Legend of the Conquistadors or the St. Bartholomew's Day Massacre, memories of which the Terror invoked for British radical dissenters. The Terror eventually become mythologized across the political spectrum as a founding event of secular history, the sort of phenomenon theoretical astrophysicists now call a "singularity."

The notion that the Terror is the first world-historical violence for which human beings could take full responsibility was elaborated first by conservative and eventually by liberal thinkers, and finally even in some versions of radical culture. Orthodox reactionaries of the time, of course, merely condemned the Revolution as satanic will that reaped what it sowed. In a related way, secular humanists would later take the Terror as human corruption that inevitably erupts with the excessive dismantling of social controls. Fear of the animal hiding behind religion or of the one hiding behind civil society is ultimately fear of the same animal. Reaction in the 1790s to the Terror was the first stage in an intellectual attitude that would later enable the writing of Conrad's *Heart of Darkness*, the locus classicus of a modern Hobbesian critique of the horror that occurs

trans. Mary J. Gregor (New York, 1979), 153. I have discussed radical reaction and these texts more extensively in "Holy Savagery and Wild Justice: English Romanticism and the Terror," *Studies in Romanticism* 28 (1989): 365–95. For a summary of radical reaction, see Emma Vincent Macleod, *A War of Ideas: British Attitudes to the Wars against Revolutionary France, 1792–1802* (Hampshire, England, 1998), 114–34 (the book is reviewed in this volume by Michael Smith).

3. John Calvin, *Institutes of the Christian Religion*, trans. Ford Lewis Battles, ed. John T. McNeill, 2 vols. (London, 1960), 1:241–49.

when humans are completely unrestrained. Indeed, the 1790s had its version of a Conradian vision of "horror" in the confluence of the terrorizing "individual" and the self-conscious terrorist state. The British confronted their own version of contemporary terror as recounted in parliamentary reports and newspaper stories concerning the East India Company that appeared throughout the 1780s and '90s. The behavior of Lord Clive and the suspected terrorizing policies of William Hastings in India, conflated with disdain for a new Nabob class of capitalist entrepreneurs and state factotums, were connected in the mind of Edmund Burke with the kind of terror that had shocked him in the Jacobins. But despite resemblances between French terror at home and British terror abroad, Burke, in *Reflections on the Revolution in France*, had in 1790 already called the French Revolution "the most astonishing thing that has hitherto happened in the world."[4] On their side, revolutionary orators agreed, for they often claimed that, however it looked backward to traditions of the Roman republic, the Revolution was completely new. For the Committee of Public Safety, the Terror's exterminating violence was a virtuous and rational recuperation of human authority long ago surrendered to imaginary gods. But the implications of the Terror itself as something new do not begin to take hold of the thoughts of radicals and sympathizers until late in the 1790s.[5] Once that happened, it was impossible to avoid thinking of the Terror when thinking of the Revolution. If, as Shelley said, the French Revolution was "the master theme of the epoch in which we live," the Terror was its master nightmare.[6]

But why should the Terror have such special historical status? It is hard to imagine any historical period that does not, in one way or another, have its particular confrontation with violence, as if in each era violence must be elevated anew as an object of social and metaphysical attention. These confrontations

---

4.   Edmund Burke, *Reflections on the Revolution in France*, ed. Conor Cruise O'Brien (Hammondsworth, England, and New York, 1969), 92; cited henceforward in the text.

5.   The question of what was to be considered historically unique in the French Revolution is a complicated one. One reason it took longer in Britain to address the idea of its uniqueness, culminating in the opinions of Carlyle (which I discuss below), is that the British did not assimilate the French Jacobin theory of terror as a manifestation of virtue. British writers, reactionary as well as sympathetic, took a less exalted view; they portrayed the Revolution as a new kind of beginning, an awakening day, in which the principal emotion was *hope*, a word that suggests the ameliorative tone even of many British radicals. The French did not need the concept of hope, since the Revolution was already in the process of being established. What it needed was terror, to keep what had already been accomplished from being destroyed; this terror came to be seen as unique among all the terror in modern history, for it arose from republican virtue. For those in Britain who soon fell away from the revolutionary cause, it was precisely terror that destroyed the hope—an old historical thing that had killed the new beginning. For discussion of how the asserted uniqueness of the Revolution affected the French view even of the uniqueness of their terminology, see Philippe Roger's essay in this volume.

6.   *The Letters of Percy Bysshe Shelley*, ed. Frederick L. Jones, 2 vols. (Oxford, 1964), 1:504.

have taken many forms—Machiavellian acceptance of useful violence, the Calvinist or Hobbesian sense of the order guaranteed by state terror, or simply the horror conveyed by a Euripidean chorus crying out at human, all too human cruelty, of a kind that shocked even the gods. The Machiavellian, the Calvinist, the Hobbesian, and the Euripidean are striking, but not unique, moments of human self-consciousness that were revived in the revolutionary and reactionary violence that continued with only brief interruptions from 1792 to 1815.

Still, there are many reasons why the position that anyone took toward the Terror from the 1790s on implied much more than any previous attitude to violence—too many even to enumerate here. One important reason that I shall focus on turns on the fact that actual terror in the 1790s both blended and clashed with what had developed in aesthetic and psychological discussion during the previous century. If the Terror set the terms of this preoccupation with violence from the 1790s on, the actual political terror of 1793 occurred in a culture that had already designed a complicated rhetoric of terror. Eighteenth-century culture had its own way of entwining the grand thoughts—about infinitude, eternity, and godly power—with thoughts of death, submission, and annihilation. Because the eighteenth century had so tightly linked the psychological qualities of the sublime and of terror, it was especially necessary for revolutionaries and their radical descendants, from the 1790s to the 1820s, to be cautious in associating them. Some found it useful to fill the sublime with terror, others to empty the terror out of it. To be sure, not all European radical cultures cultivated the same traditions. The Jacobin interpretation, which treats the Terror as self-defense, can proudly resonate a century after the Revolution in a single word, as in the title of a book such as *Robespierre terroriste*.[7] The word *terroriste* here evokes the virtuous revolutionary. Few British sympathizers could refer to terror in this sense after the 1790s, and by the middle of the nineteenth century—along with the disappearance of the sublime as a significant psychological and political category—the honorific use of terror or terrorist grew impossible except in French.

The need to guard against the facile association of terror and the sublime is immediately apparent in the language of that revolutionary who notoriously wove them together—Maximilien Robespierre, often taken to be the consummate terrorist, for he both authorized executions and authored the rhetoric of their terrifying purpose. It is, of course, too often forgotten that his declarations were arrived at by majority vote in the Committee of Public Safety and the Convention and that it was Robespierre who often tried to prevent terrorist excess. Still, he became in the 1790s—and has been ever since—a popular personification of terrorist evil. In one of his most important speeches on the policy of

7.   Albert Mathiez, *Robespierre terroriste* (Paris, 1921).

terror (5 February 1794), he proclaims its adoption with republican pride. He knew full well the resonance of the word used to elevate violence to transcendent significance. In the sense here employed, *terror* is a manifestation of *vertu,* a republican quality sacralized in the nation:

> Si le ressort du gouvernement populaire dans la paix est la vertu, le ressort du gouvernement populaire en révolution est à la fois *la vertu et la terreur*: la vertu, sans laquelle la terreur est funeste; la terreur, sans laquelle la vertu est impuissante. La terreur n'est autre chose que la justice prompte, sévère, inflexible; elle est donc une émanation de la vertu; elle est moins un principe particulier qu'une conséquence du principe général de la democratie, appliqué aux plus pressans besoins de la patrie. [If the moral force of popular government during peace is virtue, then in revolution it is both virtue and terror—that virtue without which terror is crime, that terror without which virtue is powerless. Terror is nothing more than swift, severe, and inflexible justice; it is hence an emanation of virtue. Terror is less a particular principle than a consequence of the basic principle of democracy applied to the most pressing needs of the nation.]

Robespierre knew that, in the cultural symbolism of the day, where terror was, there also was the sublime. Hence he emphasizes the terror as policy with a religious aura of justice, goodness, and virtue. But he also at times de-emphasizes it as a necessary part of the sublimity of the French nation: however necessary terror may be at the moment, it will eventually be transcended in the political sublime of republican peace and order. Some of the hesitation in Robespierre's association of the two suggests his awareness of how he both spiritualizes terror by means of the sublime and tries to avoid its repressive implications. Nevertheless, Robespierre often reverted to the rhetoric that associated the sublime grandiloquently with terror. The combination of the two is difficult to avoid when he universalizes the call to Terror in an imaginative complicity of all those individuals, even those in other countries, who feel the sacredness in the Revolution. In this mode, he figures himself both as a foreigner and as a Frenchman, blended into one universal figure transformed in a sacrificial moment of sublimity:

> O ma patrie! si le destin m'avoit fait naître dans une contrée etrangère et lointaine, j'aurois adressé au ciel des voeux continuels pour ta prospérité; j'aurais versé des larmes d'attendrissement au récit de tes combats et de tes vertus; mon âme attentive auroit suivi

avec une inquiète ardeur tous les mouvemens de ta glorieuse révolution; j'aurois envié le sort de tes citoyens, j'aurois envié celui de
tes représentans. Je suis Français, je suis l'un de tes représentans
... O peuple sublime! reçois le sacrifice de tout mon être; heureux
celui qui est né au milieu de toi! plus heureux celui qui peut mourir
pour ton bonheur! [O my country! if destiny demanded that I be
born in a foreign country far away, I would still have continually
prayed to heaven for thy prosperity. I would have tenderly shed
tears upon hearing the stories of your combats and virtuous deeds.
My soul would have attentively followed with an unquiet ardor all
the progress of your glorious revolution. I would have envied the
fate of your citizens, I would have envied that of your representatives. I am French, I am one of your representatives.—O sublime
people, accept the sacrifice of my being. Happy is he who has been
born in your midst and even happier he who can die to further
your happiness!][8]

What Danton, Marat, St. Just, and above all Robespierre did in symbolic or-
chestrations of terror and the sublime was not at first alien to the vocabulary of
British radicals. Much of their rhetoric during the 1790s, however, was drawn
not from the psychologized sublime but directly from seventeenth-century
revolutionary Puritan traditions. This vocabulary was shaped by biblical language, the violence of a righteous God who wielded retribution in plague, fire,
famine, and slaughter for the good of humanity. But what Robespierre and other
terroristes added to the rhetorical mix was more than the sacred, secularized. In
appeals to political will, Robespierre portrays a world-historical moment as world-
historical imagination. A revolutionary ideology of Reason obviously appropriated the imaginative authority of the sacred; but it also furnished the idea of
terror, before the shedding of blood, adopted *by the mind* in exalted, virtuous
complicity.

❧ ❧

The French appeal for universal assent to the Terror is one of the marks of the
transformation of the eighteenth-century violent mob, the many-headed beast,
into the nascent idea of a consciously violent human mass. In this mass, revolutionaries and sympathizers far away could recognize themselves and imaginatively participate. But this kind of association of terror and the sublime carried

8.   *Oeuvres de Maximilien Robespierre*, ed. Marc Bouloiseau and Albert Soboul, 10 vols. in 11 (Paris, 1967),
      10:357, 445.

with it dangers to the imagination. Robespierre's metaphorical maneuver and the actual violence of the Terror awkwardly merged with the British tradition of violent biblical prophecy. The consequences of imaginative complicity and its expression in Protestant prophetic terror can be seen in a painful experience recounted by Coleridge.

In 1817 Coleridge felt called upon to explain and justify the violence expressed in his political poem of 1798, "Fire, Famine, and Slaughter." Coleridge recounts a conversation he had nearly twenty years before in the presence of Sir Humphrey Davy, Sir Walter Scott, and other friends. Scott had come upon "Fire, Famine, and Slaughter," a bloody poem indeed, anonymously published in the *Morning Post* in January of 1798 (also discussed by John Barrell in this volume, in the context particularly of British politics). When Scott read it aloud to the assembled company, Coleridge's host, William Sotheby, commented that whatever the merits of the poem, "they could not have compensated for that malignity of heart which could alone have prompted sentiments so atrocious." Shaken by the remark, Coleridge noticed that Humphrey Davy (the only other person in the room aware of the author's identity) was also made uncomfortable. Coleridge summoned up, he says, "presence of mind enough to take up the subject without exciting even a suspicion how nearly and painfully it interested me." He then reports how he responded to the charge of thinking cruelly and what he has since thought about the subject of violence, quoting himself in passages from *The Friend* of 1810.

The real subject of the "Apologetic Preface" to "Fire, Famine, and Slaughter" is the contamination of metaphoric by actual historical violence. Here is Coleridge's defense, offered after years during which the Terror had been sinking even deeper into European consciousness, now more fully elaborated as a special occurrence of violence in the history of civilization: "Could it be supposed; though for a moment, that the author seriously wished what he had thus wildly imagined, even the attempt to palliate an inhumanity so monstrous would be an insult to the hearers?" After making careful psychological distinctions, he goes on to defend writers and poets of the past, as if the contamination he must now defend against can be too easily projected back upon them. Dante, Jeremy Taylor, Milton—those who spoke with terrible imprecation of the imaginary horrors of eternal justice—should not be thought, Coleridge insists, to be devoid of "humanity, or goodness of heart." He distinguishes Milton's violent seventeenth-century republican language from any "modern" associations with revolutionary "violence": "Milton became more and more a stern republican, or rather an advocate for that religious and moral aristocracy which, in his day, was called republicanism, and which, even more than royalism itself, is the direct antipode of modern jacobinism" (*CC* I.i.429–40). Coleridge is arguing against those who, he suggests, see in poets of the past a horrifying complicity that these poets could never have intended.

That Coleridge had to distinguish between barbarous intentions and his metaphors indicates how profoundly writers could be affected by a culture whose violence can no longer be contained in coherent symbolic form. His defense of himself is historically specific; his defense of his poetic predecessors is a defense of *all* political poetry in the face of history. How could the mantle of the prophetic poet be worn comfortably if the Romantic poet had to point out that Milton's seventeenth-century republican wrath was not proleptic Jacobin excess? As John Barrell points out, discussing the "Apologetic Preface" in his essay for this volume, Coleridge had the immediate legal problem of having written a poem vulnerable to the charge of treason, not because he acted but because he dared even to imagine political assassination. Coleridge defends his poem in the "Apologetic Preface" with the claim that such violent poetic language is only cathartically expressive and not an actual call for political violence. It is likely, as Barrell points out, that this defense is related to the prohibition of such imaginative catharsis in English law. The immediate object of the violent menacings in the poem is, after all, Pitt; and, if Barrell is correct, perhaps even the king, figured in the shadow of Pitt. Coleridge was, of course, not a revolutionary with fever in his brain and fire in his eyes. By 1798 he had already several times condemned the violent excesses of the *Terroristes*, especially the slaughters in the Vendée (*The Watchman, CC* 2:212–14; 246–47). But he commonly both condemned violent excess and symphathetically explained its real origin, which was, he thought, in the terrifying violence of Pitt and his allies. Coleridge's careful distinction between English republican and French Jacobin violence suggests also how he had become in the 1790s the kind of sympathizer Robespierre had called for—one who, though distant in another land, was mentally complicit in "tous les mouvemens" of France's "glorieuse Révolution." One of those essential movements involved a call to virtuous terror, which was justified as self-defense by many British radicals in the 1790s.[9] The official British version of treasonable political imagination was, in its French version, a mental act of universal liberation. Coleridge was not the only British radical of the time who enjoyed participating in the imagination of that liberation and who later regretted that imaginative complicity. "Fire, Famine, and Slaughter" was eventually published with epigraphs, indirectly asking, in the words of Claudian and Ecclesiasticus, forgiveness for his offending tongue and his poetic sin. Not long after 1798, and certainly by 1817, poetic sins had become his admitted political sins. And yet not

9. I have borrowed here from my essay "Holy Savagery," 391–93.

quite—that is, if the sins could be turned back, as he argues they should be, into something to be imagined as *only* poetry.

One major English poet who did use the vocabulary of biblical terror with relative comfort even after it had been invoked by the terrorists of 1793 is William Blake. In his epic poem *America,* Blake casts the sense of totalizing violence of the French Revolution backward over the American Revolution. Despite its extreme violence, it had little in it resembling the legendary material of the Terror; Blake's poem, however, is filled with the imagery of the terrible, the terrifying, and the terrific, as Blake appropriates the old dissenting, godly violence for the poetical and political imagination—to some extent just as Robespierre did for the new humanly founded state. Unlike the Tory Coleridge, who because of his early radicalism is uncomfortable in this poetic tradition, Blake, an unregenerate radical, remains at ease with biblical images of terror, writing as French violence reaches its height. In any case, Blake is the last English poet of the late eighteenth and early nineteenth centuries to use the language of terror on such a grand poetic scale in order to give a face to political liberation. The effect, then, of the Terror upon poetic/political language of the nineteenth century was, at least in one semantic field, to impoverish it. The connection between violence and inspiration would be renewed during the American Civil War in such hymns as "Onward Christian Soldiers" and in the image of the prophet adopted by John Brown, but he was, after all, only a marginal figure. For Americans as for the British, Brown resembled those superannuated dissenters and rebels who spoke the language of biblical terror, as Calvinist fanatics do in Sir Walter Scott's *The Heart of Mid-Lothian, or, Old Mortality*—people of the "deep past" who could give voice to prophetic violence precisely because they lived *before* the French Revolution. It was Scott who had read aloud in the company of Coleridge's literary friends that furious poem "Fire, Famine, and Slaughter," which embarrassed its once radical author. For whatever reasons Scott chose to call attention to this "anonymous" poem, it created the gloomy impression pronounced by Sotheby of a mere "malignity of heart." In his own fictional creation of violent, revolutionary rhetoric, the conservative Sir Walter would never make that mistake. He knew quite well when he could allow characters to speak with such fury, and, as an anti-revolutionary writer, he also knew that the old language of Terror spoken by Scottish rebels of 1745 would be read directly through the recent memories of 1793. For Scott, the native prophetic tradition of violence could be used and even imaginatively enjoyed, yet it could also be taken to be historically exhausted. He could write such language only because it was to be taken as language of a spirit that the modern world must repress. The French Revolution had used up, or at least contaminated, any contemporary use of the metaphoric power of terror for both revolutionaries and reactionaries.

✌ ✌

Thus there was in the 1790s an uncomfortable confluence of a Robespierrist, Terrorist link to the sublime and the long-established violent rhetoric of the British dissenting tradition. The confluence of similar vocabularies with different purposes—as we see in Coleridge's defense of his poem—gave urgency to the task of emptying terror out of the sublime. Two interesting versions of this rhetorical sensitivity to the mixture of terror and the sublime can be seen in Tom Paine's *The Rights of Man* and *The Age of Reason* and in Percy Bysshe Shelley's *Mont Blanc*. Before considering them, however, we need to turn to Edmund Burke's *A Philosophical Enquiry into the Origin of our Ideas of the Sublime and the Beautiful* (1757), which, though written long before the Revolution, had become implicated in the clash of radical and reactionary cultures. In these texts, we have an influential British analysis of the sublime, filled with terror; and two radical versions of the sublime, emptied of its terror. These are different kinds of writing, with different rhetorical expectations and political contexts—an essay on aesthetics, two political/philosophical polemics, and a political poem about epistemology. But however different in kind, and regardless of opposing political viewpoints, all speak within a similar discourse made up of a generally coherent middle-class ideology that they expect their audiences to understand. *The Rights of Man* and *The Age of Reason* employ traditional British deistic language; *Mont Blanc* is a poem about "power" and its relation to the human mind. But all these texts are obliged to engage that version of middle-class and deistic psychology of Burke's *Enquiry* and its repressive political implications. Both Paine and Shelley steer clear of the associations with terror that had embarrassed Coleridge so much. Even more important, both texts embody radical forms of perception antithetical to the psychology of terror, so strikingly exaggerated by Burke.

In order to appreciate the terrorist leitmotif of the *Enquiry*, however, it is important to remember the many texts that lie behind it, both of stern Protestant theology and secular deistic writing. These texts of the previous century made up a large part of any educated reader's sense of what was psychologically universal. This is not the place to survey the intricacies of that vast body of writing. Suffice it to say that Calvin's *Institutes*, as I have already mentioned, provided a Reformation version, widely echoed thereafter, of necessary terror in the apprehension of God and the necessary repressive fear to be implemented by civil government. The *Institutes* opens with the reminiscence of those who feared the sight of God and knew that even to look upon him meant death. Bowing to sacred terror—common, as he says, to all religions—Calvin sets aside a pagan cynicism, particularly that of Cicero, who thought that supernatural fear was self-consciously devised by rulers to keep people in check, an idea revived by

Enlightenment thinkers such as Voltaire, Diderot, Paine, and Godwin. Calvin rejects any notion that terror is invented rather than being an essential part of the universe; nonetheless he modulates terror when he incorporates it into our second, or fallen, nature. Constant fearfulness in the fallen man prevents the sinner—that is to say, everyone—from properly conceiving of splendor, magnitude, and true godly power. All of us are the children of wrath, he says, and our fearlessness of God caused original disobedience. But God's wrath, which continually inspires fear and trembling in the sinner, is not all that the believer can at moments apprehend in him. Calvin, master of accommodation, subtly confirms throughout the *Institutes* the idea that original sin was *occasioned* by our not being fearful enough; but he also designs a lesser kind of fear as more properly part of sin, not of the essence of God nor of our possible imagination of him, which is more properly built upon a willed "reverential" fear. That is why the civil order must be repressively fearsome—it must deal with the material life of sinners and ensure the peace necessary to the contemplation of the greater glory of the godhead. But this civil fear and even terror, necessary in keeping the children of wrath in order, is always of the second nature.[10]

Another very different kind of moral thinker can find God's terrifying wrath modulated otherwise, in the foundation of both religion and the civil order. Consider Lord Herbert of Cherbury's *De Veritate*, a founding text of deism, usually designated the first completely philosophical work written in Britain. Herbert, like Calvin, is drawn to careful distinctions between *fear* in the origin of religion and manifestations of *power* in the civil state and in the mind. He never imagines the self trembling before this power. And Herbert is in no way restrained when he speaks of ultimate freedom from most forms of terror.

> [T]he most fearful senses of all are those which relate to the future. All degrees between doubt and despair are found in them, such as anxiety, fear, dread, alarm, shock, consternation, horror, fright, trembling, agony, panic, stupefaction, paralysis and hysteria. . . . The unruffled mind . . . can ignore such feelings. It can contemplate objects within the body or outside it with calm detachment. The schools are unreasonable when they deny freedom its own home while permitting its existence outside its doors; for our mind, I maintain, has the power of contemplating all things without difficulty and is not compelled to perform any task it does not like. In this respect it resembles the Prime Mover, which moves all things

10. *Institutes*, 1:35–47. On civil repression and the fallen nature in Calvin, see Michael Walzer, *The Revolution of the Saints: A Study in the Origins of Radical Politics* (Cambridge, Mass., 1965), 30–57.

without itself being moved. Our mind does not itself change, but wills change in the body, that is to say, in its own world, by means of its Common Notions. In this way it is not passive but is active throughout its entire domain, since the mind cannot be passive except under the wrath of God.[11]

Like Calvin, Herbert speaks of humans metaphysically as the children of wrath (Ephesians 2.3), but the primary interest of the theologian and the philosopher is in the world of that power, where from day to day the fallen human being paradoxically shares some aspects of the power of God. Along with Calvin's insistence on the righteousness of the bloody sword—like that of Luther and Catholic counterreformers before him—we should not forget that Calvin does reserve a vision of peace in the apprehension of God's creation, and there is no hint of the terrible sublime in Calvinistic earthly splendor. Herbert goes much further. He sounds almost blasphemous in suggesting a human sharing of energy with the Prime Mover, first felt as power over one's physical being.

In turning from these writers to Edmund Burke's *Enquiry* with regard to the concept of power, the regression to a terrorist vision is immediately striking. This vision of power is also productive of a mastery of the self, but it is mentally inescapable, portrayed hyperbolically as a determining inward force, one that sometimes seems more essential to the constitution of the self than it does in Calvin, Herbert, or Hobbes. Ideas, we know, do not function in the same way over time, even from decade to decade; we are nothing today if not sensitive to history as isolatable discourses. But Burke's *Enquiry*, which is in many ways unlike most other writings on the sublime, can be considered within two distinguishable discourses that overlap, one on the sublime, the other on terror. The first led to several problematic relationships with contemporary aestheticists, who were also his critics. The second completes, in Enlightenment terms, a discourse of terror that begins in the Reformation.

Burke begins with the idea of "power" in his definition of the grand effects of the sublime, the essential form of which is always "terror." Anyone reading the *Enquiry* from the eighteenth to the early nineteenth centuries would have been habituated to the alternating words *power* and *terror* that we have seen in the semantic nuances of both conservative Protestant and "progressive" deist arguments. Each word was used in accordance with the degree to which a writer emphasized the primacy of metaphysical terror or its civil and psychological manifestations. Power, unburdened by the shadow of metaphysical terror within it, allows room for that subjected self still to be rationally defined. Burke is clearly

11.   Edward, Lord Herbert of Cherbury, *De Veritate*, trans. Meyrich H. Carré (Bristol, 137), 196–97.

on the side of those who insist on the primacy of imaginative terror, in the acts of God or of the state, and in both there is always implied our most exalted and most frightening thoughts of eternity, punishment, and pain. As he puts it:

> Now, though in a just idea of the Deity, perhaps none of his at-tributes are predominant, yet to our imagination, his power is by far the most striking. Some reflection, some comparing is necessary to satisfy us of his wisdom, his justice, and his goodness; to be struck with his power, it is only necessary that we should open our eyes. But whilst we contemplate so vast an object, under the arm, as it were, of almighty power, and invested upon every side with omnipresence, we shrink into the minuteness of our own nature, and are, in a manner, annihilated before him. And though a con-sideration of his other attributes may relieve in some measure our apprehensions; yet no conviction of the justice with which it is ex-ercised, nor the mercy with which it is tempered, can wholly re-move the terror that naturally arises from a force which nothing can withstand.[12]

The traces of Protestant theological discussion of a simultaneously vengeful and loving God are apparent here. Burke's deity is, to be sure, one of justice and of mercy, but ultimately he must insist on the efficacy of terror in our emotional re-action to sublime spiritual presence. Our real nature, responding to the essential reality of God, responds to power, and that power is defined primarily by its ter-rifying impingement:

> It were endless to enumerate all the passages both in the sacred and profane writers, which establish the general sentiment of mankind, concerning the inseparable union of a sacred and reverential awe, with our ideas of the divinity. Hence the common maxim, *primos in orbe deos fecit timor*. This maxim may be, as I believe it is, false with regard to the origin of religion. The maker of the maxim saw how inseparable these ideas were, without considering that the no-tion of some great power must be always precedent to our dread of it. But this dread must necessarily follow the idea of such a power, when it is once excited in the mind. It is on this principle that true religion has, and must have, so large a mixture of salutary fear; and that false religions have generally nothing else but fear to support

12. Edmund Burke, *A Philosophical Enquiry into the Origin of our Ideas of the Sublime and Beautiful*, ed. James T. Boulton (Notre Dame and London, 1968), 68; cited henceforward in the text.

them. Before the Christian religion had, as it were, humanized the idea of the divinity, and brought it somewhat nearer to us, there was very little said of the love of God. The followers of Plato have something of it, and only something. The other writers of pagan antiquity, whether poets or philosopher, nothing at all. And they who consider with what infinite attention, by what a disregard of every perishable object, through what long habits of piety any contemplation it is, any man is able to attain an entire love and devotion to the Deity, will easily perceive, that it is not the first, the most natural, and the most striking effect which proceeds from that idea. Thus we have traced power through its several gradations unto the highest of all, where our imagination is finally lost; and we find terror quite through the progress, its inseparable companion, and growing along with it, as far as we can possibly trace them. Now as power is undoubtedly a capital source of the sublime, this will point out evidently from whence its energy is derived, and to what class of ideas we ought to unite it. (*Enquiry,* pp. 69–70)

Nothing here conflicts with theological notions that the absence of fear caused original sin and that part of our nature must always be to fear God. But there is more than this in Burke. He begins with a consideration of Christian love tempering the originary sense of dread. It is not, however, part of Burke's aesthetic project to privilege spiritual intellection or mercy. His aesthetic psychology is based on an essentialist psyche that is a mainstay of social order.[13] It is surely the case, as Tom Furniss and others have argued, that at the center of that order is a masculine gendered, productive bourgeois self that survives the imagination of his own annihilation and is all the stronger for it. At the same time, this overcoming of our imaginative destruction is a never-ending psychological process. By filling up the sublime with essentialist power and filling up power with an essentialist idea of terror, Burke completes an argument that makes clear the perversity of *not* yielding to our own psychological nature, which is to fear this

13. The discursive elements of that order have become gradually clearer, beginning with the provocative work of Isaac Kramnick, and more of its elements have been described by Francis Ferguson, Tom Furniss, Thomas Weiskel, and others, who have unpacked in Freudian, post-Freudian, or even anti-Freudian ways the class, gender, and sexual content of Burke's *Enquiry,* all of which we can now see as more clearly connected with his reactions to the French Revolution. See Isaac Kramnick, *The Rage of Edmund Burke: Portrait of an Ambivalent Conservative* (New York, 1977); Frances Ferguson, *Solitude and the Sublime: Romanticism and the Aesthetics of Individuation* (New York, 1992); Tom Furniss, *Edmund Burke's Aesthetic Ideology: Language, Gender, and Political Economy in Revolution* (Cambridge, 1993); Thomas Weiskel, *The Romantic Sublime: Studies in the Structure and Psychology of Transcendence* (Baltimore, 1976).

metaphysical presence. Yet it is a presence the fear of which we can never be allowed to forget. We do not see all of the bourgeois productivist self at the center of Burke's texts until we see the overcoming self, always blended with its humbled, terrified self.

Burke's implicit political psyche extends into the nineteenth century's productivist ideology of the self, but it is also a powerful shadow out of the Calvinist past. When Calvin speaks of assenting to terror, for instance, it is also of a willing assent and of a constant overcoming. As Michael Walzer has described it:

> Christians, Calvin thought, ought to be the subjects as well as the objects of social control. . . . Like the secular state, the Christian commonwealth would be coercive; unlike the secular state, it would be founded upon the consent of conscientious men. Calvinism brought conscience and coercion together—in much the same way as they were later brought together in Rousseau's General Will.[14]

Historians of ideology, on the basis of this assent, have linked Calvin with Hobbes and Rousseau. A further rhetorical extension of this discourse must include Burke's combination of aesthetic and political psychology. Burke accomplished an important task among those who were, like himself, neither stern Old Testament traditionalists nor pale deists who seemed to undermine the authority of religion. While his ideas on the sublime may not have been typical of all such theories, his psychology of terror can be traced all through the late eighteenth century. The most complicated of those forms is in the well-known aesthetic of gothic literature, in which terror (along with forms of the merely horrible) is released from the sublime to take on its own secularized psychological language.

It is not surprising that Burke's treatment of fear and terror was influential. It was, after all, an essentialist, modern psychology, not a theology, and it sought to account for fearful emotions that were not as dramatically explained by the first versions of empirical associationist psychology. Furthermore, this psycho/spiritual theorizing invoked neither superstitious anthropomorphizing nor cannibalistic violence of the kind that the Philosophes saw vestigially present in Christian sacrifice. Terror was now, in addition to being a quality of the godly, an essential quality of perception and thinking. Terror was now a religious concept *and* a commonly shared, eminently discussable emotion, the mental necessity of which spoke to the very nature of what it is to be human. Though today we might dis-

14. Walzer, *Revolution of the Saints,* 47.

dainfully call this a kind of pop psychology, we should note how pervasive popular psychology can be. It was Burke's version of the terrific sublime—not Baillie's, Addison's, Kames's, or Kant's—that produced the clichéd, and therefore most widely disseminated, descriptions of terror in the face of nature. Both the affirmations of and the attacks upon social forms of terror in popular gothic literature are extensions of this essentialist psychology. If we also remember the examples Burke likes to give of the resident force of unimaginable terror in our minds—such as the drawing and quartering of Damiens, the would-be assassin of Louis XV—the mix of psychic and spiritual terror with political images is hard to deny. And it is this mix of images—even more evident on the surface of his discourse than the paradigm of the bourgeois laborer who both survives and incorporates the sublime—that should probably be given primacy when we make connections between the *Enquiry* and the *Reflections on the Revolution*. Given the abundant eighteenth-century interest in terror of a kind defined by Burke, it is worth considering how much of Burke is echoed in Robespierre, along with Calvinist, Hobbesian, and Rousseauist terror. Robespierre the theoretician of terror, as we have seen, modulates the role of terror in the sublime. But Robespierre also believed that the terror exteriorized in the Revolution is something resident in the mind of every human being. In fact he uses most of the same clichéd classical arguments that Burke does to suggest the primacy of terror in the psychology of the self.[15]

Ever since Kramnick challenged readers to see the connections between the *Enquiry* and the *Reflections on the Revolution* more clearly, it has been impossible to ignore the terrors that haunted Burke's language. Kramnick notes, for example, "the giant ravaging the country, plundering the innocent traveler, and afterwards gorged with his half-living flesh," and suggests that these nightmares actually reappeared for Burke in the Revolution.[16] But in the same way that Burke's discourse is not confined to his psyche but functions in terms of the entire culture (as Frances Ferguson and Tom Furniss have showed), we can see that

---

15. An example is the defense of violence on the basis of the instinct of self-preservation, going back at least to Hobbes and important to both Robespierre and Burke. See Robespierre, *Oeuvres*, 10:357; and Burke, *Philosophical Enquiry*, 38.

16. Kramnick, *Rage of Edmund Burke*, 93–99. I have omitted in my discussion the important gendering of the sublime and beautiful as male and female; Kramnick points out that the sexual imagery is striking and insistent throughout the *Enquiry*. Most political writers identified their favorite form of government as marked by "manly" disciplined virtue rather than an "effeminate" taste for luxury, pleasure, and vice, common to tyrants. This is an ancient political cliché. It is true, however, that Burke's metaphors are more than manly; they are aggressively sexual. Peter de Bolla, in his fascinating account of eighteenth-century aesthetic theory, notes that in the work of Lord Kames the sublime does indeed bear all the marks of a powerful erection; see *The Discourse of the Sublime: Readings in History, Aesthetics, and the Subject.* (London, 1989), 95.

terror in Burke is more than a subtheme in the discourse of the sublime: it is the continuation of two centuries of religious and psychological writing in a discourse of terror that continues to enfold within itself—albeit with less and less force—the bourgeois discourse of the self. Its particular effect is to continue to preserve within the self the primacy of fear and, however vestigially, a sense of the sacred operating in the mind. The theorizing of Revolutionary terror in someone like Robespierre or St. Just is not just an example of a nightmare; it is also a historically realized form of an invented mentality of which Burke is the most popular eighteenth-century interpreter. Several years before the actual Terror, he apparently recognizes in his *Reflections* the nightmare and, more important, the mind that accounts *in itself* for the nightmare. What surprised or angered Burke was not so much the political violence of 1789 but what he saw as implied in it—a grotesque political form of what he had theorized as the most noble, heroic, and masculine aspects of the sublime.

Long before Robespierre's combination of political and metaphysical terror, it was clear at least to some that the functions of terror were so important and pervasive that they had to be analyzed and distinguished. Though useful in the metaphysical girding up of the state, of social authority, and of moral behavior, terror usually had to be reduced to human scale to keep it from crushing the very notion of the human and to restore the Christian refinements of mercy and love. How much more necessary it was, for instance, to make adjustments to terror when Milton's metaphysical epic in English needed to encompass not only terror but also mercy. In the *Enquiry*, discussion of terror in *Paradise Lost* leads to Burke's typical analysis of primal terror and the mind "hurried out of itself, by a crowd of great and confused images." This leads him to the Book of Job and to the assertion that there is in poetry the possibility of terror beyond any human description, and certainly beyond the powers of the plastic arts. It is all quite intemperate and mysterious, especially when compared with Samuel Johnson's estimation of how *Paradise Lost* finds gradations of terror reasonably fitted to the mind:

> Pleasure and terror are indeed the genuine sources of poetry; but poetical pleasure must be such as human imagination can at least conceive, and poetical terror such as human strength and fortitude may combat. The good and evil of Eternity are too ponderous for the wings of wit; the mind sinks under them in passive helplessness, content with calm belief and humble adoration.[17]

17. Burke, *Philosophical Enquiry*, 61–63; Samuel Johnson, "Milton" in *Lives of the English Poets* (1779–81), ed. George Birkbeck Hill, 2 vols. (Oxford, 1905), 1:181–82. In Hill's edition, a quotation from Cowper points up the kind of gradations that Johnson had in mind; Cowper, given his documented deep depres-

It could be said that Johnson's sense of gradation is much like Burke's descriptions of the stages of terror in the sublime, in which we imagine our annihilation and then overcome it. Burke conflates nature and art in presenting the actual delight that the mind takes in submitting to sublime terror. Johnson's poetical terror is something that, despite all its stimulation, the human can indeed combat. There is more in Johnson of Lord Herbert of Cherbury, even of Calvinist common sense, than of Burke. Johnson, like earlier religious theorists of the fearful emotions, wants to keep everything from being conflated with godly terror to avoid a collapse into one insufferable, exhausting state of fear. Johnson leaves room, like Herbert of Cherbury, for a sense of human will and the significance of resisting both external terror and our weakness before it. Complete submission is reserved by Johnson for the purely metaphysical. Burke's sense of sublime terror is the cause of much more unease. Burke is chiefly interested—at least when he speaks of the delight that terror occasions—in the process of submitting and then of overcoming. This is not really a gradation of terror but a continuous process always seeking completion.

Accepting primal terror and yet bounding it somehow, so that it could be constitutive of and not destructive to the mind, was a problem precisely because of Burke's insistence on terror. Kant, who recognized the influence of Burke in his own thinking, provided two moments of sublime terror: the first is the kind Johnson refers to, the primal and metaphysical; the second is what Kant considers the sublime and its terror contemplated transcendentally as an object of rational thought. It is the cultured mind that can attain feelings of sublimity and understand its core of terror; the uncultured, primitive mind can only shudder in lowly fear. But for all of Burke's interest in psychological aspects of the sublime, he was more interested in its effects, for these were important to a world of social order. If the active presence of the deistic God was now dissipated, there were still ways to retain the sometimes subtle, sometimes not so subtle, forms of universal spiritual authority. Most eighteenth-century aestheticists of the sublime preferred the subtle ways of sublime authority, just as Kant would prefer transcendentally sublime terror rationally contemplated. Burke clearly is aware of these differently imagined "levels" of terror, which are carefully distinguished by nearly all writers on the subject, from Calvin to Kant, and which he himself would invoke in *Reflections on the Revolution in France*. But we must not ignore

sion, convincingly describes how too much cultivation of terror was psychologically dangerous: "The first book of the *Paradise Lost* is in truth so terrible, and so nearly akin to my own miserable speculations . . . that I am a little apprehensive, unless my spirits were better, that the study of it might do me material harm" (182 n. 5). In much eighteenth-century poetry, the desire not to combat but to embrace and cultivate terror, horror, and fear is frequently expressed. For discussion of this mode, see Margaret Anne Doody, *The Daring Muse: Augustan Poetry Reconsidered* (Cambridge, 1985), 159–98.

Burke's insistence, however sublimely transcendental his language may some-times seem, on the constant presence of the *body* in the properly terrified mind. Unlike Herbert of Cherbury, who assumes that the body is where we first sense our will and control, Burke uses the body, in discussing sublime terror, as a place where we most intensely locate our primitive sense of fear. It is Burke, after all, who insists on our remembering the flesh painfully stripped away from the eigh-teenth century's most famous political assassin. Obviously Burke does not think that he is yoking two disparate things together; for him, sublime and primitive terror, though different, must inhabit the same mental place. Executing assas-sins and our delight in natural and aesthetic sublimity must be connected some-where in the psyche where we become not only middle-class laborers and producers but also—for Burke—subordinated human beings.

Burke was, of course, too brilliant a political rhetorician with a too finely nuanced mind not to see, just as Johnson or Kant did, that terror as a primary element in political order had to be kept deep within the mind's experience of it-self yet always available to memory. His best-known taxonomy of terror, however, is provided not in the *Enquiry* but in the *Reflections*. A detailed rhetorical exam-ination of how he fits the psychological terror proposed in the *Enquiry* into his vision of the ordered state would carry us far off course. But even a cursory read-ing of the *Reflections* makes clear his fundamental distinction between imagined violence and real pain, with terror as a civilizing force while violence unleashed by the Revolution is mere savagery. Terror housed in the psychic core of a reli-gious state produces order because its universality makes rulers as fearful as their subjects of going beyond certain bounds. Terror as Burke sees it in the Revolution is unmodulated savagery, cruelty, and barbarity, for the Terrorists themselves have no fear.

In the British order of an established church and citizens who cherished their fear and hope in God, knowing inwardly their complete subjection before God's wrath, there was a guarantee of order. The problem with the French was that (as in original sin) they lacked this fear. Burke, through the image of the body, con-nects shuddering primitive fear to a more refined form in sublimely apprehended terror. What, for him, should be unimaginable is no fear at all. Fearlessness is the mark of the cannibal, the savage, the madman. Revolutionary terror (and Burke is writing before 1793) is a "black and savage atrocity of mind" (*Reflections,* p. 262). This human appropriation of the terror of the godhead is a mere simu-lacrum of the barbarously fearless, who demand "abject submission to their oc-casional will"; it is an "unnatural inverted domination," the fear of God turned upside down in a hurly burly of a Hobbesian state of nature and Calvinist fear-lessness identified in the first disobedience. Burke's conceptions of mentality, published in 1757, are completely and even figuratively coherent with his political reactions in 1790. The reason he gives for the potential for horror in democracy, for example, is precisely that it has no "body"—that is to say, no place in its imaginative discourse to figure the pain and sense of annihilation that comes from primal fear. Unlike Damiens, the body politic of the terrorist republican state cannot feel itself being drawn and quartered. When interpreters of the sublime in Burke ignore this bodily aspect of his discourse or refer to it as outdated or silly, they underestimate the figuration that reveals some of the basic oppositions in his thinking and that constitutes the rhetorical scene in which he acts out—as Tom Paine could not help but be struck by—an uncontrollable rage:

> A perfect democracy . . . is the most shameless thing in the world. As it is the most shameless, it is also the most fearless. No man apprehends in his person he can be made subject to punishment. Certainly the people at large never ought: for as all punishments are for example towards the conservation of the people at large, the people at large can never become the subject of punishment by any human hand. (*Reflections*, p. 191)

Without a body the democratic mentality cannot properly figure, Burke thinks, the pain—which, he insists, must be present in some way in the apprehension of the truly sublime. The body of the assassin Damiens, then, broken and flayed, not mentioned in the *Reflections* but clearly figured in the *Enquiry*, is a very important body indeed. It bears the imprint of what true political order is, without which democracy, with either terror or the sublime, becomes only a cannibalistic savage turning inward to destruction.

❧ ❧

Given the pervasive eighteenth-century association, whether subtle or brutal, of terror with the sublime, it is interesting to see how Tom Paine distances himself from it, in both *The Rights of Man* and *The Age of Reason*. Because the political differences between Burke and Paine are so obvious and they appear so mentally and stylistically opposed, we may underestimate how deliberately Paine steps aside from all psychological predisposition to mental submission. His rhetorical maneuvers are as brilliant as Burke's and Robespierre's. They are, however, unadorned and rapid, as we can see when he places himself within a commonplace scene of grandeur. Quite aware of his culture's rapturous sublime, Paine reacts to landscape with what we might call de-elaboration. Less of the sublime means more of the human for Paine, as when he turns his eye to the vast American landscape, a form of powerful raw material that contemporary writers and painters were continually turning into the aesthetic sublime. Writing about American landscape as the sublime swirls fashionably around him, Paine guards against its sweep and avoids its repressive implications. He recognizes ontological grandeur but removes all possibility of a humbled spectator in the scene:

> As America was the only spot in the political world, where the principles of universal reformation could begin, so also was it the best in the natural world. An assemblage of circumstances conspired, not only to give birth, but to add gigantic maturity to its principles. The scene which that country presents to the eye of a spectator, has something in it which generates and encourages great ideas. Nature appears to him in magnitude. The mighty objects he beholds act upon his mind by enlarging it, and he partakes of the greatness he contemplates.—Its first settlers were emigrants from different European nations, and of diversified professions of religion, retiring from the governmental persecutions of the old world, and meeting in the new, not as enemies, but as brothers. The wants which necessarily accompany the cultivation of a wilderness, produced among them a state of society, which countries, long harassed by the quarrels and intrigues of governments, had neglected to cherish. In such a situation man becomes what he ought. He sees his species, not with the inhuman idea of a natural enemy, but as kindred; and the example shows to the artificial world, that Man must go back to Nature for information.[18]

The passage is typical of Paine—straightforward and plain. He took care to write prose that cut through what he described as mystery and obfuscation,[19] yet it is also guarded, specifically in its avoidance of sublime emotions.

The discourse of the sublime was not a very old one in modern Europe; it gave birth to common Enlightenment usage only after the late seventeenth century and Boileau's famous translation of the pseudo-Longinus's *Peri Hupsous*.[20] The rapidity with which it became intellectually fashionable is striking. But the

---

18. Paine, *Rights of Man*, pt. 2, in *Tom Paine: Collected Writings*, ed. Eric Foner (New York, 1995), 548; this edition cited henceforward in the text and notes.

19. Explaining, for instance, one reason for the delay in publishing the second part of *Rights of Man*, he says, "I wished to know the manner in which a work, written in a style of thinking and expression different to what had been customary in England, would be received before I proceeded farther" (p. 542).

20. The classic survey of the history of the sublime is Samuel Holt Monk, *The Sublime: A Study of Critical Theories in Eighteenth-Century England*, with a new preface by the author (Ann Arbor, Mich. [1960]). For a critique of previous histories and their underlying assumptions, see esp. de Bolla, *Discourse of the Sublime*.

word *sublime* in the Longinian—and above all the Burkean—sense is consciously
excluded from Paine's vocabulary. His writing always reaches past and around
the discursive sublime to the vocabulary of enlightened discussions of deity,
which recognized *power* but dissipated the mysteries of authoritarian *terror*. Paine
uses words such as *gigantic, magnitude, great, mighty*—all associated ordinarily
with sublime infinitude. But the emotional elevation is counterpointed with the
final word of the passage quoted above: man, he says, must go back to nature for
information. This word had a certain radical cachet, as we hear in the carefully
named Society for Constitutional Information. It was an important word for
Paine, who uses it in a way any modern reader would understand—information
as facts, data, and the patterns they reveal. But he also uses the word as part of
his deist challenge to the word *revelation*. Revealed religion, as Paine asserts in *The
Age of Reason*, is the source of most historical and social horrors. The deist has
nothing revealed to him; in the true spirit of science, he simply gathers information from nature, trying always to understand its power and to follow its principles of organization. His notion of information in the landscape may remind
us of an older, theological sense implied in the *in-forming* of the body by the
soul. Paine may not consciously wield the old theological word, but he does develop the idea of information in a way that sets it at odds with the religious and
psychological cast of the Burkean sublime. Paine makes this crystal clear in the
conclusion to *The Age of Reason*. Instead of taking any typically grand or sublime
scene, he describes the ultimate "sublime" scene—an imagined point of observation from which one could see the entire universe. There the observer would
be "exalted," but only because "great objects inspire great thoughts." This would,
indeed, be a scene not of revelation but of information, where what was to be
learned was not humbling fear but power as knowledge of "the system of laws,
established by the Creator, that governs and regulates the whole." In this exalt-
ing scene, the observer learns "far beyond what any church theology can teach
him, the power, the wisdom, the vastness, the munificence of the Creator." What
this kind of "sublime" inspires is the exact opposite of fear—an understanding of
the source of earthly comfort:

> He would then see that all the knowledge man has of science, and
> that all the mechanical arts by which he renders his situation com-
> fortable here are derived from that source.

Because Paine expands on the centrality of science or knowledge, not terror,
as the core of the sublime, it is not surprising that he ultimately confronts
Longinus and Burke. He consigns them to a footnote, but one that reveals the
political adversary who casts his shadow upon this text on religion. He refers to

the idea of having God say "Let there be light," a phrase he likens to the "presto" of the magician, a bit of ridicule that leads him directly to the *Enquiry*:

> Longinus, [Burke] says, calls this expression *sublime*, and by the same rule that of the conjurer is sublime too, for the manner is expressively and grammatically the same. When authors and critics talk of the sublime, they see not how nearly it borders on the ridiculous. The sublime of the critics, like some parts of Edmund Burke's *"Sublime and beautiful"* is like a windmill just visible in a fog, which imagination might distort into a flying mountain, an archangel, or a flock of wild geese.

Clearly, Paine's consistent association of the sublime with the ridiculous is intended to undermine the Longinian and Burkean terrific that leads to a sense of annihilation before its power. Through the information gathered from what Paine calls the "bible of Creation," the mind need not combine the sublime and the ridiculous, even when linking the great with the small in scientific investigation. Hence even the smallest heuristic model of the universe is a way that "man can see God, as it were, face to face." Where once looking into the face of God could not be imagined except simultaneously with violent death, for the scientist it is only a question of measurement:

> We know that the greatest works can be represented in model, and the universe can be represented by the same means. The same principles by which we measure an inch or an acre of ground will measure to millions in extent. A circle of an inch diameter has the same geometrical properties as a circle that would circumscribe the universe. (Pp. 827–28)

This is the kind of clarity by which Paine confronts the Burkean fog of the sublime, and it is a direct answer to the famously arrogant notion in the *Enquiry* that a "clear idea" is "another name for a little idea" (p. 63).[21] This famous line follows Burke's assertion that "hardly any thing can strike the mind with its greatness, which does not make some sort of approach towards infinity; which nothing can do whilst we are able to perceive its bounds; but to see an object distinctly, and to perceive its bounds, is one and the same thing." There can be no more deliberate opposition to this Burkean psychology than Paine's assertion that we can

---

21. Burke was himself aware of how easily the sublime can become "ludicrous," which he thinks occurs whenever artists try to represent the most extreme forms of terror. That is why poetry is the best expression of the sublime, confining it only to the possibilities of a mental image that cannot be bounded by actual physical lines or form (*Enquiry*, pp. 60–64).

model the universe even in the space of an inch. For Paine clarity is exciting; it is with clarity that man can conceive greatness, not in Burke's "incomprehensible darkness" or through the obfuscating mystery of the "stupid bible of the church that teaches man nothing."

In cutting through the fog associated with lightening, thunder, and Burkean terror, Paine avoids simply turning terror back upon oppressive powers of Church and state. He is not tempted by the liberation promised in science to indulge in the rhetoric of terror, as does his fellow radical Josiah Wedgwood. Writing to Joseph Priestly about some electrical experiments, Wedgwood's tone grows exalted:

> [W]hat daring mortals you are! to rob the Thunderer of his bolts,
> —and for what?—no doubt to blast the oppressors of the poor and
> needy, to execute some public piece of justice in the most tremen-
> dous and conspicuous manner, that shall make the great ones of the
> earth tremble.

Kramnick cites these lines and laconically transcribes their spirit: "Men rivaled the gods. They, too, could terrify the great of this world."[22] But Paine truly wants to eliminate the rhetorical blur that he identifies in Burke and will not indulge the urge to terrify. Unlike many of his fellow middle-class radical dissenters, whose fear of God was important in all their political discourse, Paine wants to strip the experience of grandeur of every form of fear.[23] Nothing had been more frequently argued in deistic tradition, from Herbert of Cherbury to David Hume, than the necessity of removing terror from the core of religious feeling. Yet the rhetoric of terror in religious and political discourse was so ingrained that it came naturally even to the most progressive thinkers of the day. It is this habitual rhetoric—for some only an innocent manner of speaking—that would be in-toned differently by Danton, Robespierre, and the *terroristes*, echoing, as if in dark irony, old religious force in a new, rationalized political voice. Paine's self-conscious avoidance of this rhetoric, however, reamined—two centuries after the first deist was burned at the stake in France—a constant gesture in his writing. For Paine, grandeur is not simply to be instrumentalized; it does not signify the chastening rod of violence. God is more sublime than that. Humankind is given its *form* by the mighty grandeur of what in nature is sensed as that beyond the human, which, in this liminal space, is emotionally affected by the perception of something that seems uncontainable by the mind. But the human, rather than

---

22. Kramnick, *Rage of Burke,* 65.
23. Consider the *Analytical Review,* one of the most important middle-class radical journals, which dissociates itself from Voltaire's satiric attacks on Christianity.

being diminished in that space, is finally shaped in a meeting with grandness. This is not the portrayal of an incomprehensible subject overwhelming an object, not of the submissive but of the creative social being. Paine's sublimity is of the human and the godly combined, much like the radical Blake's sense of "the human form divine," imagined in clearly outlined form, the *in-forming* of humanity by infinitude, not the humbling of it.[24] Paine was never mentally humbled, even when he was himself a prisoner under the Terror. The transformation by the French of the well-meaning Paine into a suspected enemy of the Revolution, thrown for over a year into prison, would not lead him to give substance to the idea of terror. That his body was seized and imprisoned as a result of political fears and machinations did not affect his disposition to see the mind informed by principles other than fear. As an early witness to the Terror he did not sacramentalize terror; as its imprisoned victim he did not demonize it.

～ ～

Shelley the poet writes within the same tradition as Paine the pamphleteer. *Mont Blanc* was written a year before Coleridge explained his violent language in "Fire, Famine, and Slaughter." Coleridge's antiwar poem of prophetic terror caused intellectual difficulty because he had managed to live until 1817, when the language of the Terror had long been an object of wonder and embarrassment. What Coleridge, looking back in 1817 to his youthful radicalism, came to see about the danger of association with such language, Shelley the young radical of 1816 had the advantage of already realizing. He was a late-Enlightenment poet, a student of Hume, the son-in-law of Godwin and Mary Wollstonecraft, an inheritor of the radical tradition of the 1790s. His *Mont Blanc* is a lyric of Romantic epistemology and psychology that arises out of all those influences. Here the poet is unlike Blake, who flaunts the ancient prophetic terror, and more like Paine, who leaps backward to the dissenting language of ontological order figured in landscapes of grandeur. Shelley confronts the Burkean sublime and empties it of terror by trying to reinvigorate the old theological and deistic word *power*. He forces this word to give up its Burkean content and fills it up with a sense of a grand, even "sublime," creative energy in language itself.

That the Burkean psychology cannot be far from Shelley's thoughts is suggested by his choosing Mont Blanc to refigure the content of the sublime. The

---

24. It must be said, however, that Paine's notion of human "form" is primarily intellectual; it resides in the permanent image of the rational. Blake, with his system of contraries, insists more on human physical form as a sublime image. Paine, in objecting to St. Paul's notion of an eternal immaterial body, compares humans as physical things unfavorably to animals and insects and asserts that the human body is "too mean for the sublimity of the subject [immortality]" (p. 815).

mountain and its glacier had become by 1816 one of the most popular tourist sites in the Western world. We know from travelers' letters, essays, and journals that it was one of those places where the tourist was expected to gaze upward and feel the power of the natural scene. There, the enthralling and frightening expanse drove one to feel sublime power casting its shadow over the tiny self. Though we can assume that not many tourists felt annihilated by the terrible sublime, it was certainly by cultivating this gaze that he or she delighted in testing the extreme emotions Burke portrayed. And certainly, many of those tourists speak as if they had just read the *Enquiry*.[25]

Shelley, who was once a tourist at Mont Blanc, along with Mary Shelley, takes aim in his poem at precisely this notion of subjection before the sublimely terrible. He begins by refusing to yield to the role of the mere spectator of the mountain, syntactically weaving—or, as some would say, confusing and blurring—subjects and objects in an image of the mind as both perceiving and informing the scene:

> The everlasting universe of things
> Flows through the mind, and rolls its rapid waves,
> Now dark—now glittering—now reflecting gloom—
> Now lending splendor, where from secret springs
> The source of human thought its tribute brings . . .[26]

He surveys most of the traditional attributes of the sublime scene—the mountain, its glacier, the grand ravine of the Arve—and it is filled with an awful scene of what is called "power," made up of uncontainable energy streaming through

25. Instances of the tourist's adoption of the Burkean psychology of terror would number in the thousands; many can be found in the voluminous collection of tourists' comments in G. G. de Beer, ed., *Travellers in Switzerland* (Oxford, 1949). A typical reaction to Swiss mountains is Abbé Defeller's, during a voyage in 1777: "Il ya là je ne sais quoi de terrible et d'agréable. On est charmé de voir une chose si extraordinaire, et d'avoir sous les yeux de si grandes opérations de la nature; et en même tems [*sic*] on ressent quelqu'inquiétude, comme à l'aspect de tout objet monstrueux et insolite" (p. 57). Similar sentiments are common roughly until the 1860s. The Burkean mode, however, disappears rapidly as more and more tourists actually climb high up on Mont Blanc. The primal fear of the Burkean spectator turns into the rational fear of the climber challenging the mountain; see, for example, Leslie Stephen's "Round Mont Blanc" (1872), in which the climber's sense of danger and "terrific" precipices is acknowledged, but this is no more emphasized than the blasé attitude the climber must adopt in order to survive. Consider this passage, which we might take as the indisputable sign that the eighteenth-century terror of Mont Blanc was now dissipated, or at least domesticated; Stephen is walking on one of the ascents at night: "I seemed to be continuing a peaceful dream; the moon was nothing but a dim night-light; the clouds were muslin curtains swaying sleepily in front of her; the little party silently plodding in front of me were such figures as one watches in a half-dream, moving monotonously yet never seeming to advance; and the huge glacier itself lay icebound in a slumber almost death-like, except that the booming sound of a distant moulin suggested that the monster was snoring" (*Men, Books, and Mountains: Essays by Leslie Stephen*, ed. S. O A. Ullman [London, 1956], 195).

26. *Mont Blanc: Lines Written in the Vale of Chamouni*, 1–5 (cited by line number henceforward in the text), in *Shelley's Poetry and Prose*, ed. Donald H. Reiman and Sharon B. Powers (New York, 1977), 89.

a form, stable yet changing. When in his description he comes to the climax of naming the "sublime," Shelley locates it not in the scene but in his own dream state of imaginative energy:

> . . . and when I gaze on thee
> I seem as in a trance sublime and strange
> To muse on my own separate phantasy,
> My own, my human mind, which passively
> Now renders and receives fast influencings
> Holding an unremitting interchange
> With the clear universe of things around;
> One legion of wild thoughts, whose wandering wings
> Now float above thy darkness, and now rest
> Where that or thou art no unbidden guest,
> In the still cave of the witch Poesy,
> Seeking among the shadows that pass by
> Ghosts of all things that are, some shade of thee,
> Some phantom, some faint image; till the breast
> From which they fled recalls them, thou are there!
> (Lines 34–48)

Shelley pushes the sublime far past the point to which Burke had brought it. Burke had located the understanding of the sublime in analyzing the spectators' perceptions and attendant feelings, but he also insisted on the idea of the presence of power and the content of terror in the thing itself. Here the sublime is shifted to a trance-like power in the perceiver rather than to the sublime form uncontainable by the imagination. The poet enters the scene of the sublime, the thing-in-itself of the mind, and finds vacancy that must be filled up:

> Mont Blanc yet gleams on high:—the power is there,
> The still and solemn power of many sights,
> And many sounds, and much of life and death.
> (Lines 127–30)

At the very moment that the poet locates the power in a place, he immediately dissipates it. Sights and sounds are "there," but they are of course also of the mind. The power arises out of the phenomenological activity of sights and sounds, and it is totally unlike the sense of self-annihilation that Burke insists we feel simply in confrontation with that power. The poet imagines the alternation of life and death within it, but nothing in that power terrifies with the specificity of personal death and pain—that is already understood in the transformed and transformative phenomenality in the stuff of nature flowing down the valley of the Arve. Personal disappearance in time and space has little to do with the power sensed in the actively perceiving spectator, the power of the mind itself:

> The secret strength of things
> Which governs thought, and to the infinite dome
> Of Heaven is as a law, inhabits thee!
> What were thou, and earth, and stars, and sea,
> If to the human mind's imagining
> Silence and solitude were vacancy?
>
> (Lines 139–44)

Blake instrumentalized terror in the old biblical way in order to claim human primacy in the universe; Coleridge invoked the old prophetic language as 1790s radical wrath, and in the face of actual fire and slaughter, was embarrassed by it; Paine emptied terror out of the mind so that it might be informed by the beneficence of nature. Shelley uses the old deistic word *power* but carries out the purposes of both Blake and Paine, centralizing the mind as forming the sublime, like Blake, but also emptying it of the terror, like Paine. He loosens the terrifying hold of the universe by allowing not only absorption into power but also subjective, creative continuity with it. Like both Blake and Paine, Shelley will not allow the spectator of grandeur and power to become a diminished aesthetic and psychological subject. And because the subject is not repressed in these ways, neither will it be repressed politically. The powerful mountain actually takes on a political voice, one that speaks from above, but only to give shape to thoughts that come from below:

> Thou hast a voice, great Mountain, to repeal
> Large codes of fraud and woe; not understood
> By all, but which the wise, and great, and good
> Interpret, or make felt, or deeply feel.
>
> (Lines 80–83)

The sublime is not avoided but radicalized. *Power,* otherwise called the *sublime,* can produce feelings not of humbling or even annihilation but of liberation. To loosen the mind from Burkean fear may free the mind from what enforces, also *in* the mind, the world's "large codes of fraud and woe."[27]

27. For a lucid interpretation of this much interpreted poem, particularly in relation to the sublime, see Angela Leighton, *Shelley and the Sublime: An Interpretation of the Major Poems* (Cambridge, 1984), 58–72. Pointing to one manuscript version of "Power dwells apart in its tranquillity, / Remote, sublime, and inaccessible," Leighton comments on Shelley's association of the sublime with "absolute remoteness" (p. 69). Surely she is right, but in the final version of the poem he eliminates the word "sublime" and substitutes "serene." While Shelley likely had his own notions of what the sublime constitutes, and that probably included frightening things, the poem de-emphasizes what is frightening.

But just as the actual terror of 1793 affected Coleridge's sense of the limits now imposed on poetic violence in the Protestant prophetic tradition, so those limits can be seen in the radical Shelley. They are there in his poems because of 1793. His poems of political incitement, such as *The Mask of Anarchy,* take on the rhythms and tone of a call to action, with echoes of Christian apocalyptic violence; but they are really calls to another conception of political change—one that involves a modern sense of mass and nation, but not of violence. In *The Mask of Anarchy* the poet, voicing the common accusation of radical culture, casts the role of the terrorist back upon the authoritarian, repressive powers of the state. Here Shelley has no qualms about using the vocabulary of revolutionary violence of the kind employed on all sides in the 1790s. The difference is that the eaters of hearts and the drinkers of blood are not the rebels but English rulers. But this violence, usually called terror, Shelley calls "anarchy," as if even the traditional radical concept of state terror must be erased. For to introduce terror on either side risks driving the poem back to the false dialectic in the 1790s argument about who was the original terrorist. The opposition here is not of terror against terror but of anarchy against rational order, understood and spoken by the people. The restraint in his vocabulary is striking when we remember that *The Mask of Anarchy* is a poem written in response to the famous Peterloo massacre.

When the poet speaks to the victimized "people" he is obviously, as in *Mont Blanc,* dismantling rather than elaborating political violence. We hear of the sounds of volcanoes and thunder, but the emphasis is on sound not blood:

> "Ye who suffer woes untold,
> Or to feel, or to be behold
> Your lost country bought and sold
> With a price of blood and gold—
>
> "Let a vast assembly be,
> And with great solemnity
> Declare with measured words that ye
> Are, as God has made ye, free—
>
> "Be your strong and simple words
> Keen to wound as sharpened swords,
> And wide as targes let them be
> With their shade to cover ye.
>
> . . . .
>
> "Stand ye calm and resolute,
> Like a forest close and mute,

With folded arms and looks which are
Weapons of unvanquished war,

. . . .

"On those who first should violate
Such sacred heralds in their state
Rest the blood that must ensue,
And it will not rest on you.

"And if then the tyrants dare
Let them ride among you there,
Slash, and stab, and maim, and hew, —
What they like, that let them do.

"With folded arms and steady eyes,
And little fear, and less surprise
Look upon them as they slay
Till their rage has died away.

. . . .

And that slaughter to the Nation
Shall steam up like inspiration,
Eloquent, oracular;
A volcano heard afar.

And these words shall then become
Like oppression's thundered doom
Ringing through each heart and brain,
Heard again—again—again—

Rise like lions after slumber
In unvanquishable number—
Shake your chains to earth like dew
Which in sleep had fallen on you—
Ye are many—they are few."[28]

28. *The Mask of Anarchy: Written on the Occasion of the Massacre at Manchester,* in *Shelley's Poetry and Prose,*
    301–10. For discussion of several aspects of the political and literary response to the Peterloo massacre, see
    James Chandler, *England in 1819: The Politics of Literary Culture and the Case of Romantic Historicism*
    (Chicago, 1998).

The animal most commonly invoked in the 1790s to allegorize the Terror was the bloodthirsty tiger. Shelley prefers a lion who needs only to roar words; but the lion must roar them again and again. The poet cautiously measures the traditional political and poetic rhetoric of prophetic violence, just as he asks the "many" he addresses to speak in "measured" words. Nothing could be further from both the Burkean sublime and revolutionary Terror than the idea of measurement. That Shelley chooses such a word, however, is not simply a sign of the rhetorical restraint imposed upon the inheritors of 1790s British radicalism; they had no choice but to yield up to reactionary culture all the symbols and finally even the words of the "new" French mentality of terror, and even of violence itself. Even as Shelley invokes apocalyptic rhetoric, in this and his other political poetry, he turns the images of explosive, rebelling violence upside down. What is most "powerful" in the mass of the people is their unmovable mass, their resistance to violence. As an early example of the concept of civil disobedience, this poem stages a reversal of the old theological idea of the source of original sin—the absence of fear. The people imagined by Shelley will consciously not obey because ultimately they are without fear. Terror is irrelevant to them.

Here Shelley is being as rhetorically cautious as Tom Paine was *before* the Terror, and it could be said that he writes within an already clearly established *rationalist* rhetoric of violence. Such a rhetoric reacts to terror and violence with a cultivated semantic reminiscence of old Puritan fury while simultaneously dismantling it. This rhetoric depends on an obvious elision, one that asks the reader to shift quickly from the images of imagined violence into the imageless completion of an abstracted mental and historical process. As soon as Paine employs a prophetic terrorist image he softens it, and he finally erases all its qualities, as if catching himself in a drift into old prophetic violence that he must guide toward beneficence and reason. His revolutionary flames are of this strange, silent kind: "From a small spark, kindled in America, a flame has arisen, not to be extinguished. Without consuming, . . . it winds its progress from nation to nation, and conquers by a silent operation" (p. 596). This is a fire that does not burn, whose flames do not even crackle. Rational transparency and good will are difficult to metaphorize in fire, let alone slaughter.

Mary Wollstonecraft's descriptions of French revolutionary violence are similar, because they depend on this figurative elision of violence and thought. For her the Bastille was essentially taken by the mind: "The accounts of the slaughter . . . were certainly very much exaggerated; for the fortress appears to have taken by *the force of mind* of the multitude, pressing forward regardless of the danger [italics added]." She means that the violent crowd took the Bastille more by its mass and determination than by killing the keepers. But the phrase "force of mind" is just the right kind to elide the historically violent act with a mental process. Her metaphors of fiery violence are made with Paine's kind of fire, itself only a metaphor of enlightenment. Tyranny is burned away with light—not really, or only secondarily, with actual fire:

> The irresistible energy of the moral and political sentiments of half a century, at last kindled into a blaze by the illuminating rays of truth, which throwing new light on the mental powers of man, and giving a fresh spring to his reasoning faculties, completely undermined the strong holds of preistcraft and hypocrisy.[29]

Shelley's call to the mass of oppressed English protesters is then, in its way, an already traditional radical appeal to the mind, like Paine's or Wollstonecraft's. But even more distantly it echoes Christian apocalyptic vocabulary, and in so doing it goes beyond that tradition by completely expunging even the image of radical fury or destruction. Shelley carries radical reasonableness and radical rhetorical decorum one step further. He turns caution into daring in a poem that has two origins, one in the Peterloo massacre of 1819 and another in the violence of 1793—a poem born in blood and terror yet struggling to transcend them. Shelley's combining of the imagining self and linguistic creation is within a tradition that goes back to the Enlightenment, as can be seen in the recognition by some aesthetic theorists of the psychological subject as the source of the sublime. But to locate Shelley within both these traditions—the rational rhetoric of violence and a subject-creating discourse of the sublime—does not explain completely what seems psychologically urgent in all his poetry.[30] His is one of the most difficult of Romantic tasks: to write traditional prophetic poetry, both of epistemology and of political action, by removing its most traditional source of power, the core emotion that had been central in both domains since the sixteenth century—the primacy of fear.

I have given just a few examples of rhetorical maneuvers in the cultural history of terror. More examples, especially from the vast literature of gothic romance, would have led us to other strategies, not only ways of emptying terror out of the sublime but also of isolating it, preparing the way for radical writers such as Godwin to isolate terror completely as the primary controlling device of what a class-dominated society was supposed to recognize as grand and sublime. The isolating of terror in gothic narrative, along with the kinds of disassociation

---

29. Mary Wollstonecraft, *An Historical and Moral View of the Origin and Progress of the French Revolution,* 192, 12, as cited by Brian Rigby, "Radical Spectators of the Revolution: The Case of the *Analytical Review,*" in Ceri Crossley and Iam Small, eds., *The French Revolution and British Culture* (Oxford, 1989), 83.

30. Peter de Bolla, *Discourse of the Sublime,* passim.

of terror and sublimity that I have discussed, left the sublime with a severely diminished psychological content. It would not survive very far into the nineteenth
century as a psycho-political term; but it did become grandly operatic before it
finally expired.[31]

~ ~

Consider what two historians of the French Revolution did with their operatic
thunder. Michelet, in his monumental *Histoire de la Revolution française,* and
Carlyle, in his equally influential *The French Revolution,* are the last great
nineteenth-century writers who, in one way or another, take the terrible sublime
seriously as a concept with which to describe historical events. Reading Michelet
in French is in many ways like reading Carlyle in English. Though Michelet has
none of the syncopated irregularity of the Scottish sage, both are writers who
cultivate mysterious senses of history as epical energy. And both writers are fascinated by the human and political reappropriation of godly terror. Michelet, in
the Jacobin tradition, still recognizes the principle of terror as an enthralling element of revolutionary consciousness. When, for instance, he describes national
celebrations of the republic, he lyricizes over the scene that he describes as sometimes charming, sometimes terrible, where the word *terror* invokes an essential
part of the sublime, now located in the state. In the case of Michelet, the secular sublime need not be emptied of terror, because for him the all-embracing
community of the republican state must be defined by its plenitude of human
power. The shock of recognition in the violence of 1793 did not erase the necessity for the state to reserve to itself its plenitude, and hence all its potential
for terror.[32]

In the large, epical narrative of Carlyle's *The French Revolution,* however, it
is not the secular sublime that derives part of its energy from terror. Rather, it is
terror that has completely absorbed the sublime. In the famous chapters on Paris
in 1793, Carlyle seems to pound at the reader, driving him to realize the significance of it all. His prose typically shouts and thumps:

> History, however, in dealing with this Reign of Terror, has had
> her own difficulties. While the Phenomenon continued in its pri-

31. Because I have focused primarily on radical writers, there is no place here to discuss the important re-
designing of terror in, for instance, Wordsworth's poetry or De Quincey's prose. For an interpretation of
revisions in *The Prelude* that complicate the nuances in his reaction to Robespierre and the terror, see my
"Holy Savagery," 379ff.
32. Jules Michelet, *Histoire de la Révolution française,* ed. Gérard Walter (Paris, 1952), 622–71.

mary state, as mere "Horrors of the French Revolution," there was abundance to be said and shrieked. With and also without profit. Heaven knows, there were terrors and horrors enough: yet that was not all the Phenomenon; nay, more properly, that was not the Phenomenon at all, but rather was the *shadow* of it, the negative part of it. And now, in a new stage of the business, when History, ceasing to shriek, would try rather to include under her old Forms of speech or speculation this new amazing Thing; that so some accredited scientific Law of Nature might suffice for the unexpected Product of Nature, and History might get to speak of it articulately, and draw inferences and profit from it; in this new stage, History, we must say, babbles and flounders perhaps in a still painfuller manner. . . .

But what if History were to admit, for once, that all the Names and Theorems yet known to her fall short? That this grand Product of Nature was even grand, and new, in that it came not to range itself under old recorded Laws of Nature at all, but to disclose new ones? In that case, History renouncing the pretension to *name* it at present, will *look* honestly at it, and name what she can of it! Any approximation to the right Names has value; were the right Name itself once here, the Thing is known henceforth; the Thing is then ours, and can be dealt with.[33]

Carlyle wants to give two names to this new "Thing." He calls it first of all "transcendental despair." But making terror into despair is the ultimate removal of terror from the sublime, for despair sees only dark emptiness at the center of what was once godly infinite, manifested in an earthly, aristocratic state. And in understanding the spectator's despair at all that was supposed to be great, Carlyle argues that terror as despair became terror as action, and in this aspect 1793 becomes an enunciation of truth. He goes on to describe dramatically the oppressed poor rising up to tear down what is "altogether a Lie," in the pomp and the grandeur of the oppressor. In this shouting out for truth, all the intellectual superstructure of France dissolves:

[A]ll creeds, intentions, customs, knowledges, thoughts and things, which the French have, suddenly plump down; Catholicism, Classicism, Sentimentalism, Cannibalism; all isms that make up

---

33. Thomas Carlyle, *The French Revolution* (1837), ed. K. J. Fielding and David Sorensen (Oxford, 1989), ii, 332–33; cited henceforward in the text.

man in France, are rushing and roaring in that gulf; and the theorem has become a practice, and whatsoever cannot swim sinks.
(P. 334)

The theorem Carlyle refers to is the Rousseauist call to fraternity. As this theorem tries to turn itself into practice, all grand mental structures fall before this
frightening new thing, the Terror. It will not be surprising that in the grotesque
mixture of psychological and aesthetic categories now completely dominated by
Terror is the sublime itself. At times its light is intense, but the light is now only
transitory, and no brighter than the light given off by the ludicrous:

> Terror is a sable ground, on which the most variegated of scenes
> paints itself. In startling transitions, in colors all intensated, the
> sublime, the ludicrous, the horrible succeed one another; or rather,
> in crowding tumult, accompany one another. (P. 336)

Like Paine in *The Age of Reason*, Carlyle jumbles the sublime and the ludicrous,
but the effect is altogether different. The mixture does not simply dismantle the
Burkean sublime; it leaves the Terror standing by itself. Carlyle's naming of the
Terror as both transcendental despair and a call to truth pushes him to a point
paradoxically beyond the sublime. Terror, no longer felt only in the metaphysical, in the aesthetic, or even as social control in any given state, is now introduced fully formed and unto itself in history. This description of the Reign of
Terror records the death of the sublime as both a psychological and political category. We end where we began. For it was in Carlyle's *The French Revolution* that
Dickens found historical theory for *A Tale of Two Cities*, the novel that Prime
Minister Thatcher seems to have been thinking of at the bicentennial celebration
of the Revolution. As far as British political culture of the nineteenth century is
concerned, this completes the story of the successful designation of terror as a
mental collapse in revolutionary and radical culture.

The ideological manipulation of terror has continued to thrive into the
twenty-first century. It has been commonly imagined as an inevitable form of
human horror in totalitarian states of the fascist kind and grand mechanisms of
state capitalism in the former USSR or today's People's Republic of China. No
one, as far as I know, found anything identifiably sublime in the balance of nu-
clear terror. If the nineteenth century completed the emptying out of terror from
the sublime, the twentieth managed to empty out all vestiges of the sublime
from terror. Perhaps that is why some European critics—one thinks of Michel
De Guy, François Lyotard, Luc Nancy, and others—are now tempted to return,
however hesitatingly, to the sublime and explore it once again. Like spectators
gleaning a vast field after the battle waged upon it is over, cultural critics poke

at what remains, at what perhaps is still useful.[34] Whether or not cultural critics will be able to revive the idea of the sublime as a useful category of psychology and poliltics remains to be seen. It is, however, certain that contemporary terrorists are far ahead of the critics in giving, by means of horrific images of death, new life to old ideas. Whether inspired by American militia groups or Islamic fundamentalists, mass violence will continue to deliver up the primordial ideal of fear as a moral force. Surely terror, which has a much older history than the sublime, has a very long life ahead.

University of California, Los Angeles

---

34. For some recent theoretical considerations of the sublime, see Jean-François Courtine et al., *Du Sublime* (Paris, 1988), translated by Jeffrey S. Librett as *Of the Sublime: Presence in Question* (Albany, N.Y., 1993). For a detailed history from a phenomenological point of view of the political sublime up to the middle of the nineteenth century, see Marc Richir, *Du sublime en politique* (Paris, 1991).

Review Article

The French Revolution, British Cultural Politics, and Recent Scholarship across the Disciplines

———————————————— Michael S. C. Smith

Kevin Gilmartin, *Print Politics: The Press and Radical Opposition in Early-Nineteenth-Century England*
Cambridge: Cambridge University Press, 1997. xiv, 274 pages.

Paul Keen, *The Crisis of Literature in the 1790s: Print Culture and the Public Sphere*
Cambridge: Cambridge University Press, 1999. xii, 299 pages.

Robert Ryan, *The Romantic Reformation: Religious Politics and English Literature*
Cambridge: Cambridge University Press, 1997. xi, 292 pages.

Emma Vincent Macleod, *A War of Ideas: British Attitudes to the War against Revolutionary France, 1792–1802*
Aldershot, England: Ashgate Publishing, 1999. vii, 240 pages.

Marilyn Morris, *The British Monarchy and the French Revolution*
New Haven, Conn.: Yale University Press, 1998. vii, 229 pages.

I. R. McBride, *Scripture Politics: Ulster Presbyterianism and Irish Radicalism in the Late Eighteenth Century*
Oxford: Oxford University Press, 1998. xi, 275 pages.

Of the members of Parliament who resisted Charles James Fox's enthusiasm for the French Revolution, none was as audacious in arguing this position as Edmund Burke, Fox's lifelong friend. The antagonism between the two men, allies in the leadership of the Whig party for years, increased sharply in the months after 1789, with Fox celebrating the fall of France's old order and Burke warning of the horrors to come. At first, few in the Whig party endorsed Fox's seemingly "radical" response to the Revolution, but even fewer supported Burke's apparently alarmist "conservative" reaction, and the growing rift in the leadership did not bode well for the Whigs.

In an oft-quoted remark to Lord Grenville, Fox declared the French Revolution to be "by much the greatest Event that has ever happened in the world,"[1] and he told the House of Commons that the new French constitution was "the most stupendous and glorious edifice of liberty, which had been erected on the foundation of human integrity in any time or country."[2] He was certainly not alone in these sentiments. Many Britons were enthusiastic or at least quietly content about the demise of the traditional French state, and Burke's outrage, which he announced in his *Reflections on the Revolution in France* in 1790, seemed to many to be misplaced. Fox condemned Burke's *Reflections* as "mere madness." Burke admonished Parliament that the Revolution would wreak havoc throughout Europe, and in December 1792 he stood on the floor of the House of Commons, threw down a dagger, and warned that such a gesture was the very thing to expect from the Revolution. Yet Fox, not Burke, eventually found himself banished to a political wilderness. By the end of 1794, Burke had "gone over," as it was phrased, to Pitt, as had other Whig leaders, including Earl Fitzwilliam and the duke of Portland. Fox was left with a coterie of supporters in the House of Commons totaling less than sixty members—not even Lord Grey or the Friends of the People (the reform organization founded by Grey in 1790) allied with him. For the rest of his life, the causes Fox espoused, including peace, retrenchment, and reform, seemed lost amid the tumult of the 1790s. Part of the reason was that disillusionment over the bloodshed became widespread, even among the Revolution's most ardent English supporters. English reformers and radicals were branded as Jacobins and reform quickly lost its cachet. Fox's banishment also had to do with his own political temperament. He loudly and continuously advocated peace and reform though both were increasingly unpopular, tirelessly ranting about such issues as the encroachment of the executive and the persistence of corruption and patronage. That was overfamiliar political language of the 1760s, 1770s, and 1780s. He failed to understand that political discourse and politics, and indeed the stakes in the entire political game, had been transformed in a very short time.[3]

The Revolution's impact on Britain was more profound than the embattled Fox was able to grasp. It inspired, among other things, aristocratic Whigs to form the Friends of the People and to promote reform; the shoemaker Thomas Hardy to found the London Corresponding Society; John Reeves to form his loyalist as-

1.   Quoted in L. G. Mitchell, *Charles James Fox* (Oxford, 1992), 110.
2.   Quoted in L. G. Mitchell, *Charles James Fox and the Disintegration of the Whig Party* (Oxford, 1971), 160.
3.   Eric Evans has summed up Fox's political character succinctly: "No man was ever more prisoner of the Whig legend than Charles James Fox"; *The Forging of the Modern State: Early Industrial Britain, 1783–1870*, 2d ed. (London, 1996), 64.

sociation for "preserving liberty and property against republicans and levelers"; "Church and King" mobs to riot in defense of the state; Dissenters to move for the repeal of the Test and Corporation Acts; and a host of other perhaps more surprising developments, including burnings of Tom Paine in effigy, food riots, attacks on George III, treason trials, volunteer militias, pamphlet wars—and the largest and most expensive war to date in British history.

Historians and literary scholars working on the period over the past several decades have not repeated Fox's mistake. If anything, they have exaggerated the transformative nature of Britain's experience in the 1790s. E. P. Thompson, in his pioneering study of class formation in the late eighteenth and early nineteenth centuries, argued at great length that "something like an 'English Revolution' took place," which "was of profound importance in shaping the consciousness of the post-war working class."[4] Thompson's study of working-class radicalism not only transformed the discipline of social history, or "history from below," but also opened the door for studies of English radicalism and radical culture, including Albert Goodwin's monumental study and the concise and informative work of Edward Royle and James Walvin.[5] H. T. Dickinson, Ceri Crossley, and Mark Philp have edited volumes of essays devoted to the impact of the French Revolution in Britain in relation to politics, culture, and social and economic history.[6] Other historians have examined the importance of the 1790s in the history of popular political associations, public opinion, and popular contention; according to Charles Tilly, the movement away from local, particular forms of contention to national, organized, and cosmopolitan forms accelerated during the last decade of the eighteenth century.[7] Even studies not specifically focusing on the French Revolution often urge its importance to English history. David Hempton has written that the decade subsequent to the Revolution was a "watershed in the fortunes of the Church of England."[8] Not only the religious revival of the late eighteenth century and the spread of Methodism but also the example

---

4. E. P. Thompson, *The Making of the English Working Class* (New York, 1966), 177.

5. Albert Goodwin, *The Friends of Liberty: The English Democratic Movement in the Age of the French Revolution* (Cambridge, Mass., 1979); and Edward Royle and James Walvin, *English Radicals and Reformers, 1760–1848* (Lexington, Ky., 1982). See also H. T. Dickinson, *British Radicalism and the French Revolution* (London, 1985); J. R. Dinwiddy, *Radicalism and Reform in Britain, 1780–1850* (London, 1992); and Malcolm Thomis and Peter Holt, *Threats of Revolution in Britain, 1789–1848* (London, 1977).

6. H. T. Dickinson, ed., *Britain and the French Revolution, 1789–1815* (New York, 1989); Ceri Crossley and Ian Small, ed., *The French Revolution and British Culture* (Oxford, 1990); and Mark Philp, ed., *The French Revolution and British Popular Politics* (Cambridge, 1991).

7. Charles Tilly, *Popular Contention in Great Britain, 1758–1834* (Cambridge, Mass., 1995). See also E. C. Black, *The Association: British Extraparliamentary Political Organization* (Cambridge, Mass., 1963).

8. David Hempton, *Religion and Culture in Britain and Ireland from the Glorious Revolution to the Decline of Empire* (Cambridge, 1996), 23.

of the French in toppling traditional institutions utterly changed the place of the Church in English society.

Studies of political, cultural, and social change and of radicalism led to a methodological counterstroke, arguments for continuity. J. C. D. Clark's work has placed the era of real change in the 1830s, urging that the Anglican, aristocratic, monarchical, divine-right culture of the ancien régime survived throughout the eighteenth century until it finally yielded to Repeal, Emancipation, and Reform.[9] Other historians revised the focus on revolution by turning to loyalism. Robert Dozier's study of the loyalist association movement provided the groundwork for this shift, and Ian Christie took the case one step further by arguing for the ideological superiority of British conservatism. H. T. Dickinson argued for a "populist conservatism" that swept the countryside in the 1790s,[10] and Linda Colley's view that loyalism, patriotism, and Protestantism combined in a successful social as well as political dynamic against the "Other" gained considerable ground—also demonstrating that historians needed to undertake interdisciplinary approaches.[11] In recent years, British loyalism and reactionary politics have continued to attract scholarly interest, but much of the focus has shifted to larger issues of national identity.[12] The most important consequence of recent historiographical developments is that historians are analyzing in a much more nuanced fashion the varying cultural and political preoccupations of late Hanoverian Britons.[13]

Like historians, scholars of English literature have long been fascinated by the 1790s and British radicalism. Romanticism has been the focus of some of the most important critical and theoretical work of the last thirty years, but partly as a result of New Historicism and similar interpretive perspectives, many literary

9. J. C. D. Clark, *English Society, 1688–1832: Ideology, Social Structure, and Political Practice during the Ancien Régime* (Cambridge, 1985), extensively revised and updated in *English Society, 1660–1832: Religion, Ideology, and Politics during the Ancien Régime* (Cambridge, 2000).

10. Robert Dozier, *For King, Constitution, and Country: The English Loyalists and the French Revolution* (Lexington, Ky., 1983); Ian R. Christie, *Stress and Stability in Late-Eighteenth-Century Britain: Reflections on the British Avoidance of Revolution* (Oxford, 1984); and H. T. Dickinson, "Popular Loyalism in Britain in the 1790s," in E. Hellmuth, ed., *The Transformation of Political Culture: England and Germany in the Late Eighteenth Century* (London, 1990). See also Thomas Philip Schofield, "Conservative Political Thought in Britain in Response to the French Revolution," *Historical Journal* 29 (1986). Schofield contended that Burke and other "conservatives" created "a vigorous and eclectic intellectual milieu."

11. Linda Colley, *Britons: Forging the Nation, 1707–1837* (New Haven, Conn., 1992).

12. Tony Claydon and Ian McBride, ed., *Protestantism and National Identity* (Cambridge, 1998); and J. C. D. Clark, "Protestantism, Nationalism, and National Identity," *Historical Journal* 43 (2000).

13. See, for example, J. E. Cookson, *The British Armed Nation, 1793–1815* (Oxford, 1997); and Nicholas Rogers, *Crowds, Culture, and Politics in Georgian Britain* (Oxford, 1998), particularly chap. 6.

historians have recently turned to extensive analysis of historical frameworks. British Romanticism, after all, found its inspiration in the French Revolution and prospects for a new social order, offered a philosophical outlook at odds with the European Enlightenment and traditional forms of belief and behavior, and was inextricably tied to socioeconomic issues and radical political ideologies.[14] In recent years, cross-disciplinary work combined the tricks of the historical trade with the theoretical perspective of literary scholarship, focusing on texts, discourse, symbols, images, rituals, and "performances." In this respect, the work of James Vernon, John Belcham, and James Epstein has been of particular importance.[15] Vernon fashioned his study of nineteenth-century political culture as a "remedy for the deficiences of the current narratives of nineteenth-century political history, with their triumphalist accounts of the development of England's democratic and libertarian constitution." Influenced by postmodernism and the linguistic turn, Vernon's "anti-Whig" or "anti-Liberal" account eschewed "orthodox political history" in favor of ballads, cartoons, handbills, ceremonial forms, and uses of time and space, all to "acknowledge that the languages, categories, and identities of nineteenth-century politics were both shared—in that they all drew their authority from the same constitutional master narrative—and different—in that each individual or collective subject appropriated those languages, categories,

14. On English literature during the age of revolution, see the work of Marilyn Butler, esp. *Romantics, Rebels, and Reactionaries: English Literature and Its Background, 1760–1830* (Oxford, 1981); and, as editor, *Burke, Paine, Godwin, and the Revolution Controversy* (New York, 1984). See also Raymond Williams, *Culture and Society, 1780–1950* (New York, 1960); Howard Mumford Jones, *Revolution and Romanticism* (Cambridge, Mass., 1974); Ronald Paulson, *Representations of Revolution, 1789–1820* (New Haven, Conn., 1983); Michael Scrivener, *Radical Shelley: The Philosophical Anarchism and Utopian Thought of Percy Bysshe Shelley* (Princeton, N.J., 1982); Nicholas Roe, *Wordsworth and Coleridge: The Radical Years* (Oxford, 1988); John Mee, *Dangerous Enthusiasm: William Blake and the Culture of Radicalism in the 1790s* (Oxford, 1993); David Worrall, *Radical Culture: Discourse, Resistance, and Surveillance, 1790–1820* (Detroit, 1992); Marcus Wood, *Radical Satire and Print Culture, 1790–1822* (Oxford, 1992); and James Chandler, *England in 1819: The Politics of Literary Culture and the Case of Romantic Historicism* (Chicago, 1998).

15. John Belchem, "Radical Language and Ideology in Early-Nineteenth-Century England: The Challenge of the Platform," *Albion* 20 (1988):247–59; "Republicanism, Popular Constitutionalism, and the Radical Platform in Early-Nineteenth-Century England," *Social History* 6 (1981); and *'Orator' Hunt: Henry Hunt and English Working-Class Radicalism* (Oxford, 1985); James Vernon, *Politics and the People: A Study in English Political Culture, c. 1815–1867* (Cambridge, 1993); and, as editor, *Re-Reading the Constitution: New Narratives in the Political History of England's Long Nineteenth Century* (Cambridge, 1996); James Epstein, "The Constitutionalist Idiom: Radical Reasoning, Rhetoric, and Action in Early-Nineteenth-Century England," *Journal of Social History* 23 (1990): 553–74; *Radical Expression: Political Language, Ritual ,and Symbol in England, 1790–1850* (Oxford, 1990); and "Our Real Constitution: Trial Defence and Radical Memory in the Age of Revolution," in Vernon, ed., *Re-Reading the Constitution*. See also the important work of Dror Wahrman, *Imagining the Middle Class: Representations of Class in Britain, c. 1780–1840* (Cambridge, 1995).

and identities in different ways."[16] Such investigations, however, have occasionally been hampered by their anachronism. James Epstein, for example, has sought to "relocate" Tom Paine in the twentieth century by characterizing him as a "quintessential modern theorist," while suggesting that there was such a thing as the "literary Left" in 1790s Britain.[17] The capitalization of "Left" amplifies the anachronism. Nonetheless, such theoretical work has had a particularly beneficial impact on the scholarship of late-eighteenth- and early-nineteenth-century cultural politics, as historians have fruitfully focused on the discursive practices of both radicals and loyalists.[18] Mark Philp's 1995 article on conservatism offered one of the most thorough reassessments of 1790s loyalism: the "overemphasis on the intellectual vigour of conservative doctrine" had skewed our historical understanding of the period, as had the neglect of the rhetorical strategies and language embodied in the activities and publications of the loyalist association movement. According to Philp, loyalist ideology and practice changed depending on circumstance and place and on who was doing the talking. There was a lack of coherence to the association movement and to conservative doctrine, and the reception of that doctrine was far from univocal. Philp treated loyalist writing and activity as "performances" and "texts" that offered multiple meanings and that have to be "read" cautiously by historians in drawing conclusions about political ideologies and culture and about the dominance of particular loyalties.[19]

❧ ❧

Of the studies reviewed here, those by Kevin Gilmartin and Paul Keen are the most conspicuously cross-disciplinary and theoretical in their approaches, but all of the books share common themes. Each focuses on ideas, historical context, and ideology, especially radical ideology, and has as its vantage point the intersection between culture, politics, identity, and discourse. There is a consensus that the French Revolution had a profound impact on English politics and culture and that political discourse changed dramatically between the closing years of the eighteenth century and the first three decades of the nineteenth.

Gilmartin's *Print Politics: The Press and Radical Opposition in Early-Nineteenth-Century England* is a study of the language and strategies of London

---

16. Vernon, *Politics and the People*, 1.
17. Esptein, "Our Real Constitution," 25, 29.
18. In addition, historians in recent years have been drawn to sources beyond the typical archival material, including visual media, symbols, rituals, clothing, and linguistics. In *Remapping Early Modern England: The Culture of Seventeenth-Century Politics* (Cambridge, 2000), Kevin Sharpe has urged historians to move to a "broader politics of discourse and symbols, anxieties and aspirations, myths and memories" and away from "an uncompromising English empiricism" (pp. 3, 18).
19. Mark Philp, "Vulgar Conservatism, 1792–93," *English Historical Review* (1995): 42–69.

radical journalism in the first three decades of the nineteenth century, offering a "sustained analysis of radical culture from a perspective informed by, though not wholly limited to, the methods of literary scholarship" (p. 1). Gilmartin confesses that his approach belongs to the "plebeian school" (like E. P. Thompson's), and a significant portion of his book is devoted to analyzing what he calls an "alternative public sphere" or a "counter–public sphere" (p. 3). In their efforts to champion popular rights and liberties against the oppressive rule of English elites and the dominance of the two traditional political parties, London radicals fashioned a counter–public sphere through the press and printed material, which included pamphlets, broadsheets, and tracts as well as periodicals and newspapers. Gilmartin numbers radical exponents as Richard Carlile, William Cobbett, William Hazlitt, John Wade, T. J. Wooler, and John Hunt, and the printed material he considers includes such radical publications as the *Black Dwarf*, the *Yellow Dwarf*, Cobbett's *Political Register*, and Leigh Hunt's *Examiner*. Not only did these radicals address the English working classes, but their productions were also typically cheap enough for the working man to afford. Radical print was aided by the radical public, in that local clubs, associations, and communal groups could meet to discuss issues and to read radical literature aloud. Like many recent studies of radicalism and loyalism, Gilmartin's also emphasizes the often contradictory, fragmented nature of political discourse and of the radical counter–public sphere, focusing on the rhetorical strategies of radical writers and examining the radical commitment to public deliberation. Radicalism was a "free-press" movement opposed to the political dominance of both the Whig and the Tory parties, the oppressive nature of the early-nineteenth-century state, and widespread corruption. On the whole, Gilmartin is less concerned with radical ideology itself than with the rhetoric, strategies, constructions, and discursive practices of the movement as seen in the press. In many ways Cobbett is the prototypical radical of Gilmartin's book: Cobbett formulated an ideological "counter-system" at odds with the corrupt "system" of dominant elites and set examples for his radical brethren by, among other things, issuing unstamped versions of his *Political Register*. Radicals who followed Cobbett's lead in evading newspaper duties were, like him, fighting the "web of repression" spun by the English government.

Paul Keen's *The Crisis of Literature in the 1790s: Print Culture and the Public Sphere* has a number of affinities with Gilmartin's study. In particular, he too is interested in the intersection of Romantic literature and the construction of political identities. Pointing out that the Romantic period saw a profound social and economic transformation in which "literature became a site of ideological contestation," Keen examines the battle for the public sphere among England's radical literary world and finds that "the ideal of the bourgeois public sphere was a dominant but highly contested position that was most closely associated with the reformist middle class" (pp. 1, 6). Literature has always been a form of political expression, he argues; it has always therefore been in a state of flux, and the age of revolution was a particularly important moment in the ongoing contestation over literature's role. The European Enlightenment propelled print into the forefront of culture, especially with the development of reading rooms and societies, lending libraries, and cheap printed books and periodicals. This "information revolution," as Keen sees it, made the public sphere a deeply contested public space and, with major social and economic change, resulted in the development of "subaltern counterpublics" made up of lower-class radicals who simultaneously challenged and sought inclusion in the largely middle-class public sphere. Print symbolized freedom, the late-eighteenth-century republic of letters was inherently political, and the public sphere had a "democratic ethos"— but ultimately that public sphere was virtually as exclusive and class-bound as its aristocratic nemesis. Because this space was appropriated and dominated by middle-class men, "subaltern counterpublics," as Keen designates them, never found inclusion in it. The public sphere always emphasized reform but also attested the supremacy of reason, which, to most of its "members," was a "masculine" characteristic. And this is where the political importance of the public sphere truly lay, for even if it was dominated by specific class and gender constructions, it also fed the reformist impulse in a very broad sense of the term. Female radical writers, as Keen so adeptly shows in his chapter on "masculine women," sought to prove that they too could be "rational" without having to deny their femininity entirely.

The real novelty of Keen's study is the elusiveness of his object, an ephemeral, abstract phenomenon: "the shifting cultural geography within which literary texts are inscribed" (p. 2). His focus is not so much on the ideology and activities of radical writers in the age of revolution as on the "long history of the changing status of literature as a public sphere," and he chooses the 1790s because that was when the "contradictions inherent in this discourse were most dramatically foregrounded" (p. 10). What the poets and writers of the period might have contributed to the political modernization of England is not something that interests Keen as much as the ways in which these writers transformed their conceptions about their roles and the role of the public sphere in the political and cultural life of the nation. With so much political and social change going on around them, radical writers and poets waged a fierce battle for and within the public sphere so that they might one day fulfill their hopes of being the "unacknowledged legislators of the world."

From a historical and conceptual standpoint, the studies by Gilmartin and Keen have some problems in common. Although they do not accept Habermass's work uncritically, they do assume that something like a public sphere existed and that it was fully formed by the late eighteenth century.[20] They do not satisfactorily indicate what specific forms "public culture" took in the eighteenth century, why the public sphere was so central to political and cultural discourse, and who made up the "public" in the first place. The term "rational" itself is often employed rather loosely to describe late-eighteenth-century cultural discourse; thus it is not clear how appeals to emotion, ad hominem attacks, political exaggerations, demonizing of enemies, religious rhetoric, and other apparently less "rational" tactics that characterized the debates of the 1790s should be classified in this scheme. There is also an extent to which these studies of the public sphere privilege printed books and periodicals. The authors must be commended for their wide reading of printed sources; but if the public sphere as they envision it did in fact exist, other sources of information and ideas must have been integral to that public sphere, including political caricatures and other visual media, broadsheets, the occasional manuscript, and discourse carried on in public spaces. Pubs, meeting houses, street corners, parishes, stages, and even Parliament itself were locations where ideas were contested and the public sphere was "in process." Social spaces—that is, locations in which social relationships, class and gender identities, and political relationships impinged upon the exchange of ideas— should be studied as having shaped the ideas expressed in them.

Whatever impact these two studies will have on academic discussions of literature and the public sphere, their implications for the study of British radicalism are perhaps more important. In some ways, it is true, Gilmartin and Keen do not offer fully viable definitions of radicalism in the age of revolution: In Gilmartin's words, early-nineteenth-century radicalism was "a protest against the dominance of two political parties" (p. 11). English radicals defended popular right against oppressive rule, desired parliamentary reform, and wanted an end to corruption. In Keen's view, English radicals were caught in an unresolvable paradox: in forming "subaltern counterpublics," radicals protested the exclusiveness and social elitism of the bourgeois public sphere and yet desired to be part of the public sphere or at least harness the power of print to emancipate individuals. But radicalism was more complex than either study suggests; it was more than a platform to attack the two-party system and, while it had a fairly coherent ideological structure, it was, perhaps paradoxically, varied in its expression of political and economic aims. Although by and large English radicals

---

20. Keen, for example, remarks that "Habermas underestimates the complexity of the relations between the political and literary public spheres" (p. 15).

promoted male suffrage, annual elections, the redistribution of parliamentary seats, payment of M.P.s, and similar political positions, other versions of radicalism, such as that of Godwin, tended to be much more economically oriented and class based, as seen in radical attacks on hereditary property and the promotion of an agrarian law. Of course, implicit in one form of radicalism were the aims of the other, so that purely political radicalism and economic radicalism were not mutually exclusive. Nevertheless, the metropolitan radicalism of men such as Francis Burdett was a far cry from the working-class radicalism of the Luddites, whose main concern was the loss of a specific form of life and not the particular habits of pensioners in Parliament. However, even if Gilmartin and Keen may be working with a too monolithic notion of radicalism, they do raise in new ways the persistent question of why it did not achieve its aims.

Despite its variety of expression, radicalism of the late eighteenth century as a whole was limited by the linguistic, conceptual, and rhetorical categories of the political climate in which it existed. As James Epstein has pointed out, and as many eighteenth- and nineteenth-century radicals made very clear, radicalism was deeply constitutionalist and sought to work within the tradition of English legal and political practice.[21] The target was not so much a parliamentary system with two parties, two houses, and a monarchy but the corruption and devolution of government and the ascendancy of oppressive elites. Like Charles James Fox, many radicals perceived a dangerous encroachment by the monarchy over the rights and liberties of the freeborn Englishman but did not necessarily want to overthrow the institution. As a 1795 "dictionary" of political terms put it for the entry "enquiry": "In the old English dictionary, it was held a CONSTITUTIONAL PRIVILEGE, derived from MAGNA CHARTA and the BILL OF RIGHTS, for the people to *enquire* into the conduct of kings or ministers, and into the errors of their government; but all things now seem in a state of revolution, and, according to Mr. P-tt's new code, which is implicitly adopted by all the legal courts through the three kingdoms, *enquiry* implied disloyalty, sedition, or treason, and they who are *audacious* enough to claim this ancient *obsolete* privilege, expose themselves to the penalties of fines, pillory, or imprisonment, and if in Scotland, of transportation for fourteen years to BOTANY BAY."[22] The Scottish antiquary and historian George Chalmers, who advocated freedom of the press, wrote that "it is . . . happy for the security of our persons, and fortunate for the privilege of free discussion, that the distance is great between bad writing and criminal writing; between the purpose to exercise a constitutional right, and the design to do ill." He also argued that the right of free thinking and free publishing was "the com-

21. See Epstein, *Radical Expression*, chap. 1.
22. Anon., *The Voice of the People, &c. Consisting of Extracts from Pigott, Gerald, &c. Printed for Citizen Lee, at the British Tree of Liberty* (London, 1795), 3.

mon law right, the Magna Charta right."[23] Chalmers and the anonymous author of *The Voice of the People* detested Pitt's ministry, the extended treason and antisedition laws, and political corruption, but they wanted to reform England from within its own constitutional and legal tradition. In this sense, radicalism was tempered by the conceptual limitations of its constitutional and political discourse. This is part of the reason for radicalism's nonviolent nature and, perhaps, for its ultimate failure. It could not escape the political and cultural worlds it was designed to transform.

Historians have often disagreed about why radicalism did not succeed in its political aims, and the explanations have ranged from government repression to the popular appeal of conservatism, from the lack of organization and effective strategy on the part of radicals to the shift of the majority of public opinion in favor of the government in a time of war. Gilmartin's and Keen's studies raise the questions about the failure of radicalism again. If the counter–public sphere was so viable, why did it not fulfill its aims? If print was such a powerful, transforming medium and there was an "information revolution," why did the overwhelming reformist impulse of most Hanoverian publishing fail in bringing about political and social reform?

The real importance of Gilmartin's and Keen's work is that their approach and their findings underscore the inadequacy of the conventional explanations for radicalism's failure. The authors acknowledge that, when measured in conventional political and historical terms, radicalism did not succeed; but it did not fail completely. When measured in terms of the public sphere and of rhetorical and literary impact, radicalism was deeply influential, even if it did not immediately transform the structure of Hanoverian politics. As William Stafford has pointed out, one consequence of the "linguistic turn" is recognizing that the objective of radicals was not reform or revolution but access to the public sphere. This argument is implicit in Gilmartin's and Keen's studies. "The questions," Stafford argued, "will not be about how numerous [radicals] were, or how large their following, or how suitable their ideology as a means of mass mobilization. They will be about the extent to which, against all the odds, they expanded what could be said, where it could be said, and by whom it could be said."[24] By extending the boundaries of what could be said and who could do the saying, and by extending the limits (in real numbers as well as in conceptual and literary terms) of what could be printed and read, radicalism was not only successful; its legacy also led to the expansion of the role of public opinion in politics in the

23. George Chalmers, *A Vindication of the Privilege of the People* (London, 1796), 20–21.
24. William Stafford, "Shall We Take the Linguistic Turn? British Radicalism in the Era of the French Revolution," *Historical Journal* 43 (2000): 588.

nineteenth century and to the growing diversity of print. While these two studies do not address later periods, these developments may very well have had an
impact on Victorian political reforms. At the very least, British literature and
public political culture were transformed: the purview of public debate had expanded, and the boundaries of what could be said and printed broadened significantly between the 1790s and the 1830s.

~ ~

The polarization of political opinion in the age of revolution and reform is an indication of the immense power of ideas, and Robert Ryan and Emma Vincent
Macleod consider the nature and impact of political and religious ideology. While
the politics of Romantic writers has been known and thoroughly studied, few
scholars have concentrated on the religious roots of Romanticism. More typically, they have seen the movement, as in Shelley's case, as an embrace of athe-
ism, or, in the case of Byron, Keats, and Wordsworth, as the striving toward
freedom from traditional orthodoxy and the adoption of non-Christian transcendental ideals. Despite Coleridge's religiosity and the efforts of at least one
historian to make Lord Byron into an evangelical, Romanticism has traditionally
been seen as a non-Christian, even nonreligious, ideology that gave primacy to
the individual and to the need to transcend codified systems of belief.[25] In Ryan's
view, this orthodoxy has prevailed for far too long. He aims in *The Romantic
Reformation: Religious Politics and English Religion* to examine the religious milieu
"wherein English Romanticism acquired its distinctive character"; to show that
"Romantic poets accepted the role of religion as a dynamic ideology behind social and political action"; and to prove that "all poets committed themselves to
this work of cultural critique and rehabilitation," which entailed examining
the "religious principles cementing the social order" and then changing them
(pp. 1–4). Analyzing the writings and thought of Blake, Wordsworth, Keats, and
the Shelleys, Ryan argues that Romanticism did in fact have a substantial religious
foundation that informed its ideology from beginning to end. Ryan drew inspiration for his approach from Jonathan Clark, who argued that all political and
cultural discourse in Hanoverian England was essentially religious and that
Anglican cultural values remained dominant well into the nineteenth century.
Ryan rightly sees little or no separation between the religious and political
spheres. Instead of discarding traditional religion as an obscurantist philosophy,

25.   In his study of the influence of evangelism on social and economic thought, Boyd Hilton contended that
even the rebellious Lord Byron was evangelical in his heart; see *The Age of Atonement* (Oxford, 1988), 29.

Romantic poets fought to establish an entirely new religious "reformation," not unlike the one inaugurated in the 1530s. These Romantics' religious concerns were certainly tied up with their political and social ones; they wanted to reform and liberalize traditional, established religion, which, like the secular government to which it was attached, was not progressive, liberal, or free enough.

In *A War of Ideas: British Attitudes to the Wars against Revolutionary France, 1792–1802*, Emma Vincent Macleod surveys the reactions and responses to the war against Jacobin France and finds that firmly held ideas and principles guided official policy and loyalist reaction, as well as public opinion and radical enthusiasm. While not a particularly novel argument (H. T. Dickinson, Robert Hole, I. R. Christie, and others have proposed the same), Macleod's study does make a thorough case for the persistence of ideology in the age of revolution. Her loyalists were populist, pragmatic, "committed activists" who defended the British constitution against French ideas and were profoundly disturbed by the impact of those ideas on the British social and political order. Inspired by Burke, who set the tone for the entire conservative-radical debate, the loyalists became die-hard war crusaders who based their support of Pitt's anti-French efforts on their detestation of Jacobinism. Pitt and his ministers might have sympathized with the loyalist cause but were less tied to such flagrant ideology; instead, they were motivated by balance-of-power considerations and the need to stop the French from attacking British interests across the Channel. They were opposed by two main groups: the Foxite Whigs and domestic radicals. The Opposition Whigs and their extraparliamentary allies throughout the country opposed the war because of their early sympathy for the ideals of the French Revolution. The same held true for English radicals, whose calls for peace and reform were predicated on their affinity for mainstream Jacobin principles. In her concluding chapters, Macleod considers the ideological makeup of churchmen, women, and the public in general. In her view, the "majority of churchmen tended towards quite a Burkean loyalist position, but all the major political stances on the conflict had their clerical proponents and theological underpinnings" (pp. 136–37). Loyalist churchmen were primarily afraid of immorality, irreligion, potential anarchy, and the erosion of the relationship between Church and state, although, as Macleod argues, individual perspectives on France and the war often depended on theological orientation. Dissenting churchmen, for example, interpreted the specter of France and the impact of Jacobin ideas in a more favorable manner than did their Anglican counterparts. Finally, women, at least those who made their voices heard, tended to be antiwar but also anti-French and stressed the importance of moral vigilance. On the whole, the British public, which could not avoid the debates of the era because of crowd activity, the presence of local militias, and ubiquitous pamphlet wars, proved to be somewhat xenophobic and deeply anti-Gallican.

Ryan and Macleod make strong cases for the centrality of religious and political principles, but their studies do not always fulfill the aims they set, and the arguments do not go as far as they should. In Ryan's view, the Romantic poets' "authority in the religious sphere was widely acknowledged" (p. 6). Blake, Wordsworth, Keats, and the Shelleys were certainly Britain's leading literary figures, but they held no political offices, tended no dioceses or parishes nor held other offices in the Church, were not theologians, did not deliver sermons, and were not generally recognized among the Anglican or the Dissenting elite as authorities on religion. Ryan does not examine the readership of these Romantic writers to determine how deeply their religious ideas seeped into the culture, or even to document how much of the public was attending to their work. Ryan's argument raises numerous questions about the arena of public discourse and, especially, about the use of the term "power structure." Does he mean the Anglican establishment, which was never homogeneous to begin with; or the political elite, which comprised stalwart defenders of the established Church as well as friends of Dissent and supporters of political and religious reform? Are the Nonconformist and Catholic gentry included in this power structure as well, or is it simply an enclave of land-owning Anglican elites?

It is therefore unclear just what Ryan's phrase "the system of religion that was increasing its hold as the dominant ideology and idealism of its time" refers to (p. 7). Religion and politics had never been separate spheres in England in the past, but by the 1790s they were, in fact, beginning to diverge. Reform, for example, was a strictly political issue, not a religious one, and the arguments for Repeal were typically based on political suppositions about rights and liberties, not on ringing endorsements of theological heterodoxy. It is also unclear just what the "dominant ideology" was in the first place. If it was that meeting ground between politics and religion, it also had much to do with property, commerce, and trade. If the dominant ideology was traditional Anglicanism, it had extremely powerful contenders, not only among Dissenters, whose number increased as the years went by and who became increasingly active and organized, but also from within the establishment. The battle between Low Church latitudinarians and High Churchmen continued, while the Established Church itself contributed significantly to the English Enlightenment.[26] Philosophical radicalism emerged in the early years of the nineteenth century, and intellectuals such as

---

26. B. W. Young, *Religion and Enlightenment in Eighteenth-Century England: Theological Debate from Locke to Burke* (Oxford, 1996).

Paley pursued a "rationalized" form of Christianity. Ryan makes a thoroughly convincing case for the religious basis of much Romantic thought; it is the institutional relevance of such thought that remains open to debate.

Macleod's thesis is clearly formulated and repeatedly presented in a variety of registers, although she is not always attentive to the subtle relationships between political principles, theological persuasions, and political practice; nor does she engage with current theoretical approaches to ideas, culture, and discourse. *A War of Ideas* essentially overstates the role of ideology, suggesting implicitly that each ideological group fit into its own neat box and that, most of the time, the lines between ideological positions were clearly drawn. While tried-and-true ideologues can be pointed to—Burke, John Reeves, and John Bowles on the loyalist side, and Thomas Spence, John Thelwall, and Thomas Paine on the radical— there were varieties of loyalists and radicals alike. Not all Dissenters, for example, cheered for the Opposition; many joined loyalist associations in the early 1790s and were entirely unenthusiastic about the French Revolution.[27] Thomas Francis Sheridan detested French revolutionary principles, domestic radicalism, Tom Paine, and any argument for universal manhood suffrage, but urged the repeal of the penal laws against Catholics. As he put it, "I would repeal every penal, every disqualifying statute regarding the Catholic—The very names of Catholic or Papist, or indeed of any other religious sect, I would expunge from our statutes."[28] The Friends of the People is mischaracterized by Macleod as being primarily motivated by the members' sympathy for the Revolution. While Grey and his cohorts were inspired by the example of the French to create their club and promote parliamentary reform, their political platform and modes of action had English pedigrees. Forming extraparliamentary associations to promote parliamentary reform had become an important practice in the 1780s, and it was in this climate that Grey received his political education. And while it is true that radicals opposed Pitt because of their ongoing sympathy with French ideas, this was not the case for all of them throughout the 1790s. The London Corresponding Society, for example, was deeply motivated by the Revolution, but the radical activity of the mid-1790s had much to do with more immediate concerns, especially with growing economic distress—high prices, food shortages, bad harvests, and taxes.

Macleod's study therefore raises interesting questions about the relationship between ideas and historical context and about the extent to which ideas shaped

27. Dissenters in Hawes, for example, formed a loyalist association in January 1793 and pledged to defend the monarchy and the constitution; British Library, Add. MS. 16929 (Reeves Papers).
28. Charles Francis Sheridan, *An Essay Upon the True Principles of Civil Liberty, and of Free Government, Occasioned by the Levelling Doctrines of the Day, in Which is Also Discussed the Roman Catholic Claim to the Elective Franchise in Ireland* (London, 1793), 5.

political and social action. Xenophobia, for example, definitely informed much loyalist thinking and, as Macleod argues, hastened the development of a modern form of national identity and, to an extent, unity. *A War of Ideas* vividly illustrates just how "English" the English could be in a time of war and social upheaval. The argument, however, could have been balanced with a consideration of the powerful local and regional factors in political ideology and action. Moreover, in her informative account of loyalist war crusading, Macleod's case would have benefited from a more cross-disciplinary approach, for one major facet of pro-war pamphleteering was its rhetorical impact. The heavily politicized extremist discourse embodied in the writing of crusaders such as John Bowles demonized Opposition and radical ideas and set up rhetorical bogeymen, characterizing calls for peace as advocating the destruction of Britain's social order. Reformers such as Grey never advocated a complete overhaul of Britain's political order or a revolutionary change in the branches of government, but their loyalist opponents argued that they did; as one writer put it, the object of Grey's association "is not to reform but to destroy."[29] In a political climate as contested as that of the 1790s, rhetorical strategies were just as important as ideas. The super-heating of political discourse is one reason why even the most moderate reformers were branded as Jacobins, levelers, or, worse, traitors; and it partly explains why reform remained a pipe dream for thirty years and why radicals could not fulfill their goals.

❧ ❧

If Macleod's study of the war of ideas in the age of revolution at times lacks sufficient historical perspective, Marilyn Morris's fascinating study of the British monarchy during the same tumultuous period perhaps provides too much. Drawing on approaches as diverse as those of Linda Colley and Clifford Geertz and going back to studies of seventeenth-century theories of divine-right monarchy, Morris's *The British Monarchy and the French Revolution* insists that the Revolution's impact in Britain resulted in renewed support for the institution of monarchy. The political debates of the 1790s played a significant role: "the dialectic between democratic reformers and supporters of the political status quo produced a species of kingship that melded patriarchalism with egalitarian republican ideals" (p. 2). The monarchy strengthened its role as the central institution of the nation but was forced to alter its place in political and social life because

---

29. Anon., *Remarks on the Proceedings of the Society, Who Style Themselves "The Friends of the People:" and Observations on the Principles of Government, as Applicable to the British Constitution* (London, 1792), 7.

of the influence of republican and loyalist thinking. "In the decade of the French Revolution," writes Morris, "the monarchy regained its place as a focal point in political argument, but, no longer politically absolute, the monarch's palace at the head of the social hierarchy took on new importance" (p. 11). Seventeenth-century divine-right theory and the ideology of patriarchalism survived well into the eighteenth century but had to contend with emerging republican ideas; the result was that loyalist and radical discourses became centered upon a common ideological front that espoused responsible, balanced, honest government: "The main difference was that loyalists claimed that this model already existed, while reformers saw it as an ideal that would be realized only through parliamentary reform" (p. 100). In the final analysis, then, loyalists and radicals desired the same type of polity but differed drastically on methods. George III was the guardian of English religion, the sanctified embodiment of the law, and the inspiration for a largely loyalist public that, whatever reforms it might have desired, did not endorse France's response to Louis XVI as a solution for England.

Morris's wide focus provides a long historical lesson, but it too often comes at the expense of the more relevant eighteenth-century context. One-third of a chapter on court culture in the reign of George III is taken up by detailed considerations of the courts of James I, Elizabeth I, Charles I, Charles II, James II, William III, and the first two Georges (chap. 7, esp. pp. 134–42). In the introduction and first chapter, Morris is so intent on providing broad context and a sociological approach to monarchy that she overlooks relevant historiographical debates. But the argument is intriguing and provocative and, like Linda Colley's work, greatly contributes to our understanding of the formation and power of national identity in the late eighteenth and early nineteenth centuries.[30] The strengthening of a Protestant national identity unified British culture, in terms broader than local, regional, sectarian, and familial continuities. This line of argument has made historians more aware of the centrality of the monarchy to political culture and of the unity as well as the divisiveness it could inspire.

Not every Briton, however, apotheosized George III or had regard for the safety of his person. The opening day of Parliament in October 1795 was an infamous moment; as the king made his way from Buckingham Palace down

30. Important evidence for the emergence of a national culture can be found in the electoral practices of English voters. By the early nineteenth century, national, as opposed to local, issues often influenced voters' decisions and the outcome of elections; see Frank O'Gorman, *Voters, Patrons, and Parties: The Unreformed Electoral System of Hanoverian England, 1734–1832* (Oxford, 1989); John Phillips, *The Great Reform Bill in the Boroughs: English Electoral Behaviour, 1818–1841* (Oxford, 1992); and Phillips, "Popular Politics in Unreformed England," *Journal of Modern History* 52 (1980): 599–625. For a challenge to these studies, see Edwin Jaggard, *Cornwall Politics in the Age of Reform, 1790–1885* (Woodbridge, England, 1999).

Pall Mall toward the House of Lords, he was greeted with boos, hisses, and, worse, pebbles and stones. A mob of angry Londoners surrounded the king's procession in St. James's Park to assault the king's ears with cries of "Bread! Bread! Peace! Peace!" When the tumult died down and arrests were made, some of the harshest punishment was reserved for one Kyd Wake, who was detained for hissing at the king and shouting, "Down with George, no war."[31] Wake was tried in May 1796 and defended unsuccessfully by Thomas Erskine. He was sentenced to hard labor in a Gloucester gaol for five years, the first three months of which were to be spent in pillory on a public street for one hour each day.[32]

The case of Wake, as well as that of other Britons who refused to pay due deference to their social betters or to the king, demonstrates that no matter how beloved the king might be, and no matter how many citizens rallied to his support in a time of crisis, numerous individuals did not allow the public image of the sanctified monarch to displace their disaffection toward the government, the aristocracy, Parliament, and the prime minister. Loyalists and radicals might have shared a common love of balanced government, but their common ground was the constitution more than the monarchy. Certainly, mainstream figures on either side would not have imagined a constitution and a Parliament without a king (or queen), but late-eighteenth-century loyalist and radical discourses contain little royalist rhetoric. The loyalist associations of the early 1790s, for example, explicitly state in printed declarations, advertisements, accounts of meetings, and pamphlets their support for the constitution and to "King, Lords, and Commons" as a whole.[33] Theirs was a heavily constitutionalist language, and this was true of English radicals as well.[34] Royalism was not an essential element in late-eighteenth-century political discourse.

❧ ❧

Irish radicals, however, were a different story, and it is surprising to find that Gilmartin, Keen, Ryan, Macleod, and Morris do not consider Irish radicals or the "Irish question" in their studies. The Irish were a significant problem for the

31. *The Annual Register* (1795), "Chronicle," 38.
32. Ibid., 6, 17.
33. The papers of the Reeves Association in the British Library contain numerous references to the ancient and balanced constitution and the three branches of government but, by and large, do not single out the person of the king, the royal family, or the House of Hanover. Given that the Crown and Anchor Association and its numerous offspring were at the forefront of loyalist public opinion, this is a telling indication of loyalism's relationship to the monarchy; see Reeves Papers, British Library, Add. MSS. 16919–16931. See also Philip, "Vulgar Conservatism," passim; and Michael S. Smith, "Anti-Radical Expression: Counter-Revolutionary Thought in the Age of Revolution" (Ph.D. diss., University of California, Riverside, 1999), chap. 2.
34. See Epstein, *Radical Expression*, chap. 1.

English in the late 1790s, not only because of their own radical, sometimes violent, agitations, but also because Irish radicals befriended the French, who believed that a successful invasion of England would come by way of landing in Ireland. Ian McBride studies the relationship between Ulster Presbyterianism and Irish radicalism in the late eighteenth century. *Scripture Politics: Ulster Presbyterianism and Irish Radicalism in the Late Eighteenth Century* is a lucid, penetrating work, balanced and judicious in its assessment of the radicalization of Presbyterian politics and the essential role of theological opinions in the formation of political ideologies. Ryan made a provocative case for the religious elements of Romantic thought but took the argument too far in stating that Romantic poets were therefore authorities in religion. Macleod stressed the importance of religion to political ideas in the 1790s but implied that one's theological opinions could almost readily predict one's political positions. McBride offers a subtler analysis. He pays attention to what he calls the "distinctive cultural formation of the Dissenting north" and analyzes several significant elements in the development of Irish republicanism: the gradual development of national consciousness, the political resurgence of Catholicism, and the rediscovery of a Gaelic past (pp. 3–4). Republicans were "pro-religious," radicalism was the result of mingling "alternative" theologies with politics, and the United Irish Society was brought about partly by a series of radical initiatives that emerged out of Belfast in the eighteenth century (p. 11). A variety of political and cultural developments were at play in the north. The political resurgence of Catholicism compelled many Catholics to adopt Whig constitutionalist ideas, while the Enlightenment brought toleration and similar liberal ideas to public debate. Presbyterianism played the greatest role. The ecclesiastical structure of the religion (bishops in the Church were equal, for example), the legacy of early-eighteenth-century rational Dissent, the fact that ministers were elected, and the historical refusal to subscribe to oaths led Irish Presbyterians to attack the confessional state, critique the aristocracy's control of the lower house of Parliament, favor equal representation and parliamentary reform, and defend contractarian politics. While much of McBride's book is devoted to the varieties of Presbyterianism and radicalism between the age of Wilkes and the 1780s, the closing chapters on the United Irishmen are the culmination of the story. The revival of radicalism brought on by the fall of the Bastille led to the formation of the Irish Whig Club in 1789 and the Northern Irish Whig Club in 1790, the rise of Wolfe Tone, and the "transformation from commonwealthsmen to United Irishmen" (p. 169). Prior to the 1790s, Irish radicals employed characteristically Whig discourse, taking aim at patronage and the executive and defending the virtue of independent liberty against the corruption of the elite. But it was the rise of millenarian thought in the face of revolutionary change that transformed the cause into a mass insurrectionary force. Irish

Presbyterians often interpreted the events of the 1790s in biblical terms and prophesied that the time of redemption was at hand, but, paradoxically, this made them "enlightened" thinkers because their millenarianism reinforced their belief in civil and religious liberty and individualism. The eighteenth-century confessional state, which had withered by the 1790s, had, in a sense, already made them this way, and the events of the 1790s fueled the fire.

The Irish radical movement was decimated by the failure of 1798. The radicals' defeat and widespread alienation over the course of the French Revolution once Napoleon took the helm meant that they were reduced to pursuing oppositionist politics in the north. Some secret societies survived into the early nineteenth century, but the great republican moment, the closest Britain came to real insurrection in the 1790s, was over. McBride's study reminds us that Irish radicalism did not die by 1800, if only because many of the few remaining Irish radicals shared basic political tenets with their English brethren: annual parliaments, equal constituencies, universal manhood suffrage, and payment of M.P.s.

Once again, the question of why radicalism did not succeed in real, immediate political terms arises, and McBride's study offers a particularly harsh explanation. First, as others have suggested, while antiradical pressure, repressive legislation, a successful volunteer movement, and insufficient organization certainly hampered British radicalism, the limitations resulting from most radicals' reliance on traditional constitutional ideology and discourse meant that radicalism could not overthrow the system—it was part of the system. But further, despite radicalism's eighteenth-century and, in some cases, seventeenth-century antecedents and its relative ideological coherence, much of it rested upon passion, hysteria, and short-term goals and commitments. Radical activity and allegiance, in its varying forms, therefore appeared and disappeared rapidly across the countryside, and this was equally true of loyalist allegiance. Only the most ardent practitioners of each movement continued the struggle in the long term. As David Eastwood has argued:

> The most serious threat to the conservative order in Britain in the 1790s would have come from a radical politicisation of the plight of the poor, from food rioters in England following their French counterparts into the temples of Jacobinism. That most, although not all, food riots reflected the frustrations of temporary hardship rather than any deep-seated ideological alienation from the governing elite was crucial to the survival of that elite.[35]

35. David Eastwood, "Patriotism and the English State in the 1790s," in Philp, ed., *The French Revolution and British Popular Politics*, 162.

So the problem was essentially twofold. The inability of radicals to harness successfully the plight of the laboring poor contributed, as Eastwood believes, to the survival of the traditional ruling class. That radicalism was tempered by the limitations of its constitutionalist discourse and operated within a constitutional tradition meant that, ultimately, it had to be evolutionary in its political designs if it ever hoped to succeed. British reformers and conservatives alike accepted change it if came piecemeal, as the political and social reforms of the nineteenth century were to do. And in a period when sudden change inspired anxieties about insurrection and revolution, the need for evolutionary politics was all the more pressing. By the nineteenth century, reformers understood that gradual change was all that the political climate and the constitution would really allow. From the perspective of aristocratic reformers and the traditional elite, gradual change was all they *could* allow, not only to avoid massive disruptions in the social order but also to secure their own interests.[36]

As Gilmartin, Keen, and others have rightly insisted, at the core of radical discourse was the debate between virtue and corruption, a defense of a system of values that pitted populist government against the corrupt, vested interests of the landed elite and the forces of finance.[37] But although the outcry against corrupt government was heard increasingly after 1789, it had been expressed by reformers for decades, particularly in the 1760s as a result of the John Wilkes affair, and other ideological polarities existed prior to the 1790s. The Church and King mobs that descended on Joseph Priestley's house in 1790 were not expressing ideas new to the decade but, as Nicholas Rogers has pointed out, were letting loose an old sectarianism that had extensive roots in the Birmingham region.[38] Long-held principles were, as Macleod argues, crucial to the events of the 1790s but were often not more important than other elements, especially social grievances and local influences. Many who joined loyalist associations in the early 1790s, for example, did so from social coercion, and many who enlisted in local militias toward the end of the decade had overriding employment, material, and social concerns.[39] No matter how profound the French Revolution's impact, and no matter how quickly and deeply political discourse changed, continuities existed

36. See, in particular, Ian Newbould, *Whiggery and Reform, 1830–41: The Politics of Government* (Stanford, Calif., 1990).

37. For a groundbreaking discussion of the decline of the charge of "old corruption," the persistence of the traditional elite, and the development of efficient government, see Phil Harling, *The Waning of "Old Corruption": The Politics of Economical Reform in Britain, 1779–1846* (Oxford, 1996).

38. Nicholas Rogers, *Crowds, Culture, and Politics in Georgian Britain* (Oxford, 1998), 182.

39. J. E. Cookson points out, "The volunteers were certainly encouraged to regard themselves as national defenders, and they were increasingly organized as a force for national defence. However, their localism was always more conspicuous than their readiness to serve the state on the state's terms"; *The British Armed Nation, 1793–1815* (Oxford, 1997), 91.

at both the local and the national levels. Fox's mistake was believing that such continuities prevailed, but it would be a mistake of equal magnitude to assume that all was new after 1789.

Nevertheless, the studies by Gilmartin, Keen, Macleod, McBride, Morris, and Ryan succeed in arguing for the French Revolution's transformative influence on British politics and culture. The rise and growing influence of public opinion, the polarization of politics, the contestations over religious authority, the changing role of the monarchy, the unprecedented size of the war with France and the local call to arms, the creation of radical and loyalist societies, and the impressive expansion of the press and of public discourse in general—the development of the "public sphere" or something like it—meant that when the smoke cleared in the 1820s and 1830s, politics was no longer the same, nor was the social and cultural makeup of the nation. Most of the studies critiqued in this review do not discuss the nineteenth century in detail, but all argue that the cultural and political contests of the late eighteenth century were volatile and profoundly significant, while a few imply that such contests necessitated progress toward democracy. Most of all, these studies, and in particular those by Gilmartin and Keen, illustrate both the importance and the inherent difficulties of cross-disciplinary approaches and point to the need for more studies in this vein. British historians must move beyond a traditional English empiricism without abandoning the rigorous evidentiary standards that such empiricism entails. Even a cursory glance at the period's political and cultural history shows that symbols, rituals, discourse, memory, and other subjects of cross-disciplinary investigation were essential aspects of eighteenth- and nineteenth-century life. Burke had his dagger to throw on the floor of the House of Commons; radicals had their liberty trees; loyalists had their effigies of Tom Paine; writers and caricaturists employed exaggerated language to discredit their opponents; clergy continued to give sermons on 30 January to commemorate the martyrdom of Charles I; and no one let anyone forget about the legacy of the Glorious Revolution of 1688, although many differed on how to interpret it. The linguistic turn, the turn to the public sphere, the use of nontraditional sources, and the examination of cultural symbols and practices has enriched an already rich historiography of late Hanoverian Britain.

California State Polytechnic University, Pomona